FROM A[illegible]GLE

TO [illegible]ADEMIA

PADDY MCMENAMIN

Published by Rivers Run Free Press

ISBN: 978-1-3999-1615-8

A catalogue record for this book is available from the British Library.

CONTENTS

The cover photo shows a door handle from Cage 18 found in the rubble by the author, Paddy, after the burning of Long Kesh in October 1974!

PROLOGUE

The years 2020-21 will always be remembered as a time when the whole world was hit by COVID-19 — a pandemic of proportions unseen since the Spanish Flu of 1918.The modern, super-efficient world effectively closed down. Paradoxically, as a nation and a people we found ourselves again, and what we had lost in our greed was suddenly replaced by a greater need for community spirit, a desire to reconnect with family, realizing that our children and our old people were more important than any materialistic gain. It was a time in which we reclaimed what is important in life.

In the preceding years I have had a difficult time health-wise: three open-heart surgeries, an infected Aortic valve, and to top it off, a brain haemorrhage. During the recovery period, my partner, Mary, encouraged me to 'Write the book'. We had talked about it over the years but there's nothing like a crisis in your life to bring out the creative side, and so the period of recuperation then followed by Covid-19 gave me space and time to sit down and put these words together.

My story is of an ordinary working-class youth who became involved in something extraordinary; a story of 'armed struggle', death, prison ships and prison camps. This morphed into life in Donegal, family and work, and then a return to academia, graduating as a 'Teacherman', and a new life in Galway. In writing this memoir, I've found it to be a story representing those I grew up with, those who embraced conflict on the streets in the '70s and the years in Long Kesh; they were friends for life with an unbreakable bond. Many didn't survive the conflict and others succumbed to the passage of time in recent years. It's a story which needs to be told, a story from the streets and not a revisionist history from those who rewrite to suit an agenda. Between recuperation after surgery and the COVID-19 lockdown, I have taken the opportunity to proverbially put pen to paper. It has been a journey with many twists and turns but thankfully, I'm still here to write it all down.

One of the early articles I scribbled while in Long Kesh was about the power of advertising and the use of symbolism in automotive advertisements. The English teacher who came into the Cages was very impressed and actually brought it around the 20 odd cages and read it out to the attentive classes of Provos, Officials, INLA, UVF and UDA men, maybe even to some of the 'Screws', I was a bit embarrassed and got a bit of a slagging from the boys, but one thing stayed in my mind, afterwards she said to me: "When you get out of this place, write about it, in 30 years, every media hack, political observer and academic will be writing about the conflict without any knowledge of what actually happened."! Almost 50 years later, I'm finally getting around to doing just that, I hope you find it as interesting as it was living through it!

'The most fortunate of us all in our journey through life frequently meet with calamities and misfortunes which greatly afflict us, to fortify our minds against these calamities and misfortunes should be one of the principal studies and endeavours of our lives'

—Thomas Jefferson

DEATH IN THE AFTERNOON SUN!

One Saturday morning back in 1988 we were preparing to head back to Donegal, the family having spent a week in Belfast for the first time since I left it a decade earlier. It wasn't a normal week by any means; my brother-in-law Kevi had been shot dead by British soldiers near his home in Turf Lodge, then Caoimhin MacBradaigh was killed along with two mourners by UDA gunman Michael Stone at Milltown during the Gibraltar funerals of Mairead Farrell, Sean Savage and Dan McCann. Old Rita (my mother-in-law) wanted to visit MacBradaigh's house and as we paid our respect, we got talking to his mother who, as it turned out, was from the Donegal Gaeltacht and a fluent gaeilgeoir. It was sad to see the two mothers who had lost sons consoling each other but each also had a pride which resonated with everyone. We took our place then in the funeral procession. Once again, thousands were in attendance. The coffin was covered with the tricolour, beret and gloves attached, the cortege took off down the Andersonstown road towards Casement Park. We were about 50 yards behind the hearse, Rita, Stevie, my ex-wife and I, we chatted as we walked along, it had been a long stressful week at that stage and I just wanted to get back to Donegal. My close friend Gerry had headed down to Dublin earlier and I was sorry we had not headed straight back to Donegal.

A British Army helicopter flew overhead but the RUC/Army stayed away and there was no colour party on display. Shots had been fired in tribute earlier close to MacBradaigh's home, a final salute to a brave guy who gave his life chasing down a psychopathic killer at Milltown. Suddenly, there was the sound of a car swerving, gearbox engaged then reversing up ahead of the cortege; there was utter confusion and a certain feeling that it was another loyalist attack on the funeral. The crowd surged forward as the car stalled and then we saw a guy on the roof of the car with a wheel brace battering at the side windows. We watched in amazement from about 20 yards as the crowd attacked the car. Just then, one of the guys in the besieged car fired a shot from a pistol scattering the crowd for a moment but it only delayed the inevitable.

The two men in the car were dragged out and as they were right outside Casement Park, they were manhandled through the gates of the stadium away from the glare of the public. It was still felt to be a loyalist attack and there was no sympathy for those caught in the car. The two men were beaten and half-stripped. At this stage IRA volunteers took control of the situation and identification found on the men showed they were members of the British Army: from that moment their fate was sealed.

A black taxi was commandeered and the soldiers were thrown over a low wall into the street below as the funeral cortege started to move off. The soldiers were thrown into the back of the taxi and driven away, passing us as they did. The driver waved a clenched salute as they passed by, whilst above, the army helicopter observed everything but no effort made to help their fellow soldiers. The black taxi drove up the Andersonstown road and turned off near 'Penny Lane' through to open ground behind 'Biddy's' pub and a bookies, disappearing from view. At this stage, I suggested to my father-in-law, old Steven, that we get out of there as the army was bound to saturate the place and would lift anyone at the scene. The four of us decided to head off home rather than follow the funeral to Milltown, and so we headed up the road from Casement and, as fate would have it, we turned into the same entry we thought the taxi had driven through, a taxi we didn't imagine we would be seeing again so soon. As we walked through the entry, two guys came running by us from the direction of the waste ground behind the pub. Above us, the helicopter was hovering about 100ft in the air. As we quickly walked by, we noticed a black taxi parked right in the middle of the waste ground. As we passed it, I peered inside and there lay the seemingly unconscious and almost naked soldiers in the back of the taxi.

Suddenly, the door of the taxi flew open and the first soldier jumped out: the taller one, who I later found out to be Derek Wood — virtually fell into my arms and to be honest, my first instinct was to grab hold of him. I knew right away who they were and self-preservation kicked in. They were covered in blood and I didn't want it on my clothes in case we were stopped by the army. I stepped back; I was about 2 inches from his face for a few seconds. He was naked except for a pair of short, white boxers. The other soldier, David Howes, jumped out, a man of smaller frame than the well-built Wood who had fired the shot from the car outside Casement. Both, barefooted, ran for their lives like rabbits in headlights. We watched in astonishment as the scene developed in front of our eyes, the men running hither and thither, when the two guys who we had passed earlier came running back and started grappling with the two soldiers. Howes more or less gave up and fell to the ground whereas Wood, the physically stronger of the two, started fighting for his life with the IRA volunteer. To be honest, it was a difficult scenario, these two men with just seconds to live. The IRA vols. shot Wood in the chest to break his valiant resistance and then as they stood over both soldiers we witnessed a 'public execution'. It all happened right in front of us before both IRA volunteers made their getaway.

A few old women who were also walking by started to scream. My ex-wife was screaming as events unfolded, other soldiers had killed her brother earlier in the week. She was caught up in the emotion of the moment. Above us, the army helicopter still hovered; apparently filming whilst in contact with other undercover soldiers on the ground but no effort was made to save the soldiers' lives. Steven and Rita, I think, were in shock. Their son had been killed by soldiers six days earlier. The whole paradox and pathos of the situation was spellbinding, I felt certain sadness as a result of what I had just witnessed as I would for any human being. This was a public execution in broad daylight on a Belfast street. It felt like a horrific stretch of time yet it was only minutes. I had no sympathy for the soldiers on a purely military level as I'm sure they had no sympathy for Kevi, but they were undercover soldiers armed with Browning weapons operating in a republican area. The army claimed later they innocently drove into the IRA funeral but that lame excuse didn't hold water. No-one in West Belfast believed anything the British Army said during the conflict. There was a dirty undercover intelligence war going on to try and defeat the IRA. Derek Wood and David Howes were either unfortunate, extremely naive, unlucky, or just plain stupid to drive into an IRA funeral in West Belfast. Whatever way we look at it, it has to be said that it was a sad day for everyone.

It was tragic for the two soldiers who lost their lives and their families, tragic that the republican community in West Belfast were vilified and demonised afterwards by the media. They were treated as if they were subhuman, animals, 'murdering bastards' to paraphrase the pathetic British tabloid, the 'Sun'. Over 40 people would be charged, eventually, with various offences including murder. The government punished the whole community, and the fact that what happened was a direct result of the loyalist attack in Milltown was conveniently overlooked by the media. I might have been arrested, like most of the 40 who were convicted by association of just being at the funeral, but we had returned to Donegal the next morning and never set foot in the place for a long time, I had placed myself out of harm's way. One of the guys clearly seen on television driving the black taxi that day later got life, he died himself in the last year or so, at one stage he was the youngest guy ever interned in the torrid history of the northern statelet, he too was a victim of conflict!

The republican community were held up as barbarous savages and blood thirsty animals, yet three from that community were murdered in Gibraltar, Kevi by a British soldier, and three mourners by a loyalist gunman, possibly with British connivance during that week, and all overlooked. The soldiers' deaths were the main newsworthy item on the agenda but conflict and death affect everyone. Saying all that, I felt something for the soldiers killed near 'Penny Lane' in South Link. They were someone's sons; they were in a foreign land and British undercover soldiers. I've thought many times over the years what it was like in that car that day as they reversed from the funeral to find their way blocked with thousands all around them — none of them friendly faces. They were strangers in a foreign land. Even though they were trained soldiers — possibly in a special elite unit — they must have been terrified in those last moments as they realised they were doomed. The faces of Wood and Howes are imprinted on my mind even now 33 years later. Their semi-naked blood-splattered bodies lying prostrate on the waste ground will always stay with me as I'm sure Kevi's body lying similarly in the entry a few days earlier will stay with the women who came to help him.

These few weeks were a hell that brought the horror of the Irish conflict to a world community on Sky/CNN/Al Jajeera. What made it unusual was that it was virtually all live on TV; the Gibraltar deaths, the killings at Milltown, and the soldiers' deaths. Usually, you would hear it on the morning news but that week, it was brought live to a worldwide audience. The British Army has even more video clips filmed from the helicopter: they know more about that day than they're prepared to say. Years later we were watching a documentary which showed the film from the army helicopter and you can see us walking by the black taxi. It was a horrendous week, possibly the worst of the whole conflict. And it felt as though it would never end. Ultimately, the events of that week possibly played a big part in bringing about the peace process and the Good Friday Agreement. The killings possibly brought society to its senses, we were so close to a complete breakdown of human values on all sides — the British, the Loyalists and the IRA — but society stepped back from the precipice.

Afterwards we reached old Rita's house in Turf Lodge courtesy of a nurse who gave us a lift in a wee Red Mini. As we drove up Bernagh Drive the army raced by in troop carriers and we swept our brows with relief, at the house we just sat and talked through what had happened. It was really hard to fathom everything that took place in that week of weeks. Rita's house was a wake house that week in 1988, as was the homes of the Gibraltar 3, also the three killed by Stone at Milltown and finally the homes in England of the two soldiers killed at the last funerals, it felt as if we were heading to an Armageddon but thankfully we avoided it!

The conflict was in its 20th year, more or less. War weariness was a feature but the IRA had been armed by Gaddafi and a form of 'Tet Offensive' was in the making. There were many within the IRA who believed they were operating from a position of strength when Fr. Alec Reid brought Adams to engage with John Hume and kick-started the Hume-Adams talks. The shift from 'armed struggle to politics' wasn't apparent at all — it was in tandem between 'the Ballot box and the armalite', but many in the IRA disagreed with a political strategy. Adams worked miracles to deliver the peace process as much as, if not more than John Hume: Hume risked losing face, Adams risked losing his life. Bobby Storey et al became supporters of the new strategy and only for that supportive cohort Adams could never have kept others on board.

Saying that, the week of Gibraltar, Milltown, and the soldiers' deaths definitely brought a certain realisation that we were getting close to a total breakdown of society.

Mairead, Dan and Sean, Kevi, Kevin Mulligan a friend's brother, Caoimhin MacBradaigh, McErlean and Murray, Wood and Howes — all lay dead. Some were killed by the SAS, some by the IRA, others by Loyalists: the conflict had taken its toll in the most horrific way possible. It had been a week which beggared belief: After a week of Irish funerals the soldiers' funerals would take place in the relatively peaceful English countryside, their families also in shock as they tried to understand what happened. But they couldn't comprehend why there was a conflict in Ireland. With time, they might understand that if their soldiers hadn't been in Ireland they wouldn't have died on a Belfast street; there was nothing personal in it. Their untimely deaths due to bearing the unwelcome uniform of a foreign army on Irish streets.

Moments after we left the scene of the killings, Fr. Alex Reid arrived and the pictures of him kneeling as he prayed for the dying soldiers became the iconic image of that week. His genuine comforting presence in their hour of death must have meant a lot to their families. The press, of course, exploited the images creating a Christ-like crucifixion scene amid words of xenophobic hatred. Fr. Reid rose above all that. He would have done the same if he had been in Gibraltar or Milltown. There can't be a hierarchy of victims, everyone is a human being. Fr Reid's experience led to his involvement in a way out of the conflict by talking to Gerry Adams and the leadership of the movement — helping to bring them in from the cold. Fr. Reid was the main mover in getting Adams and Hume together after that horrific week, but there were others like former priest Denis Bradley. But the real middle man, or 'Mountain Climber' as he was known, who facilitated the 'back channel' was Derry man Brendan Duddy who brought messages from the Army Council via Martin McGuinness to Michael Oatley, former Director of MI6 in the Middle East and the most important British agent in the six counties at the time. It was a precarious job for the Derry businessman, especially when he once brought a disputed statement from the Army Council saying they 'wanted a ceasefire to end the conflict', a controversial communiqué apparently doctored by MI5. I actually met both Duddy and Oatley at a conference in the National University Ireland Galway in 2010. Duddy was recovering from a stroke and he shed a tear when I told him I was in the Cages with Billy McKee, former Belfast IRA leader, who he also worked with in the '70s. Michael Oatley also empathised with me when I told him I had been in the Kesh.

He said, "It can't have been easy?"

We chatted for ages and recognised that at one time we were on opposite sides of the conflict. Nell McCafferty was also there, a well known Derry woman, writer, feminist, who during the debate queried Oatley facetiously, asking: "Did you know when you were in contact with Gerry and Martin via Brendan Duddy that they were both on the Army Council?"

He declined to comment.

The events of that week in March'88, while horrific in their 'execution', accelerated a peaceful conclusion to the conflict. It might be an oxymoron but the deaths and pain brought life and gain. We didn't know it then but we were at the beginning of the end game. That Sunday morning in Belfast I said to old Stevie:

"Thank God we're getting out of this place."

It was nothing against the place or the people who are the salt of the earth. And it's where I grew up, but I could never contemplate living there again; little did I know that it would be on the agenda again within a few years. We drove back to Donegal that afternoon, brought the kids to the Giants Causeway at Portrush on the Antrim coastline on the way; it was a bit surreal for us. There we were, still in the six counties but it, too, was a different world from the streets of West Belfast. When we crossed the border, for sure, we were definitely in a different world, to be honest, a different planet!

A LITTLE BIT OF HISTORY!

My parents were both born just after partition on either side of the new illegal British imposed border: Annie in Donegal in 1924 and Patsy in Tyrone in 1926. In a personal way, they personified the partition of our country. They both grew up in rural Ireland. Annie was born in Termon, near Letterkenny, and her father, Johnny — the local blacksmith. Patsy grew up in Plumbridge, near Omagh; his father was a small bicycle shop owner. Their childhood was as idyllic as it could be in rural Ireland at the time. Whether the partition of the country had any major effect on them as kids growing up in the new statelets is an imponderable? On both sides, as far as I know, there was little interest in politics; I never heard it mentioned as to which side of the civil war split the Russell family were on, or indeed on the McMenamin side, I never heard mention of their position vis-à-vis the northern unionist statelet but I presume, as a nationalist family west of the Bann, they just kept their head down and got on with it. They would have reached their teens during the days of the Great Depression and the 'hungry 30's. In the south, the Fianna Fáil Government had become the first-ever political party defeated in a civil war of horrendous proportions then taking power through the ballot box, an extraordinary event that paved the way for the new state to become a symbol of democracy. This, at a time when much of Europe was losing ground to the fascist threat, personified in the Free State by Eoin O'Duffy, former Garda Commissioner, President of Fine Gael, and leader of the Blueshirts!

In the six counties, nationalists had to accept partition. That a unionist statelet had become the de facto regime led to any aspirations of unity being dead in the water for the foreseeable future. In fact, during the 1930s there was more emphasis on class politics than national identity. Catholic and Protestant workers joined together in the 'Food Riots' of 1932, but unfortunately, it petered out as Unionists played the Orange card to get their constituency 'back on trend', to use a modern term, and by 1935 sectarian riots prevailed in Belfast once again!

During the 1930's, the 'Free State' engaged in the economic war with Britain in which de Valera refused to pay back levies to the British but, in turn, left the Irish economy in tatters. Unlike today, we were then tied economically to Britain and a rural backwater, whereas as the Economist observed recently, '....no other country in the rich world has seen its image change so fast', and with growth rates double the EU average including the UK! But back in the depression times of the 1930's there was a theory in Westminster that we would come crawling back to Britain with our tails between our legs but thankfully, it was not to be. To highlight how bad things were in the 'hungry thirties', I have some anecdotal evidence from my mum who once told me that when they were kids they always had plenty to eat. Living on a small 3-acre farm, they had their own cows, hens, and ducks, thus they would have milk and eggs, make their own butter, and a chicken or duck for Sunday dinner, occasionally. Her dad — my grandfather — was the local blacksmith and so had regular work shoeing horses that worked the hayfields and pulled the ploughs. Apparently, he was also a dab hand at a spot of illegal fishing and the odd salmon would find its way onto the dinner table. His wife, my granny, was great at making the old scone bread and eight different varieties would spice the palate. All in all, mum said life from that point of view wasn't too bad but there was one problem: a lack of hard cash! Despite the regular work shoeing horses and other work in the forge, payment was usually in the form of Meitheal, paid in kind: a day in the bog or cutting the hay in return for the services at the Blacksmith's cottage. That was fine, a form of communism if you like where the whole community would work together, but however, it lacked that one vital ingredient: the filthy lucre! My mum told me she remembered how one time my granda couldn't rent the adjacent field next to their farm, 'Micky Mór's meadow'. It was set at £1 a month for six months but he couldn't manage it, hard for young people nowadays to comprehend that stat!

In their late teens, my mum and her sisters headed off to Derry to work in big Protestant houses and hotels. It was WW2 time and Derry was a base for American soldiers. The attraction of the all-American boys from Detroit and Boston was probably akin to young teenagers swooning over boy bands in the modern era. These 'Yanks' brought excitement — unique Uncle Sam style: money and temporary romance. Indeed, many women in Derry would end up post-war back in some mid west industrial American city married to one of the G.I's, a far cry from the images in films. Many returned disillusioned and heartbroken but as many more made new lives across the Atlantic. My mum and her sisters had a plan to take the traditional Donegal route by the Derry boat to Glasgow, a well-worn path since Famine times as the Irish Diaspora spread its wings worldwide. They used to say if you had £2 you could head to America, if you had six shillings then Glasgow would be your destination, or maybe some of the industrial revolution cities throughout the UK. For most Donegal people, the west of Scotland was the preferred destination. It was closer to get there, to Strathclyde, the old Dalriada: it was twelve nautical miles at its closest point from Inishowen to Kintyre, and much cheaper of course. So the hills of west Donegal, Glenveagh and Muckish were swapped for the tough streets around the east end of Glasgow; initially as 'tattie hokers' in the early 20th century down the west coast, then factory workers, tunnel tigers, clippies (bus conductors) for the women, and some men even building big ships on the Clyde.

This is the scenario my mum faced as she worked in a hotel in Portrush après WW2, along with the sisters. The plan was to raise some money and take the Derry cattle boat — bovine passengers almost mixing with humans! The old boat would take all night, arriving at the Broomielaw in the morning with its Irish cargo — cows and people with weary heads — disembarking into the streets around the east end of Glasgow, the Gallowgate, Royston, Bridgeton, London Road, the poorest areas in the city. The conditions probably weren't much better than what they left behind in Donegal, indeed worse, but there was work post-war. But the best-laid plans and all that! One night my mum and sisters were going to a dance in Dungiven. Afterwards, they booked the same taxi driver to ferry them to a dance a few weeks later in the Co. Derry town. Many years later, the taxi driver related to me the story of that night at the dance in Dungiven; he had taken a shine to one of the sisters, my mum. But to complicate events, she was with another boy. To uncomplicate things, the taxi driver dropped the boy off first so he had a chance to talk to the girl. They hit it off so much that she delayed her trip to Glasgow and let the sisters head on, intending to meet up with them in a few weeks, but fate plays a massive part in our lives.

In a quirk of fate that would have major ramifications in not only their lives but mine too, the taxi driver suggested that there was work in Belfast and so Annie, the hotel maid, and Patsy, the taxi driver, headed to Belfast and made it their home for the next 50 years as her sisters would do likewise in Clydebank and the Isle of Bute. Patsy, the taxi driver, would marry Annie in Donegal a few years later and after the wedding 'breakfast' in the old blacksmith's cottage they returned to the divided city to spend their lives working hard like all country people. They reared a family, two daughters and one boy: myself, named after the Tyrone taxi driver Patsy, or Patrick Joseph to be exact, born a few months after Queen Elizabeth's Coronation, just before Germany defeated the great Hungarian 'Magyars' in the World Cup, and just eight years after the end of the greatest conflict ever known to mankind: World War 2. I emerged into the world just a few years after Germany, Britain, Russia, America, Japan, and a host of allies contributed to the greatest loss of soldiers and innocent civilian lives in a world not unfamiliar with conflict over the centuries: fascism, Nazi anti-Semitic racism, holocaust, Dresden, Leningrad, Nagasaki, Hiroshima, Pearl Harbour, Hitler, Churchill, Stalin, Roosevelt, and Hirohito. The world was devastated, but it would create almost 80 years of peace in Europe through which I have lived my entire life. However, Vietnam, Kenya, Aden, Cyprus, Afghanistan, Iraq, Palestine, Syria and Ireland would show the world that peace without justice and foreign interference would still only be a limited version of peace.

BELFAST, A WHOLE NEW WORLD FOR ONE LITTLE BOY!

I grew up in a part of Belfast known as Tiger's Bay which during the later conflict would become an area controlled by loyalist paramilitaries. In the 1950's, it was a mixed area, although predominantly Protestant, yet we never had any trouble with our neighbours in Mountcollyer. It was also close to the home of Crusaders who took the place of the famous Belfast Celtic who withdrew from football a few years before I was born: But Belfast was changing. Partition was beginning to take on a somewhat permanent look about it. The Free State had declared a Republic four years before I was born and the UK Government had declared the six counties a permanent part of the UK. Post-war Belfast was rebuilding and there was a feeling that unionists and nationalists could live together in the truncated statelet. Brookeborough had once declared 'NI' as a 'Protestant state for a Protestant people', but a new realignment was taking place and as Terence O'Neill would say in 1969: "If you give Catholics a good house they will live like Protestants, if they are jobless and live in a ghastly hovel they will have 18 children'! The hope was that nationalists would gradually accept the state and drop the aspiration for Irish unity. It was a forlorn dream.

We lived in Tiger's Bay for my first five years before moving to the Annadale flats on the embankment and near the Ormeau Road in South Belfast, another overwhelmingly Protestant area. My country parents didn't do well in their school geography exams. The four years we lived there were as normal as any childhood could be. I had loads of young Protestant friends and we played football and street games as all kids do, my parents worked away, both with two jobs. My dad was a bus driver and taxied at weekends, my mum, a hotel worker and a house cleaner at weekends. They had no time for the politics which always existed in the six counties, working 51 weeks of the year, then a week in Donegal. This happened around the 12th of July when most Belfast Catholics would head south to avoid the nonsense. Grown men would wear orange sashes to commemorate a battle 300 years previously between two foreign Kings on Irish soil. The Boyne victory for William III, or 'King Billy', would be the only cause of trouble for me in Annadale as, for a few days around the bonfire time, I would be told in a rather unpleasant manner to 'fuck off you Fenian bastard', not by my friends but some bigger guys; I didn't know what a Fenian was at the time.

On the other hand the world was changing for the better, or so we thought: The Second Vatican Council had brought ecumenism to the fore;

Martin Luther's 95 theses were nearly all absorbed into the modern church 400 years after it formally rejected the change; Fidel and Che Guevara had overturned the US-backed Batista regime in Cuba to become the first communist state in the Americas. Still, the Irish Catholic President Jack Kennedy almost brought us to WW3 before common sense prevailed, and when my mum brought her Protestant neighbour into our local chapel we were told not to mention it on the street, proving that ecumenism still had a way to go in the north, and world peace a way to go as well. For a 9-year-old boy, all this of course would go over your head. Schoolboy days in Sunnyside St, long summer evenings in the sun, football on the streets, and Superman and Batman comics were the order of the day, innocent times which wouldn't last. We moved from Annadale at the end of 1962 to the new Turf Lodge estate on the western edge of the city. Nestled beneath the Black Mountain, just across the Whiterock from Ballymurphy which, even at that stage, was gaining certain notoriety as a tough area, the residents in both estates arrived mostly from the overcrowded lower Falls, Markets, and Carrick Hill; the City Council had created, unwittingly, a sort of reservation on the slopes of West Belfast for inner-city nationalists with no amenities, no jobs, no educational prospects, and no hope, at one stage the estate was referred to as the 'Ponderosa' after a popular cowboy show on the box based in the 'wild west' how apt!

We had been allocated a corner house in Norglen Gardens with a back and front garden which suited my dad, being green-fingered. It had three bedrooms, a nice kitchen, bathroom and living room. For working-class people, it was like moving from Ballymun to Ballsbridge. For my mum and dad, country people to the core, this would be their domicile for the next 40 years. They adapted well as rural country folk, embracing urban working-class life. But, then, if you really think about it, all big cities are made up of country people if you go back far enough, all economic migrants who made the transition with ease whether it was Glasgow, London, New York, Melbourne or Belfast.

My parents were always conscientious, hard-working people: Dad drove trolley buses, later big trucks and taxis at weekends; mum worked in hotels, and then for 20 odd years as the school patrol woman at St Teresa's, the 'lollipop women' as they used to call them. Both were non-drinkers although my dad liked a wee smoke or 60 Players plain which came back to haunt him in later years. They were not big socialisers; they kept their energies for the annual trip to Donegal. For some reason, we never really went much to my dad's place in Tyrone; I think there was something about the freedom of getting across that bloody border! Neither had any interest in sport, although my dad liked a wee flutter on the horses or dogs and could be found at the old

Celtic Park or the Dunmore greyhound track on an evening; he left more often licking his wounds rather than celebrating. But they toiled every day of their working lives, rarely missing a day as they reared the family. And though this was an area of high unemployment, their rural upbringing stood to them; gathering spuds, fitting turf, and turning hay was a great 'apprenticeship' for life, and whilst those particular skills mightn't have been required in an urban setting, it was a good preparation for life.

In the 60's I went to school over at St Teresa's Primary. We had to walk down the 'new road' which attached our estate to the Glen road, about a half-mile walk. The estate was still a work in progress: the footpaths hadn't been laid outside our house; while we had a house there were blocks of flats being constructed at the top of the estate; and then there was nothing in the way of things. No taxis, no buses, no church, no school, no pubs, no youth club, no telephone boxes, just four shops: the bakery, the 'sweetie' shop, the butchers, and a small supermarket. Of course, as in any newly built development, these things would all arrive in time.

In June, 1965, I was eleven and sitting the 11+ exam after the controversial academic division of children at the tender age of eleven. I was fairly confident as I was doing ok at school. I had a love for English, reading, and writing, but not so hot on Maths and Science, the other side of the equation. The exam day came and we trooped in. Mr. Hamill, our teacher and future principal, directed us to the correct seats and tables and we were ready to roll. A few hours later, it was all over, our whole future life decided by some 'A's' and 'B's'. We were either heading to a grammar school and theoretically to university, or to the local secondary and maybe an apprenticeship if lucky, life on the building sites awaited others, or worse still, joining the dole queue in an area where the unemployment rate was much higher than average. Saying that, of course, I know millionaire builders who left school at 14 but could build a 50-storey business tower in Dubai, at the same time, PhD's who could quote verbatim Molly Bloom's soliloquy but mightn't know how to change a flat tyre?

Anyway, every year of my childhood I was packed off to Donegal for the summer holidays as was the tradition. We would make a pilgrimage to the hills to my granddad's old blacksmith cottage near Doon Well, a Holy Well and rock where the last chieftains of Ulster were crowned in the early 1600s before the Flight of the Earls from nearby Rathmullan. From 1960, my Uncle had become a publican in the nearby, aptly named 'Mountain Bar', just a few miles from Doon. So, from the early '60s that was my destination as the last of my mum's family had taken the migrant ship to the UK and the old cottage was temporarily closed up, although occasionally, another uncle would still shoe a horse in the forge for a neighbour. So, I'm down at the bar working away as you would in those days at eleven. I was on holiday but, you know, living on the farm there was always something to do: turning hay, cutting turf, moving cows, collecting eggs from the henhouse. So, as well as serving bottles of Phoenix and Double Diamond to the locals, we were hired help without pay and supposed to enjoy it. Midway through the holidays during the Glasgow 'Fair', my aunts, uncles and cousins would arrive from Clydebank and Rothesay on the Isle of Bute, and then the fun would begin.

We were city kids let loose in rural Ireland and we loved it. It was so different from our own environment in working-class Belfast and Clydebank near Glasgow. Other cousins lived on the little holiday Isle of Bute. In those innocent years of youth, life was one big party for two summer months in the '60s. My mum and dad would come down during the 12th of July; it signified in the six counties a time when Loyalists, Orangemen, Blackmen (an Orange institution), Apprentice Boys (yet another Orange institution), and well-to-do middle-class unionists would mix for one day in the year with ordinary working-class loyalists, unemployed Shankill men, Orange Lil's, and golf club Cedric's and Walter's, to celebrate William of Orange's victory over Catholic King James at the Battle of Boyne in Louth in 1690. These foreign Kings used Irish infantrymen to slaughter fellow Irishmen, and according to popular legend, William of Orange received a blessing from Pope Clementine VI, before achieving victory and the throne in Britain. Protestants celebrated this historic event as if it happened yesterday, while the nationalists were on the first bus to Donegal to escape the 'Billy boys' and the 'kick the Pope' bands. Yes, even then, it wasn't a cultural festival unless you compared it to Rangers fans celebrating winning the league in George Sq. singing, 'up to their knees in fenian blood'? Unionism is no longer a monolithic single-issue section of society. During the conflict, the UDA and UVF were more embracing of working-class politics, seeing through people like Paisley and Robinson. The reason the second Ulster Workers Strike failed was due to the paramilitaries who didn't give it their backing. They had realised that it would lead them only to gaol while the middle-class unionists didn't give a damn about them, in fact, they despised them, but all that was in the future.

1966 AND ALL THAT

So I happened to be at the Uncle's farm and pub in the summer of 1965 when my mum and dad arrived with the great news that I had indeed passed the 11+. The realisation that I was heading to St Mary's Grammar school, a bastion of Belfast Catholic elite academia and knuckle-duster wielding Christian Brothers, was probably lost on me as I shook the hay, gathered turf and served bottles of beer in the wee pub. In reality, I suppose it was a bit like LC students today getting the points required for 3rd Level. My path to academia had just opened up. If you passed this exam, like everything in the six counties, it divided us. Young kids at eleven either progressed via 2nd Level to university and a future career as a doctor, teacher, or university lecturer. If you failed, it was off to the local secondary, and then, a life working in a pub, bus driver, or on a building site, or if you were lucky, an apprenticeship as a plumber or electrician. I was lucky to have passed the first big test in life. In fact, I was the only one of my friends to pass the dreaded exam; the rest headed down the road to St Teresa's on the Glen road while I took the bus downtown to St Mary's. My mum was so happy. She valued education and was so proud telling the uncles in Donegal, her, a wee hotel cleaner, but she knew that the only way to get on in life was to get an education. She had left Termon national school at 13 as was the way in those days, walking to school in her bare feet in early summer, bringing turf to keep the fire burning, to heat the classroom. Her education was limited, but she understood the values of life.

Returning to Belfast at the end of the summer, I started in St Mary's down in Barrack St. at the bottom of the Falls Road, almost in the city centre. It was run by Christian Brothers and, contrary to popular opinion, I never had a problem with them except when you got a rap across the knuckles with a glantóir — a block of wood used for cleaning the board. The Catholic Church in the modern era has been implicated in abuse scandals which have damaged the Church worldwide, but for me, the Christian Brothers were great educators. They taught us English, History, Maths, Science, Irish etc., while also bringing us their love of Gaelic games, the language and, of course, Irish history. There was no 'Britannia rules the waves' on the radio during lessons for us at nationalist schools. I adapted quite well during 1st year and began 2nd year in 2B; all was going along nicely, but that was to change. As well as starting a whole new experience at 2ndlevel, I also 'found' football —though not the GAA which I would come to love in my later years through my sons' involvement. There was actually no GAA club at the time in Turf Lodge but Gort na Mona was formed in the late 70's. The GAA is a wonderful organisation which promotes gaelic games and the largest sporting organisation in the country; until '71 there was a ban on playing 'foreign games' but in our youthful absence of gaelic games we took to the 'beautiful game'. It wasn't so beautiful then, however, with heaving, run-down stadiums, heavy pitches, pie and Bovril: it was far from the Premiership.

In our little group of friends who played street football till the cows came home, there was a guy originally from East Belfast: Jimmy Bell. He was the eldest of our 'wee gang'. He was slightly bigger, a year or two older, and the fastest guy on his feet I've ever seen until Usain Bolt came along. Jimmy had roots in Ballymacarrett in the east of the city and suggested we go 'over the bridge' to see his team, Glentoran, one of the 'big two' in Belfast. They were the perennial rivals of Linfield who were based in the 'Village' at Windsor Park just a stone's throw across the new motorway from where we resided. But for loads of historical reasons, no kids from our area could even contemplate supporting 'the Blues'. Linfield were the traditional 'Protestant' club in Ireland. Their modus operandi was similar to their 'cousins' Glasgow Rangers. For a century, neither considered Catholics good enough to select them, and their fan base was 99% loyalist with a vitriolic sectarian hymn book. In 1948, a riot developed during a Linfield/Belfast Celtic match and the Linfield crowd invaded the pitch and attacked the Celtic players, threw Jimmy Jones down on to the terraces, attacked him and broke his leg. Belfast Celtic withdrew from football after this and never played in the Irish league again.

From 1965 until 1969, a group of us trooped over to Dee St. off the Newtownards Rd to watch Glentoran — sometimes up to twenty of us, all 'fenians' — the derogatory term used by loyalists for people of a Catholic faith. The term 'Fenians' actually stemmed from the name given to the 19th century Irish revolutionaries, the IRB. We would travel over from West Belfast to stand in the middle of a predominantly Protestant crowd, but never once in four years had we ever any trouble from anyone. In fact, the only trouble would be when we had regular battles with the Linfield fans when they visited the east end of the city. Linfield had been the top dog since Belfast Celtic exited football after the riot at Windsor in 1948, but football moves in cycles. Glentoran arose out of their 12-year slumber and won the League in 1966 with an ex-Celtic youth prodigy John Colrain as manager, and just as Jock Stein had done in Glasgow, power was transferred across the city. Simultaneously, across the water in Glasgow, events were entering a whole new scenario; again, after over a decade of despondency, Celtic under Jock Stein had won the Cup in '65 and then the first of nine league titles in a row in '66 and, incredibly, went on to be European champions in 1967. — to paraphrase Bob Dylan: '...the times they were a-changin.'

And the times did change. The swinging '60s continued a movement that crested into the Beatles and the Rolling Stones. Vietnam was the war of the ages, the civil rights movement was well under way, and the assassination of JFK, Bobby and Martin Luther King rattled earth as the Space Race took off into the skies. The only moment in history most Irish people would like to forget was when England won the World Cup in 1966. I was in Donegal that summer and bad and all as it was for Donegal to lose the first televised Ulster final to Down, watching Geoff Hurst and Bobby Moore lift the Jules Rimet trophy was akin to Collins signing the Treaty! Coincidentally, a few months later I was part of the crowd, 60,000 large, at Windsor Park to see England play their first game after the World Cup. They won 2-0 with an imperious style about them, their dazzling white jerseys emblazoned with three Lions, but strangely my memories are of the loud shrieks of teenage girls at the match every time Georgie Best touched the ball. It wasn't long after he had announced himself to the football world after a master class at Benfica, and 'El Beatle' became the star of the show despite defeat that day.

Georgie Best — 'the Belfast Boy', the genius from the Cregagh —was simply the greatest player we ever saw. His life became the story of the times, his genius a paradox for his alcoholism. Yet through everything he was loved. Every young guy wanted to be Georgie Best, and every teenage girl just wanted Georgie Best. For the next four years, we crossed the city to follow Glentoran and down the road to Windsor for internationals; they were different times in the six counties. The times were relatively peaceful. We went to the Oval without any problems. Glentoran won leagues and cups galore and played great European games against Benfica, Rangers and Arsenal. I saw Georgie Best in all his early international games where he might have been a shining jewel within a mediocre group, but it was something special to see him in the flesh. Especially, one famous day in '67 against Scotland (and half the Celtic team who had just won the European Cup.) Best was outstanding as he led the Scots on a merry dance. I've seen many great players in the 50 years since but nobody compares to Georgie Best. Well, maybe 'Jinky' Johnstone or the little Argentine genius Messi, but the difference was that Georgie was our Messi.

1966, of course, wasn't all about school and football. 50 years earlier an event had taken place which changed the course of Irish history forever — the Easter Rising in Dublin 1916. I didn't grow up in a republican family and there would never be talk about politics in our house. Even though we lived in what became a strong republican area in later years, I don't recall much fanfare about the commemorations of the Rising except in Ardmonagh which had tricolours flying: but, then, twelve-year-olds aren't really interested in things like that. There was a massive march up the Falls Road by thousands of republicans and tricolours were flying all along the Falls to Milltown. More sinister events also took place on the loyalist side of West Belfast where a revamped UVF killed several innocent Catholics in what could be regarded as the first killings of the conflict: this was to dominate events for most of my young life. Gusty Spence and others murdered two barmen on the Shankill and an old Protestant woman was burned to death after they threw petrol bombs at a Catholic pub. They received 'life' imprisonment for their sectarian murders, and Gusty became a name associated with loyalism for a long time to come. In gaol, he would eventually enact his own road to Damascus in his encouragement of younger loyalists moving away from a sectarian path. All this went over our young heads as we got on with doing what young people do: school by day, street football at night, the Oval on a Saturday, and Donegal in the summer. It mightn't have been an idyllic childhood but it wasn't too bad.

My first peer group were gradually growing up: Jimmy, Joseph, Kieran, Norman, and Tiny. We all loved football and as we morphed into our early teens we started to take note of their sisters and friends: Ann, Deirdre, Olive, Catherine et al. We guessed they were different and had a certain attraction but football still had our first love! I mention these names as a sort of starting point in life as we progressed into adulthood. As we move further through the pages and chapters of this tome, the many names of people I recall— those who have been part of my life — will appear scattered through the narrative, amid the collective 'quirks of fate' of growing up in Belfast. Our young lives were soon to change in the most dramatic way. In a few short years we would face a conflict that would be life-changing for many of us. Many of the young men who will be mentioned would not survive. Many were killed in their teens, others becoming involved in the ensuing 'armed struggle'. A large number sacrificed long years in gaol. Of course, everything looks different in hindsight, no one pictures a 68-year old golfer with a fondness for red wine and golf involving himself in armed struggle, but the times decided much of what happened. But before all this in 1967 we had the football as we walked down the Falls Road carrying tricolours, celebrating Celtic winning the European Cup with eleven guys from within 30 miles of Parkhead. It was a magnificent achievement for the 'Irish team' in Britain. Gerry Fitt, our local MP, led the celebrations like a good politician played to the crowd

'We did it'!

As natural amenities go, we weren't badly off where we lived on the edge of the city. We had the Black mountain hovering just above the estate; Sundays would be spent climbing it, up the 'loney', a lane which led to the hatchet field and finding a free-flowing stream over rocks. This, on a hot day, was like coke on tap to thirsty mouths if you closed your eyes. We also had the Falls Park, and in the centre were 'the Coolers', an open-air swimming pool in Belfast. You went in for a dip and like Billy Connolly observed, his mother put them in the North Sea as kids on holiday and they came out blue. Otherwise it was on the streets that we took most enjoyment. In earlier days, it was with 'Guiders', a mode of transport made up of a plank of wood and a set of pram wheels and 'ball bearings' requisitioned from the nearby bus depot. They created a din as we roared down the hilly streets of the estate. But it was the football that most of our endeavours were concentrated. After school with homework done, we headed out re-enacting Celtic v ManU on a street corner with street name signs as goals and maybe ten a side playing with a tennis ball, or an old ball if we could find it. We could play till eleven at night under the street lights. It was great stuff and it created many talented footballers, a fact lamented by Alex Ferguson recently when he said that modern big-time football lacked the intricate skills created by street football back in the day. The park, of course, was the other main venue for football. With no proper pitches or goalposts, we created our own with coats or jumpers for nets. 20 a-side playing the beautiful game. The highlight of our week would be some nights when the older men were playing and they might be a man short and would ask us to make up the numbers. It was like being called out by Jose Mourinho for a Champions League tie. They were great players, many of them Irish League players, and we were overjoyed to be asked to play. The most amazing thing, considering events in the near future, was when it came to 9 o'clock and the park would be closing. A wee 'Parkie', usually a wee old man with a 'game' leg would come sailing along on his bike to enforce park rules and 40 grown men would run for a hole in the railings to get out. There existed a fascinating respect for authority in those bygone days.

1968 would turn out to be the last year of normality in our young lives. Events worldwide imploded, Prague, Sorbonne, Vietnam while at home Austin Currie and others occupied a house at Caledon, Dungannon to protest discrimination in housing allocations by the local Unionist council who had given a three bedroom house to a young, 19-year-old single Protestant girl instead of a Catholic family of five. The RUC would eventually remove them but the incident, almost by accident, eventually led to what is euphemistically referred to as 'the Troubles' in the six counties. It was the first real nationalist awakening after almost fifty years of partition. For the most part, nationalists had kept their heads down, accepting the reality of the partitionist statelet, but the torch lit by Currie et al would manifest itself in the civil rights movement eventually, the marches in Derry, and ultimately, the conflagration that took place the following year in Belfast and Derry which brought the six counties to a position of no return. They were basic civil rights, but they didn't lead to uprising. Armed struggle is a different ball game altogether from hippy long haired students protesting 'one man, one vote', the Battle of the Bogside, British troops on the streets, the Curfew, Internment and finally, Bloody Sunday tipped the scales toward the long war.

Of course, all these events passed us by initially — well, at least, the housing protests and the initial civil rights marches. Still, between school and visiting the Oval on a Saturday, we were developing into a form of feral youth on a large 'reservation'. Instead of school work, homework and grinds, the streets became our education. Football became our salvation and Georgie Best our God. And needless to say, we found girls, but what to do with them? How to talk to them? How to even meet up with them was for many of us at that young crossroads of life a difficult road to manoeuvre. October 1968 would become a major influence in our young lives as we watched on TV a 400-strong civil rights march being stopped and attacked by baton-wielding RUC men in Duke St, Derry. Before that day, Duke St. to me was the train station we arrived at in Derry on our way to Donegal for the summer. Now, and for all time, it could be classed as the Civil Rights era of the conflict in the six counties. Gerry Fitt, Eddie McAteer, Eamonn McCann et al led the march where pictures of Fitt and others being batoned were captured by an RTE cameraman who smuggled them quickly by courier for the evening news: the images were shown around the world. A so-called democracy in Western Europe experiencing events which, recently, were seen in Wenceslas Square in Prague sent shock waves around the globe and had massive implications for London who, for 50 years, had been covering up a festering sore. Now, their ineptitude would bring the statelet down. A few weeks later, 20,000 marched on the same streets, and without an RUC presence, it passed off peacefully. The people had spoken and things would definitely never be the same again.

January, 1969, saw the People's Democracy students at Queen’s organise a march from Belfast to Derry. It was fraught with danger as loyalists threatened to disrupt it at every chance, and as the demographics of the six counties ensured that marchers would drift between nationalist and unionist areas, conflict was inevitable. The loyalists felt that it was their 'wee' country and while they reserved the right on all highways, they didn't believe that nationalists had that right.

The students led by Bernadette Devlin and Michael Farrell were the first of a new generation of young nationalists who would challenge the statelet. The new education system put in place post-WWII ensured for the first time that nationalists would enter the hallowed halls of Queen's which, previously, were reserved for the sons and daughters of well-to-do unionist parents from the Malone Road. Now, a new generation had emerged which not only challenged the traditional unionist/nationalist divide, but would help to retrieve the city from 1690 into the modern era of the 1970s soon approaching.

The marchers left Belfast on January 1st and were hassled and harassed on their 'long march' at various intervals as they passed near the loyalist areas. By night, they would rest and shelter in nationalist areas but during the four days en route to Derry, they were constantly barraged and abused vocally by loyalists led by the Rev. Ian Paisley and 'Major' Ronnie Bunting with a raggle-taggle band of Union Jack-waving loyalists from Cullybackey, Ballymena and Castledawson.They were met with threats that they would never make it to Derry — a symbolic city in the unionist mythology of Ulster deliverance from the papist hordes. Paisley would be a major protagonist during the conflict, but like Gusty Spence, he had his own 'Road to Damascus' experience and ended up sharing power with republicans where he and Martin McGuinness became such buddies that they were termed 'the Chuckle Brothers', an amazing turnaround.

Paisley was a modern day version of an evangelical preacher, Belfast has always had that type of bible thumper, in the 1850's we had 'Roaring Hanna' and a statue commemorates him in Carlisle Circus where the Orange Parade starts on the 12th every year. While Paisley never had 'blood on his hands' literally, his words encouraged many young working class loyalists to get involved with paramilitaries and then spend many years in Long Kesh, many of these working class loyalists eventually seen through Paisley and their backing for him waned in later years.

On the fourth day, all fears on behalf of the marchers came to the fore. They left Dungiven, a nationalist town, on the last leg of the journey, unaware what lay ahead, but several hostile areas which the marchers had to reconnoitre awaited. Whilst they had an RUC escort they didn't have faith in the custodians of law and order protecting them and as it turned out their fears were well-founded. At Burntollet Bridge, seven miles from Derry, the marchers were attacked by well-prepared loyalist demonstrators who used the advantage of hills on both sides of the road to savagely attack the young marchers with batons, bottles, stones and fists as they chased them into a river. All the while, the RUC were passive observers, but once again, an RTÉ cameraman was able to relay the pictures to a worldwide audience, it was our 'Selma'. After a long delay, the marchers finally made it to Derry, battered and bruised and once again attacked by loyalists in the Waterside area of Derry. They arrived at the Guildhall to a massive reception by thousands. They had exposed the ugly reality of a sectarian statelet, and just to enforce it, the RUC attacked residents in the Bogside that night. The conditions for conflict, if not always so apparent, were clearly developing at the pace of a speeding train, one which would involve virtually the whole nationalist community in a revolt against the sectarian statelet in which they were always second class citizens.

So in 1969 despite a liking for academic study, a love for English and history, and good grades, the Christian Brothers and I had a parting of ways. Despite being in the 'A' stream my time at school was coming to an end. Algebra and geometry did nothing for me and while I had a great time running cross country for the school team across Ireland, it wasn't enough to keep me stimulated. When it came to the second major exams of my life — the O-

Levels — my preparation wasn't nearly good enough and I exited school at the tender age of 15. This, despite my English Teacher trying to persuade me to stay on to continue English language and literature. Apparently, she had seen enough in my long essays to recognise a certain writing skill that could be cultivated. She wasn't the first teacher to suggest that, but it would take 40 years of life before I would return to University. It seems ridiculous now, but coming from working-class urban streets, it was quite normal. Unfortunately, despite all the advances in education in 50 years, there are stats that show that early school-leaving is still a problem in many working-class areas today.

In April '69, just before my O-Levels, there was a civil rights march down the Lower Falls and a few of us went down, I suppose, more for the 'craic' rather than any serious interest in the discriminatory motives of the unionist Council at City Hall, but it turned into a night of hell. It had the radicalising effect of turning young boys into would-be 'revolutionaries', even though we were far from budding Che Guevara's. As the march progressed from Divis flats towards Clonard, the RUC appeared in front and behind us and proceeded to attack the marchers and pandemonium ensued: stones and bottles flew through the air and RUC armoured cars drove through the crowds scattering everyone. At that time, there was a fear of the RUC and B-Specials, a condition created by 50 years of repressive legislation. A mythical view of the RUC and 'Specials' was prevalent, compounded by their predecessors in the 1920s who had done a good job in keeping the 'croppies' down, a term for rebels in 1798. The B-Specials were a special reserve force of the RUC, formed at the birth of partition. They were 100% exclusively Protestant and the majority of those were former UVF volunteers. They built up a fearsome reputation among nationalists as a sort of paramilitary force to keep nationalism in its place. When they were disbanded in 1970, many of them re-joined the UDR and were involved in many sectarian murders during the conflict. That particular night in 1969, there was a change in the air. The marchers were animated and when the rumour that Frank Lagan, a Catholic RUC officer of later Bloody Sunday fame, had ordered the RUC to attack the marchers it brought a reaction not seen since the riots in 1964 when the RUC attacked republican election HQ and pulled down the tricolour. The RUC were never what one might describe as a community police force. At its conception after Partition the number of Catholics in the force was never more than 20% and most were ex RIC, and by the 60's it was 12%, even in 2021 the PSNI has only 30% nationalist membership, and within the republican working class areas in Derry and Belfast it's probably zilch.

Frank Lagan was an unusual breed, a Catholic who achieved high rank in the force. The crowd responded to RUC violence with violence in kind. Riots raged up and down the Lower Falls and into the little back streets off Leeson

St. and Cullingtree Road. Running battles. And a few of us probably committed our first act of 'revolutionary' violence by throwing a large plank of wood through the windows of the Ulster Bank. The shattering of glass was akin to the shattering of our innocence. It mightn't have been an attack on the capitalist system per se, but it felt as if we had struck a blow against the police and the state. It made great conversation in school the next morning, too, as we prepared for our O-Levels which would spell the end of my education thus far. I wouldn't sit another exam for over 35 years when I would sit academic exams at NUI Galway in my 1st year at University, but that's a whole story of its own.

1969 AND THE POINT OF NO RETURN

I left school in early June 1969 and along with Paddy Smith and Jimmy McCollum, we were all working in bars within a few weeks. I was working in a trendy bar just off the city centre. Lavery's just beside the Courthouses with a mixed clientele which, in Belfast wasn't just gender based but a political and religious one. In the upstairs lounge, young things would sip cocktails in the Speakeasy lounge, a setting reminiscent of Chicago during Prohibition in the 1930s. Replica Thompson submachine guns hung on the walls along with photos of Al Capone. As Billy Connolly would say: 'for fcuk's sake, this is Belfast, they sell bomber jackets in the shops'.

In the bar downstairs, nationalists from the nearby Markets, a republican area, would share the bar with Protestant shipyard workers from East Belfast and all was well pre-conflict days. I worked in the bar for the next 18 months and while it limited my nights out with my friends, I enjoyed the craic with an eclectic mixture of customers, many who had that unique black Belfast humour. The staff were great: manager Jim, head barman Jimmy, another Paddy, three attractive girls - Mo, Jo and Rosie. They took me to my first 'adult' party on the Lisburn road that Christmas when I got pissed and woke to find a bit of free love going on. Some were smoking stuff that wasn't Players Blue, and a guy playing guitar rattling out 'Little ole wine drinker me'. As for the three young apprentice barmen from Turf Lodge, the future wouldn't pan out as we expected; within two years, one would be dead and the others in gaol.

On the streets, things were starting to get out of hand. The civil rights marches intensified, and riots were becoming the order of the day with Paisleyite counter demonstrators increasing the temperature considerably. At work one day, the other young barman Paddy showed me a headline from the Irish News, the nationalist paper in Belfast. It was a short story about a small bomb explosion near an electricity pylon which had been blamed on the IRA. In fact, it turned out to be the work of the UVF who were trying to bring down the government of Terence O'Neill. He asked me what I thought about it and the IRA. I replied that I didn't know very much about these things and he said we would talk again about it. A few weeks later, he approached me again about the same subject and said he could introduce me to some young republicans who could explain exactly what was happening on the streets and what we should do about it. I was a bit apprehensive about it all but agreed to go along with him to meet these guys. I didn't know it at the time but he was recruiting for Na Fianna Éireann, the republican youth organisation founded by Countess Markievicz and Bulmer Hobson in 1909, in its present guise, it was the youth wing of the IRA. Now, to be honest, at the time he might as well have been talking about Fionn mac Cumhaill and the Fianna from Celtic mythology than the modern Fianna and the IRA. At that stage, it was a sort of mystical organisation from the past which was going to achieve unity by uniting the working class and eradicating the sectarianism that had divided us for so long, policies inherited from the United Irishmen in 1798 and led by many Presbyterians like Wolfe Tone and Henry Joy McCracken. At least, that was the plan the new Marxist leadership had sold to the volunteers after the fiasco of the border campaign from 1956-62 which ended in a classic failure, of disorganisation, disillusionment, and an acceptance that Irish unity was as far away as ever as we entered the swinging 60's. Between the jigs and reels, Paddy brought me to a meeting in Leeson St. in the Lower Falls where a sort of trendy leftie type gave me, along with several other prospective recruits, a lecture on Irish history, including James Connolly, Russia, and a workers republic. At the end of it all, we were all sworn into the Fianna and told we would be contacted very soon to begin training. It sounded all very exciting for a 15-year-old, this thing that would consume my life for the next decade and make a major input in my thinking on events for the past 50 years. We became socialist republicans, if not budding Marxists: we recognised liberation theology. The cohort who morphed into the Provisional IRA understood that armed struggle was paramount while the Officials became side-tracked by various people with Marxist tendencies. They morphed from Official IRA to Workers Party, Democratic left, and eventually some finding a home in Labour: their politics beggared belief, to me and others at least. They became almost unionist in their thinking; how their former foot soldiers in working class Belfast embraced this thinking is beyond me. The great Leader of the Russian Revolution, Lenin, embraced armed struggle as indeed did James Connolly; they understood the path to revolution wasn't placards and free love!

For the following two months, I would combine my daily shifts at work with Fianna meetings, lectures, drilling, and firearms training, usually with a stolen RUC Webley revolver and maybe a 303 Lee Enfield rifle. It might have resembled Baden Powell's scout movement but this was one group that wasn't going camping in the country tying knots, telling stories and singing songs around the camp fire. This was serious stuff and I was part of it, a testosterone-fuelled 15-year-old becoming involved in something which was way over his head but it was exciting, and when you're 15 that's what life is all about. At this stage, my recruiter, Paddy, asked me if I thought I could recruit some of my friends in the estate into a new Fianna slua (unit), as none existed there before. I replied that I would try, and within a few weeks we had about 20 of my football mates and childhood friends seeking to become involved in something we didn't really understand, or maybe just looking for the same excitement I had promised them?

We held meetings in my wee bedroom and the back bedrooms of friends' houses while their mothers thought we were having a football team talk. We discussed the overthrowing of the capitalist system and the armed struggle to end British rule in our country. Actually, to be honest, there was more talk about whom you snogged at the weekend disco than world revolution but that would come too. Revolvers would be brought into the houses for arms training: how to load and unload it, how to clean it, how to fire it, and most important of all, how to find 'dumps' to hide it when not in use. Eventually, our Fianna slua would mostly go with the Officials after the split: a minority went with the Provos, including myself, as Turf Lodge became an Official IRA stronghold. As things progressed over the years, the Fianna became a bit side-lined as Fians started moving into the IRA quicker as arrest of volunteers' necessitated replacements. The necessities of war forced their hand.

Why did I take the path towards 'Provisionalism', I'm not sure? For a year after the 'Split' we were in a sort of limbo, our group all stayed together, selling 'United Irishman' around the estate, taking part in riots, to be honest it was hard to make contact with either IRA after the split, they were in the background, reorganising, training with what little weaponry was available, when it came to 1970 it was like a limbo period, the 'honeymoon period' as Gen Freeland dubbed it, everyone was gearing up for what lay ahead.

AUGUST 1969, WOODSTOCK, NEIL ARMSTRONG AND THE BOGSIDE

We arrived in August '69 and on the streets there was a feeling of fear that events were spiralling out of control. The main focus was on the Apprentice Boys parade in Derry, the annual ritual of the Orange commemoration of the Battle of the Boyne. And now, once again, nationalists in their own city had to allow the Orange bands to march through city streets near the Bogside with their sectarian hatred and vitriol, but the mood in the air was that enough was enough. The general consensus was that the parade should be banned or at least re-routed away from the Bogside, but that was never on the agenda for the loyal orders, or indeed the Unionist government; the parade would go ahead. In the Bogside, a defence committee was set up and preparations were made for the defence of the area in case of incursions by Orange mobs. There had been riots the previous months in Belfast, Dungiven, and Derry, and the RUC had battered two men, Samuel Devanny and Francis McCloskey. Both later died from their injuries, and both incidents infuriated the nationalist community. As a result, there was an eerie feeling of impending doom that August. On the day, the 15,000 strong parade set off as usual with their large banners commemorating various events in loyalist history: battles at Derry, Aughrim, Enniskillen, and the Boyne. The bands played loyalist tunes, 'Dolly's Brae' and the 'Sash my father wore', and the thousands of marchers were truly bedecked in their Orange sashes and bowler hats. They marched with a skip in their step as they proudly and defiantly paraded through this overwhelmingly nationalist city.

The rioting went on for two days. Bogside nationalists clashed with the RUC backed by loyalist mobs. Barricades were hastily made up to try and stop incursions of loyalists and RUC into the Bogside. Bricks and petrol bombs were flung at the police who replied with CS gas, baton charges, and armoured cars with machine guns. The battle became ferocious as youths climbed on top of the Rossville flats to drop stones and petrol bombs on top of the police lines. They gradually wore down the RUC who were flat out on their feet and short of replacements. Throughout the six counties, nationalists organised protests to take RUC men away from Derry and this began to have massive consequences when the focus moved to Belfast. On the 14th, events clearly spiralled out of control: the RUC were struggling to contain the rioting, buildings were burning, and the air was polluted by CS gas being fired indiscriminately. Loyalists in Derry responded to nationalist aggression by crossing the bridge and attempting to enter the Bogside but stiff resistance from its defenders proved effective. Meanwhile, world opinion was shifting and evolving around the pictures being flashed around the world. The six county statelet was imploding as unionism descended into turmoil. Their statelet, which had served them well for 50 years, was disintegrating before their eyes.

Over in London, the British Government was contemplating sending in troops but the Unionists objected. They felt from experience that they could control the situation but in all their years of dominance they had never experienced anything like this. Nationalist MPs were in contact with Westminster, while in Dublin the government sought to stem the rising tension by moving troops to the border and opening up refugee camps. The IRA, for their part, was prepared in a limited manner in Belfast to defend areas in danger from loyalist and RUC attack. In the Republic, the IRA leadership realised that, militarily, they were in no shape to defend nationalist areas. Indeed, under a new Marxist leadership, they had no intention of becoming involved in the conflict between working-class Protestants and Catholics. Their procrastination on the national question, however, would have serious repercussions for the organisation as a whole within the next year.

On the evening of the 13th August our Fianna group met up at a house on the Kashmir Road, close to Clonard Monastery, we were there to receive arms training but some senior figures came to the house and gave us a talk on the developing situation. We were told that the British Government would send in troops within the next few days and that the Irish Government was considering sending troops over the border. We discussed our part in defending the Lower Falls located in the immediate area and running parallel to the Shankill Road. Afterwards, we had another small arms lecture before being told we would split up and return to our own areas, but we had to keep in touch. This was easier said than done in the times that were in it, we had no iPhones, iPads, Laptops, no WWW; we relied on the 'bush telegraph'! As we left the house, we were apprehensive as RUC jeeps raced through the Kashmir area where, in 1942, Tom Williams, Joe Cahill et al attacked the RUC, killing one RUC man. The six arrested were all sentenced to death but five were reprieved as 18 year old Williams became the last IRA man to be hanged in Ireland, 'now he's marching to the scaffold, head erect he shows no fear', Belfast's Kevin Barry!

One of the young lads in our group was from the Lower Falls, Gerard McAuley, aged 15. Within 48 hours, he would find a space in history as the first republican to be killed in the modern conflict. He was the same age as the rest of us. I've often thought of him, how he never got the chance to live. I think of how much life I've experienced since his life was cut short. Close by, behind Clonard Monastery, loyalists were getting restless and making small incursions into the nationalist area. It was unusual as it had never happened previously in the 50 years since partition, but with RUC and B-Special connivance they were confident in their approach and smelled blood. It's difficult for people from other countries to comprehend but during the conflict, the RUC would collude with loyalist paramilitaries to try and defeat the IRA. They lived in Protestant areas, mixed with loyalists, and passed on information which led to the murder of innocent Catholics, It's a well-known fact. For nationalists and republicans it was a given that the RUC colluded with loyalists since partition, and when a British policeman, John Stalker, tried to investigate, they closed ranks against him and he was recalled to the UK whilst on the verge of a breakthrough. At the time, it was a strange situation: nationalists feared they were in danger from a loyalist pogrom similar to 1920, whereas loyalists felt that an IRA insurrection was about to take place. August 1969 was really the start of the conflict as a physical struggle, the first time the guns came out in Belfast, it had moved beyond civil rights. While there had been a string of incidents in the previous year, most were clashes between nationalists and the RUC and not involving guns. Now, we had both communities engaged in battle and for the first time guns appeared on the streets. With the UVF, IRA, and the RUC using arms — indeed, the RUC using machine guns on Shorland armoured cars — it resulted in the first deaths by gunfire, 9 year old child Patrick Rooney killed in his bedroom in the Divis Flats by shots from an RUC armoured car.

Marches were taking place across the six counties to take the pressure off Derry. Meanwhile, after our last meeting on the Kashmir Road we joined a protest march and attacks were made on Hastings St. and Springfield Road RUC stations. Ironically, Hastings St. was just opposite my old school, St Mary's. Loyalists had gathered at this stage on the streets running between the Falls and Shankill but held their ground, initially. On the Falls Road, the Isaac Agnew car dealership was set on fire as rioting continued, and as the night went on, barricades were erected all along the Falls. After a relatively peaceful night, the call again went out from Derry for support from other nationalist areas and crowds took to the Falls marching to Hastings St. barracks. As darkness fell, rioters attacked the RUC station with bricks and petrol bombs. At this stage, loyalists from the Shankill moved down Dover and Percy St. and a confrontation took place. Ironically, this happened not far from where Catholics and Protestants joined forces to march against the Stormont government in the 1930s in the hunger riots.

Events quickly got out of control as loyalists with B-Specials among their ranks pushed into the nationalist area and began burning houses that had been evacuated earlier. The RUC, faced up to the nationalists while, behind their ranks, loyalists burned streets to the ground. Nationalist youths on the Divis flats barraged RUC ranks with stones while the local IRA unit mobilised, albeit with limited weaponry. They tried to defend the Falls area but the RUC replied with heavy machine guns. Consequently, nine-year-old Patrick Rooney was killed in his bedroom and a local British soldier, Hugh McCabe, who was home on leave and helping to defend the flats was also killed. Riots were also taking place in Ardoyne which was particularly vulnerable as it was surrounded by loyalist areas. There, the RUC killed two more nationalists. They were desperate times and fears of a total massacre by armed loyalists with the connivance of the RUC and B-Specials had the nationalist community in a total panic. The IRA with its depleted ranks and weaponry did its best to defend the areas but hundreds of houses were burned and thousands had to flee. Many went to safer nationalist areas in the west of the city, others to the Republic where the government had organised refugee camps along the border. There has been an exaggerated urban myth surrounding the "I.R.A. I Ran Away' message painted on walls, likewise, the stories of Catholic women giving tea to the soldiers in '69, grossly exaggerated, they were a handful of women, and the reality was that if not for the handful of IRA volunteers, the Falls would have been burnt to the ground!

The IRA as a military force were badly depleted by years of inaction in the 60's and the politics of the leadership in Dublin, as streets were burned in Belfast many nationalists headed to the Republic, Dundalk, Bundoran, Buncrana, Dublin, Shannon and Cork, and created a cohort of 'nordies' which became permanent over the decades, a modern refugee crisis long before Syria!

We were back in our own area, Turf Lodge, at this stage. Barricades were erected on Monagh road — the main arterial route through the estate. The few IRA men there, Fianna boys, and any able-bodied men became vigilantes hoping to protect the area from loyalist attack even though there was relative safety in the strongly nationalist estates in the west of the city. The barricades were reinforced at all entrances to the estate and stockpiles of petrol bombs were in place. Rumours were flying that an attack might come from across the mountain during the night or that help was coming from the 'Free State'. Both proved to be just that: rumours. During the night, the RUC smashed through the main barricade and as the defenders scattered, the RUC men smashed the bottles of petrol or poured it down the steep slopes at the Monagh roundabout. While there was an eerie feeling throughout the night, it was still relatively safe in the estates of Ballymurphy, Turf Lodge, Andersonstown, St. James, and Beechmount, but the Lower Falls closest to the Shankill took the main brunt of the attack and there was more to come. During the afternoon of the 15th, loyalists attacked the Clonard area just off the Falls and while the monastery was protected by locals, several streets including the whole of Bombay Street was burned to the ground. It would eventually become a Provo symbol, the phoenix arising from the ashes. It was at this time, while defending Bombay St, that Fian Gerard McAuley was shot dead by a loyalist sniper not far from where we had attended the meeting a few days earlier. He was 15 years of age, the same age as myself. He became the first republican killed in what became 30 years of long war.

At around 6pm on the 15th of August, the first British troops arrived on the Falls Road. This temporary arrangement called 'Operation Banner' would turn out to be an almost 40-year long sojourn. Bitter decades of sectarian rioting, armed struggle, counter insurgency, 3500 deaths and almost 50,000 injured later, the troops would disappear off the streets. In their place remained a lot of pain and suffering on all sides. No conflict is nice, just death and destruction. It can corrupt everyone associated with it. There was a lukewarm welcome for British troops in nationalist areas. A handful of women gave them tea and buns, a compassionate offer from mothers to boys like their own sons domiciled in a foreign country, but it was short lived, and by Easter '70 the honeymoon period was over.

We were 15.We should have been starting to enjoy life, playing football, meeting girls, going to our first disco, maybe a little drink, holidaying in Donegal, concentrating on A-Levels, or beginning an apprenticeship. The world should have been our oyster, but instead we were thrown into an Armageddon not of our making. Our young lives would, of course, embrace events as did the kids of WWI, or Vietnam, or the War of Independence. Did we make the rational decision? Did we understand what we were letting ourselves into? Would we do it all over again if the same situation prevailed, who knows? Although, I suppose our 65-year-old selves would have a different perspective than our young 15-year-old selves, but we can never turn the clock back. It is what it is. As I write these words, I think of all the friends and comrades who didn't survive the conflict, and of all the innocent civilians who suffered and died in a conflict that they wanted nothing to do with. For all of us in a little part of the world called the six counties, we were destined to live through it as part of our domicile in that godforsaken part of the world.

We hadn't slept at all the night of the 15th, manning barricades, listening to transistor radios hourly to hear the latest news — and we were the news. Belfast was world news. The morning papers showed photos of the devastation in the Falls — whole streets burned to the ground. It was devastating and demoralising in terms of our identity. Loyalists had 'invaded' the Falls —something that had never happened previously, not even during the pogroms of the 1920s when the statelet was set up. Whilst Derry had been the focal point for the initial disturbances, they had fought the RUC to a standstill over 3 days. It wasn't until events shifted to Belfast that the guns came out. That was always the danger with the greater majority of loyalists living in the city with access to weapons through their membership of the B-

Specials and hundreds of gun clubs; there were 100,000 licensed guns in the 6 counties, mostly in loyalist hands. Eight people were killed over the few days in August '69, almost more than had been killed in the history of the northern state since the pogroms of '1920-'22. Under massive pressure from civic nationalism, the Church, and the Irish Government, the British Government sent troops into Belfast and Derry to try and stabilise events. The RUC were overrun in Derry and stretched to the limit throughout the six counties. The IRA were unable to defend nationalists in Belfast and the Irish Government had delivered a mealy-mouthed response to the predicament of nationalists with Taoiseach Jack Lynch, claiming on a live TV broadcast that 'we can no longer stand by' while nationalists were attacked, but did just exactly that. There were massive demonstrations in Dublin with people demanding guns to help nationalists in the 'north', while the seeds of a split in Government appeared as Charlie Haughey and Neil Blaney were sympathetic to the popular response from the people. Nonetheless, the government held firm albeit shedding the two ministers in the Arms trial the following year. The conflict created a major problem for Fianna Fail, the government party in the Republic more or less since partition. They claimed to be 'the republican party', the descendants of de Valera, Aiken, and Sean Lemass.They downed arms at the end of the Civil War claiming that when the time was opportune, Irish unity would be claimed again, yet now when the opportunity had presented itself, they were found wanting! Fianna Fail see themselves as the 'Republican Party' but have never made any effort to change the status quo, when the anti Treaty IRA downed arms at the end of the civil war in 1923 it was forever, three years later the majority morphed into Fianna Fail and would become the main player for the next fifty years, now they see the modern Sinn Fein espousing true republicanism akin to pre Treaty times, and FF especially condemn them constantly, afraid that what happened to the SDLP will happen to them?

The rioting ended in Belfast and Derry with the arrival of British troops. It was a strange situation here in a so called part of the UK, yet different in the extreme. We were white and English speaking, true enough. It wasn't Aden, Cyprus or Suez, about Arabs & Oil, young soldiers from Birmingham, Glasgow, and London facing up to young kids from the Shankill and Falls who looked and acted exactly the same. They probably supported the same football teams, Rangers & Liverpool, Celtic & ManU, and were into the Rolling Stones and the Beatles. Belfast, for all intents and purposes, resembled the working-class streets of Toxteth, Moss Side or Easterhouse left behind. Suddenly, they were thrust into the midst of an armed insurrection according to unionists, a loyalist pogrom according to nationalists, and virtually a civil war according to interested observers around the world.

On the 16th August, half a dozen of us, all Fianna boys, headed off down to the Lower Falls. No buses ran as many of the city buses had been burnt or used as barricades. We walked down past Andersonstown RUC station and positioned outside was a British Army Ferret armoured car. It was the first sight of this new addition to our young lives: the presence of British soldiers on our streets. Myself, Paddy Smith, aka 'Big Hack', and Marty Kavanagh et al, headed down from the estate past Andytown barracks, we went down past the bottom of the Whiterock which leads to Ballymurphy, past St James's, Beechmount, Broadway, the Royal Victoria Hospital (RVH), and then the junction of the Grosvenor and Springfield to enter the Lower Falls. What lay before us was virtually beyond comprehension: every street which led into the warren of two up, two down houses which made up the Lower Falls was barricaded. Meanwhile, on the other side of the road running parallel with the Shankill there was devastation.

At the back of Clonard monastery, Bombay St. was burned to the ground. Further down, Percy St, Dover St., and Conway St. met the same fate. It was like a scene from WW2 as people returned to try and salvage anything from their destroyed homes. It was a pitiful sight — the horror of community violence, virtual civil war, religious bigotry. Thousands moved to safer areas in West Belfast or across the border, many never came back. After 50 years, the six counties had imploded. Nationalists were virtually defenceless whereas loyalists were armed to the teeth; that was why there was little or no resistance to Stormont for 50 years. The IRA were weak before August '69, and hope for support from the Irish Army never materialised through lack of a backbone from Lynch and the Irish Government.

Partition, which had copper-fastened a sectarian unionist statelet, was staring into a day of reckoning. We went from street to street, barricade to barricade, carrying hurls with us in case of attack; they attracted strange looks from young soldiers who had never seen them before. They probably surmised them to be an offensive weapon but didn't bother us. Crowds milled around everywhere: women trying to get some bread and milk in, kids talking to the soldiers, older men guarding the barricades. On the surface, they were the defence committees that had quickly been set up. In reality, they were IRA volunteers and Auxiliaries (reserve volunteers), although many would just be ordinary civilians intent on defending their homes. The army commander would engage with them and try to talk the barricades down but for the moment they would stay in situ.

Despite the 'armageddon', our little world soon retreated into a form of ordinary life as it does when left alone. The army's arrival had ended the riots and, actually, some within the nationalist community welcomed them with open arms as saviours from the loyalist beasts, RUC and B-Specials. The kids were fascinated by the soldiers' rifles as kids would be, and the local teenage girls would just be fascinated by the soldiers, as teenage girls would be. All of this would be a massive conundrum for republicans and the IRA — especially as their raison d'être, of course, was to rid the country of British forces and create Irish unity. However, their mythical image as the defenders of the nationalist community had taken a massive hit during those weeks in August '69. The reality was that in 1969 there was no IRA worth talking about. The actions of the Army Council in Dublin who had run down the military side after the failure of the border campaign between'56 and '62, and the influence of Marxist thinkers like Roy Johnston et al, along with the lack of military capacity to defend republican areas lead to the major split in the republican movement which would take place in due course. Of course, August '69 could have been much worse if not for the defiant actions by the few IRA volunteers who were on the streets around the Falls. At St.Comgall's school and Divis flats, they passed rifles around to make it appear that a greater IRA presence was in place. That they weren't was due to their Marxist leadership, an entity that embraced the socialist politics of the Protestant and Catholic working-class in the hope of joining together to defeat capitalism and form a new workers republic. Laudable and all as these ideals were as we have seen in Bosnia, Croatia, and Serbia, when deep-seated nationalist feelings mix with religion it creates a monster. And you can't protest with your placard when your enemy has a heavy machine gun. The split in the IRA was brought about by the events of August '69. The old guys from the '40s and '50s who had left the movement after the disaster of the border campaign came back in droves. They helped form the Provos, favouring abstentionism not Marxist ideology, and their non recognition of the partitioned parliaments helped steer the politics, events in Belfast brought about the split.

Before we move off from August '69, a few significant events occurred which had as much impact on my young life as the arrival of the British Army on our streets. Around the annual bonfire, a few cans in hand, I met a pretty red-haired girl who would turn out to be my first real girlfriend, Madeleine. We were both 15, she was fun, easy to communicate with, attractive. For the next three years we would hold hands, go for walks, snog behind the flats. It was our first real relationship with the opposite sex, and she was a lovely person to know from a decent family. Her dad, Jackie, was a Republican Labour Cllr. on Belfast City Council; but as in most youthful relationships it was destined to end in failure. We've only met once in over 40 years, at her dad's wake. Funny, but it was like we had always known each other. Such is the way of friends from our youth. Coincidentally, later on the same night in '69, we called up to a house with a tricolour hanging outside and some rebel music being played loudly on the old record player, 'Sean South from Garryowen' and 'the Lonely Woods of Upton'. It was still raining, and after midnight the wee woman of the house came out and invited us in for a cup of tea and shelter from the rain. It's funny how fate can work in life. A decade later, old Rita would become my mother-in-law as I married her daughter, but there was a lot of life to live before that.

A relative calm descended over Belfast and Derry as we entered September and October '69. A re-adjusting of positions took place all around. Getting used to foreign soldiers on our streets was an interesting experience. There was a kind of 'honeymoon period' as General Freeland would dub it later. There was no aggression between nationalists and the army, but from the loyalist side aggression became commonplace. It was a strange situation with the normal positions reversed: forever and a day we were the rebels, anti-British, and they were the loyal servants of the crown. Now, there was a sense of antagonism from loyalist areas, a sort of feeling that if they had been left to it they would have sorted out the problem of disgruntled and thankless fenians once and for all. That this would have involved ethnic cleansing of Serbian proportions wasn't considered relevant to the theory. The comparison with the former Yugoslavia is relevant in terms of the Srebrenica massacre. I could also mention Shatila and Sabra in Lebanon earlier. In 1969, there was a fear in Belfast among nationalists that there could have been a mass slaughter in the Falls, thus the request for the Irish Army to cross the Border.

Nationalists were a little confused by the situation. There was a sort of grateful recognition that the army had averted a tragedy of epic proportions and the hated RUC and B-Specials were removed from our areas. Something about the situation was confusing, although it would be six months before our community would understand that the army didn't arrive to help save nationalism from annihilation but to do what armies the world over do: to preserve the status quo. In this case, the Union, as well as returning the streets to normality. Unfortunately for them, and probably for society as a whole, it would take 40 years.

Unity Flats is a small nationalist enclave at the foot of the Shankill Road, a storied loyalist area of Belfast. It was always a flashpoint since partition, and before, originally known as Carrick Hill, it was a staunchly republican area within inner-city, working-class Belfast. Regularly Carrick Hill residents would have to batten down the hatches as the Orange Order would march by, or when the Linfield fans headed to Windsor, and as each passed by the drums would beat louder. The profanities would increase as they sang 'up to their knees in fenian blood'. Saturdays in Belfast wasn't just for shopping! On the 11th of October, resentment toward the army on the Shankill increased so much that protests turned into riots, and as is the way in Belfast, the guns came out again. Loyalists had been unsettled since the turmoil of August '69 and resented the Army holding the line between both communities. Two loyalists were shot dead as, once again, Unity flats became the target for naked sectarian aggression. Loyalists gathered in their thousands and the RUC, this time with the eyes of the world on them, created a buffer zone between the lower Shankill and Unity Flats. As the news spread that the flats were under attack, four of us, all Fianna boys, decided to head over, not knowing what we could do but away we went. One of the first people I met was a young guy called 'Whitey' Bradley who previously lived in Turf Lodge, but his family were originally from Carrick Hill and moved back, as many did, over the years. 'Whitey' was also in the Fianna and along with local IRA volunteers, they were monitoring the situation in case the loyalists broke through RUC ranks. My memory of that night was the size of the loyalist crowd. I've never seen so many people in my life; there were thousands upon thousands. To be honest, it was frightening, and if they had managed to break through, God knows what would have happened at Unity flats, although a few armed men in strategic positions can soon disperse an undisciplined crowd of rabble, these were scary days. I never saw 'Whitey' again after that, although our lives would take shape in a similar pattern. He will return to the story in a tragic way 40 years later.

As the night progressed, we returned to the Lower Falls, up the Whiterock, and back to Turf Lodge. In the morning, we heard on the news that the first RUC man to be killed in the 'Troubles' — Constable Victor Arbuckle had been shot later that night, ironically on the Shankill by loyalists, they were protesting at the Hunt Report which recommended the disbandment of the 'B' Specials, disarming the RUC and creating the UDR. Arbuckle would be the first of over 300 RUC men who would be slain during the conflict. Put into context, only 90 were killed in 1920-22 as partition was introduced, although another 300 RIC men were killed throughout the country in the War of Independence. At that stage, we weren't used to death but there was a feeling that things were developing dangerously, and nobody knew what the eventual outcome would be.

I returned to work in Lavery's Bar down off the city centre and life took on a relative sort of normality. I remember clearly on New Year's Day, walking up from the shops to our estate and looking at the paper and the date was '1st January 1970'. It jumped out at me and does still as I reflect back now 50 years later. It was only 25 years since the end of WW2. To us that was history and I understood when I went back to university in later years that for young students in the 'noughties', the hunger strikes and the 1st Gulf War were history to them.

Before we leave 1969, we couldn't but remember the one event that will forever be recalled as: "one small step for man, one great leap for mankind." As Neil Armstrong became the first man from the old planet of Earth to set foot on the Moon, the Apollo Eagle landed in the Sea of Tranquillity and a few years later Alan Shepard hit a 6 Iron across the lunar 'fairway! The Moon landing was world news, and although we all watched it on television as avidly as a Cape Canaveral nerdy, the antics of the Orange Order and the imminent arrival of the heroes of Arnhem was concentrating our minds somewhat more. The 1st Airborne Division–1 Para would become major players during the conflict, especially in Derry and Ballymurphy. The Yanks achieving utopia before the Russians was heralded as a great achievement in the West; that it cost more than would have ended poverty in the 3rd world was conveniently overlooked.

In the real world, we were in awe of those wee VC fighting the Yanks in Vietnam, French students at the Sorbonne, Che dying a lonely death in Bolivia: in sport AC Milan defeated Celtic in Europe and Rod Laver lifted a tennis Grand Slam, Tony Jacklin won the Open at Lytham, the first Brit since Portrush in 1951, the last time Mayo won 'Sam'; coincidentally the Open was back in 2019 and Shane Lowry blew the world golf elite away as the 'Fields of Athenry' echoed around Royal Portrush's famous links. On the 3rd Sunday in September, just a month after the Falls burning and the Battle of the Bogside Marty Kavanagh and I made the journey to Dublin by train for the All Ireland football final in 1969 between Kerry and Offaly. There were almost 70,000 in attendance, and for our troubles loyalists attacked the train at Portadown on the way back and we had to get off at Balmoral as a large crowd of loyalists had gathered at the station in Great Victoria St. awaiting our return, ironically the same happened in 1864 as nationalists returned from a Daniel O'Connell commemoration in Dublin, loyalists from Sandy Row were waiting and attacked those leaving the train, 105 years later we were the victims of the same sectarian behaviour, two steps forward one step back!

We were also playing a lot of football ourselves, that is, the foreign game as opposed to the GAA as there was no club in Turf Lodge. On one eventful day, we played Rosario, Martin O'Neill's club, on their way to a second league title in a row. We kicked our way to a 3-2 victory, their only defeat in the whole season, but it didn't deter O'Neill from having a stellar career in the 'beautiful game' despite coming from a serious GAA background in Derry. On another occasion, which is quite funny when you look back on it, the army in that first six months were in community relations mode and asked our manager, Bob Fennell, if our team would play the army team in a spirit of sporting goodwill. We, of course, as footballers took on the challenge with enthusiasm but the match was cancelled as some budding revolutionaries cut down the goalposts the night before the game as a protest against fraternising with 'an occupation army'. James Connolly, an ex British soldier, might have turned in his grave at the perceived lack of working-class solidarity.

The following week we took it a step further and played the game at their base in Aldergrove, the old airport, where we whipped them 10-1 and kicked a few men into the bargain; we were beginning to enjoy this anti-imperialist gig. Around this time, my budding football career might have taken off. Pat Smyth and I were approached by a Distillery talent spotter who was a local referee and asked to go down to Grosvenor Park, home of Distillery, for trials. Between the jigs and the reels, however, we never made it. Football wasn't the most important thing on our minds at the time. Distillery while not exactly Real Madrid although both played in all white, were our local team since the demise of Belfast Celtic; during the 70's their ground, Grosvenor Park, was burnt and abandoned and they moved to Lisburn. One of our teammates, Brendan Tully, did make a fist of his football ability. He went on trial to Bangor where his uncle was the manager, the famous ex-Celtic player, Charlie Tully. Charles Patrick was a legend in Glasgow and a genius footballer who used to sit on the ball in games with Rangers and famously scored a goal from a corner twice after the first was disallowed. He also coined the tale about meeting the Pope on a Celtic tour in Italy where someone in the crowd in the Vatican looking up asked: "Who's that with Charlie Tully?" Whatever about that, he gave Brendan a chance in football and he had a decent career in Irish football with Portadown, Drogheda, and Donegal Celtic: the only one among us to do so.

1970 – THE TORIES ARE BACK – WE'RE DOOMED.

1970 came in with a vigour that felt like we were entering a new era as it would obviously do if you're 16. The big bad world was out there for us: work, money, girls, discos, and drink. In retrospect, it was ridiculous. We should still have been at school studying for our A-Levels but the dropout rate in working-class Belfast was high, probably similar to Ballymun today. As it was in north inner-city Dublin, the kids on the Shankill suffered as much as ourselves while the kids on the Malone Road had the same 99% progression rate to 3rd Level as their counterparts in Ballsbridge. After the disaster of August '69 for the IRA, a split took place within the organisation. A more militant tendency evolved within the group, the same group who had been side-lined throughout the 1960's split from the mainstream movement over abstentionism and the lack of military defence on the Falls. In popular history, they became known as the Provisionals while those who stayed loyal to the southern leadership became the 'Officials': in colloquial terms, they were the 'Provos' and the 'Stickies'.

In January, Sinn Féin also split and took a totally different political position from Official Sinn Fein. The split would define how events would pan out over the next decade. Ruairi O'Bradaigh became the president of Provisional Sinn Féin and the policy of abstentionism was copper fastened. Ironically, 15 years later, O'Bradaigh would lead another split over the very same issue as the IRA and Sinn Féin moved to adopt the ballot box and Armalite policy! The 1970 split wouldn't entirely be a political division and various feuds and deaths would take place in the future. Both sides, especially in Belfast, went on a major recruiting campaign with the Provos becoming the recipient of major numbers of disaffected youth who, while maybe not in the tradition of republicanism, were intent on hitting back at the state and loyalists who had inflicted terror and death on their communities with devastating results back in August '69. A more troubling aspect from a young testosterone-fuelled male point of view was the fact that our local girls appeared to find the lure of a guy in uniform very attractive. British soldiers, to wax lyrical, the ancient Saxon foe, we felt, under the guise of community relations would lure our young Catholic 'virgins' to a 'den of inequity' in a local barracks for a disco. This led to some disquiet and some girls found themselves tied to a lamppost, their heads shaved, tar and feathers poured over them and labelled as soldier lovers, bit harsh for a snog in the park but this was 1970's Belfast!

On St Patrick's Day 1970, there was a massive parade up the Falls Road, nothing unusual, you'd think, but this was Belfast. It was probably the only city council in the world who didn't organise a parade, so the community organised their own colourful show. As we marched by the Royal Victoria Hospital we noticed a Union Jack flying from a parapet on an upper floor. The parade stalled and a group of us shimmied up to the ledge to remove the 'Butchers Apron', a reference to England's colonial past, it was never flown there again. The discos continued but became a focus of protest, and at Easter 1970 the place erupted in anti-British Army sentiment. A week of riots took place in Ballymurphy with a nightly occurrence of petrol bombs, bricks, bottles, and snatch squads. Soldiers made a sortie into the ranks of rioters and like the slow guy running from the tiger in the Billy Connolly story, the guys who didn't make the cut for the 100-yard sprint at school were hauled off to the Henry Taggart barracks for a bit of a kicking for spoiling the soldiers' disco or watching Match of the Day. But the riots were a serious indication that things were changing. Bloody hand-to-hand battles with soldiers took place, along with serious amounts of CS Gas fired which engulfed the whole area. Thousands took to the streets to the consternation of a new fledgling IRA who were reorganising behind the barricades and training under the radar. To be honest, the IRA much more than the army quelled the riots by the end of the week.

People travelled to Ballymurphy from all over Belfast, similar to Derry where the Bogside was having nightly experiences similar to Ballymurphy. Rioting became a regular part of our lives, in fact, sometimes I wonder what we would have done if things had been different. But that's all by the by. It was what it was, just another quirk of fate that fed into our young Falls Road lives. We were 16 for God's sake, what else could we have done while the place became embroiled in massive street disturbances? But to be honest, the most amazing thing was our fearless response to the presence of British soldiers on our streets when, a year or two earlier, if one RUC man arrived and told us not to play football in the street we would have calmly accepted. Now, we faced up to the heroes of Gallipoli and Suvla Bay without a moment's thought. Lobbing petrol bombs; Molotov cocktails was a bit of trendy revolutionary for us. We just hijacked the milk van and took crates of empty bottles to the nearest garage. There, we'd fill them with petrol and that morning's Irish News petrol-soaked and ignited like an Apollo 10 booster as it flew through the air at the nearest squaddie. Sure, it would have made a PlayStation or Xbox game as boring as mass on a Sunday — that's if you went to mass which most of us were inclined to skip (unbeknownst to our mums.) Pope John Paul 23rd might have revolutionised the church for the 20th century, but Che Guevara and Georgie Best were our poster boys.

The Ballymurphy riots were a turning point in our relationship with the British Army; it was the point of no return. There would be no more tea, no more friendly collaboration. The IRA mightn't have been ready to take them on but on the streets, we were ready in our thousands. For the next year, it became an almost everyday occurrence: they would enter the estate on foot patrol, maybe 100 strong, and were met with the sound of women banging bin lids, dogs barking, and a feral youth launching attacks with whatever was at hand to throw at an army who were totally inept at their job of containing street disturbances. Like all armies, they were paid killers trained to fight full-scale wars with tanks, aeroplanes, heavy machine guns, and parachute behind enemy lines — but this was different: this was street-to-street rioting in a so-called democratic entity of white-skinned English speakers. We weren't Arabs or Africans, but we were different. There may have been slight amazement that the nationalist population turned against the British Army, but in reality, it was a no brainer if you know Irish history. They were never friends of nationalism — and in 1970 they returned to type and became aggressors.

Belfast was a city allegedly part of the UK, but in Ireland. We were definitely not 'as British as Finchley' to paraphrase the 'grocer's daughter' Thatcher! During the months of 1970, I combined my bar duties down the city centre with my ongoing relationship with Madeleine and the fairly regular encounters with British soldiers: the King's Own Scottish Borderers, the Royal Anglicans, the Marine Commandos, and the Royal Scots. They were a bit of a mish-mash of career soldiers and unemployed kids mixed with every scumbag who avoided a jail sentence in the UK by volunteering for service in the Armed forces. There were posters in job centres in Birmingham or Brixton suggesting that an army career would bring them skiing in the Alps or kayaking in the Algarve. In reality they would face, as Billy Connolly would say, 'the biggest laxative known to man, being part of a foot patrol on the Falls Road'.

In the football world Celtic had qualified for a second European Cup final in three years, and as I had been at Hampden for the semi-final v Leeds in a record European crowd of 136,500, I thought I might try and go to the final in Milan. In those pre-Ryanair days, the world wasn't such a small place and my £6-a-week pay packet wasn't conducive to travelling further than Donegal or Glasgow — but it was a dream. In the bar, we used to have a group of shipyard workers who frequented the back bar on a Friday evening drinking copious pints of single X, a Belfast delicacy for the working class. They complimented it with a dish which would tempt the palate of a shipwright, welder, or red leader after a week painting on those big ships — pig's feet or crubeens. The big shipyard men loved them and I even tasted a few myself. When these guys heard that I was thinking of going to Milan they said they would have a whip-round for me to pay the flight. The amazing thing was that they were all Linfield/Rangers men to a fault, but I never once sensed a bigot among them. It was a magnanimous gesture which I always appreciated in those difficult days on the streets, that I didn't make it to Milan didn't take away from their honest gesture, it highlights that sectarianism is a disgusting human condition and that it can, and ought to be eradicated.

After Ballymurphy, the commander of Land Forces, General Sir Ian Freeland, issued a warning that petrol bombers would be shot dead. It had about the same effect that Harold Wilson had when he called the loyalists 'Spongers' in 1974.The price of petrol must have increased without Saudi intervention, such was the number of petrol bombs which cascaded down on foot patrols and armoured vehicles in the ensuing months. Freeland must have thought we didn't understand plain English which was, well, partially right as we didn't accept middle-class Sandhurst graduates with their toffee-nosed approach to the natives. His troops would continue to be petrol bombed, his threat to shoot us ignored, and his patience to accept it became thin. Ballymurphy, Derry, and the New Lodge lay ahead after which his 'honeymoon' period would definitely be over. Around April, new legislation brought to an end the existence of the hated B-Specials, a reserve police force entirely loyalist in place since partition. They had a mythical status in the six counties as defenders of the status quo; their very presence in nationalist rural areas brought apprehension. Their demise brought dismay to unionists and a great welcome from nationalists.

At the same time, the RUC were disarmed and the UDR was created as a new local based British Army regiment who, not surprisingly, filled their ranks with ex-B Specials who would play a major part in sectarian assassinations during the conflict to come. Initially, it was meant to be a cross-community exercise and at the start, some nationalists joined the regiment. I actually remember one guy walking through our estate in his sparkling brand new uniform, whatever happened to him, God knows, I never saw him or anyone else wearing the UDR uniform again. In the Republic, they were having their own repercussions from August 1969. Government Ministers Neil Blaney and Charlie Haughey, Irish Army Captain James Kelly, IRA leader John Kelly et al were charged with attempting to smuggle arms into the six counties and the Arms trial became the biggest political issue ever in the Republic. It had been a delicate situation in August '69 and if those involved in the 'Arms Trial' possibly had got their way, Irish troops might have been sent into the six counties to protect nationalists. What would have happened is still open to conjecture but it would definitely have created an international situation involving the UN.

Jack Lynch got wind of the manoeuvrings and took steps to prevent it, somehow whilst 'standing idly by' — a misquote of historical significance. The anti-Treaty ceasefire of 1924 and the founding of Fianna Fáil in 1926 would leave nationalists in the six counties isolated. 45 years of rhetoric about unity from 'the Republican Party' would prove to be just that when found wanting in August 1969. Moves were made post August '69 to move Irish Army weapons closer to the border in case of a doomsday situation in the sixcounties.The whole story has been cast in mystery ever since, although a recent book by former RTÉ man, Michael Heney, and the documentary and podcast 'Gun Plot' have thrown open the suggestion that Jack Lynch was aware all along but that Haughey and Blaney were made scapegoats along with Captain Kelly. Eventually, all were cleared but Haughey and Blaney were isolated within FF. Regardless, Haughey would later become party Leader whilst Blaney would found his own Independent Fianna Fail which became a powerhouse in Donegal and an achilles heel to FF over the next three decades; Capt Kelly was ostracised by the Irish Army and vilified over the years and died without ever getting an apology from the Irish Govt; John Kelly became a future leader of the Provisional IRA during the conflict.

History is full of 'if's and but's', however, we will never know what would have happened if the two FF icons had got their way. Would we have had civil war or would we have been spared 30 years of 'armed struggle'? These are imponderables to which we can never ever know the answers. What we do know is that we had 30 years of death and destruction before peace returned with the Good Friday Agreement.

A very fragile and tense situation was soon going to be severely tested as the marching season loomed. — this unique time in which the six counties and the Orange Order commemorated the Battle of the Boyne. In early June, the nightly riots were creating a volatile situation and it wasn't helped that the Tories returned to power after a Westminster election. As it turned out, it was the last thing we needed. With the Tories aligned to the unionists as much then as in 1912 or in 2020, it wouldn't take long for the change to impact Belfast. It was like adding a detonator to the semtex.

On the weekend of the 27th June, the Orangemen were beginning the lead up to the '12th' with smaller parades taking place all over Belfast. In the New Barnsley estate facing Ballymurphy, a mixed estate, an Orange band struck up their drums and flutes and marched out of the estate to the disgust of their catholic neighbours. One thing was for sure, they wouldn't be walking back ever again. As their petty coat-trailing 'Kick the Pope' band led a few hundred Orangemen down the Springfield, while they weren't attacked, the nationalist crowds that had gathered vented their anger on the local RUC station which had been set up in a house at the front of the estate. It was intended as a temporary arrangement for the new community policing set up in recent times.

As the crowds surged towards the police station it became apparent that the place was deserted and the few RUC men inside had abandoned the place, or that was what we thought. As Fianna boys, we were in the forefront of the attack on the station. Windows were smashed, doors kicked in, and entry to the empty station was achieved with ease after which the place was ransacked. Police files, phones, caps, and jackets were tossed into the street and, funnily enough, their small portable TV to the cheers of fellow rioters. The crowd then moved further down the Springfield to the Henry Taggart Hall which had been turned into a British Army base. In these early days it just had a low wall, a far cry from the fortified structures they would become later on. The assembled masses, now thousands at this stage, attacked the base, kicking open the doors where they found the place full of soldiers off duty. A maelstrom of bottles and stones were launched at them while they scrambled to pull on army fatigues and grab their rifles. Outside, military jeeps were taken and driven out of the base and up the road. It was sort of mayhem as some people thought it was the army and attacked them before realising the mistake and then set about burning them.

The army got their act together and soon were on the road firing gas and rubber bullets as the riot intensified. Reinforcements arrived and we were scattered down into Ballymurphy and the rioting continued. Word came to us that the larger parade further down the Springfield that had left New Barnsley far earlier had come under attack. Serious rioting was taking place near the Kashmir road in Clonard — my big mate 'Hack' got hit by a rubber bullet. Then, news started to arrive that serious rioting was taking place in the Ardoyne and across the bridge in the Short Strand area, a small nationalist area in loyalist East Belfast which had been attacked every decade since partition in 1920. From news reports, it appeared that the whole city was in flames, and it literally was in Turf Lodge where the only hotel in West Belfast, the Alverno, was burnt to the ground during the rioting. The Alverno was a lovely hotel which, at one stage, would have been in the countryside before the new estates were built post-WW2, famously, the Beatles allegedly stayed there during their Irish tour in 1965, although no one actually saw John, Paul, Ringo and George?

The rioting continued around the hotel which was right in the middle between the ranks of rioters and soldiers. This led to many of the rioters entering the hotel demanding empty bottles for missiles only to be refused by the owner. As local folklore goes, the advance party of local youths then put a torch to the only 4-star hotel on this side of the city. It wasn't long before the Alverno went up in flames and that weekend's wedding was put on the backburner. Like the Titanic disappearing into the cold sea, the Alverno also disappeared from the Black Mountain skyline, never to reappear. In future years, it would be replaced by an eyesore in comparison: a British Army fort. As the day went on, the army and RUC were stretched which led to later accusations that the Short Strand was abandoned to its own devices against thousands of loyalists. As night fell, the Ardoyne and Short Strand came under serious attack; it has entered republican folklore as the night the Provisional IRA made an initial appearance on the scene. Units were sent to both areas to defend them but defence turned into an attack and in a reversal of August '69, it was loyalism that took a hit with six attackers killed as they attempted to burn down St Matthew's chapel. One IRA Auxiliary member was also killed.

This was the first time that the new Provisional IRA flexed its muscle and it helped remove any lingering doubt that the IRA were capable of defending nationalist areas. The riots and shooting continued throughout the night on into the next day. In response, 500 Catholic workers from the Harland&Wolff shipyard were expelled under the threat, a scene witnessed previously in 1920 during the pogroms after partition. Belfast was living through hell once again.

That weekend in June 1970 really saw Belfast descend into a conflict scenario. It had always been thus, of course: there had been sectarian riots in the 1860s, 1920s, 1930s, and now the 1970s. The riots took on the form of sectarian community violence but all were linked to the national question — it was an unfortunate quirk of history that religion was linked to it. Ulster like Scotland had embraced the Reformation and extremists like Jean Calvin and John Knox, their brand of religious bigotry helped create the sectarianism which bedevils Belfast and Glasgow to the present day. In the 1800's the waves of Catholic migrants to the protestant cities post Famine helped fan this situation, although the initial plantation of Ulster by Scottish loyalists must be regarded as the starting point. The Home Rule debate, the setting up of the statelet of NI, and the modern 'troubles' found both Irish nationalist and Ulster unionist communities on either side of the public debate. Partition was the literal division that would mould the modern country we live in. The division of the country had created a partitionist mentality on both sides of the border; it's an unfortunate by-product of partition.

In August '69 that sectarian history provided the powder keg atmosphere which had Protestants and Catholics clashing across the divisions in society. On a more immediate question for us, our group of Fianna members had divided along the split lines between the Provisionals and Officials, the majority staying with the latter. We would still remain friends, although it became bitter as the years went on. While people like Roy Johnston had influenced Cathal Goulding and Sean Garland towards a Marxist movement, it's forgotten that most of the young 'Official' volunteers in Belfast were just the same as young Provos. They weren't committed Marxist revolutionaries but reactionary street kids who joined and wanted to be on the streets taking on the British Army and loyalists, but their leadership would sell their soul to Dr. Faustus. Several years later, many of the committed street fighters would morph into the new INLA which the 'Stickies' tried to strangle at birth!

At the time, our focus was on the weekly, even nightly, rioting. Although we could be going around the doors selling the republican paper, the 'United Irishman', political activity was a bit scarce as both sides adapted to the new scenario. Most of my friends became 'Stickies', or Official IRA, including Jimmy, Adam, Marty, Hack et al. Many of the others just dropped away. A few of us eventually would morph into the fledgling Provo youth wing, but in those early days learning a bit of Irish history or learning to march in formation would be in vogue as well as flinging the odd petrol bomb at night. Norman, Micky and Kevi were another three friends who, while not part of the group, would be in our company fairly regularly. Kevin and Micky lived just across the street from each other and would have been part of the group who used to cross the city for the football. Norman was a good guy; he made the best 'guiders' when we were younger. His skills with his hands got him a job in construction and he had a nice girlfriend, a Protestant from across the city. Of all the boys, he was the one who didn't really get involved in any of the madness that was going on. He would rarely be involved in the rioting and definitely didn't get involved in any of the armed groups who were reorganising behind the scenes. The three of them will come back into the story later on, all with tragic circumstances.

The following week, late June '70, the city was simmering and on the verge of revolt. The Tories were back in power and Reginald Maudling, like a colonial governor of old, was making the kind of noises that suited those in favour of the Union, leaving our community dismayed. On the streets, there had been a slow re-emergence of the 'new' RUC into nationalist areas as I found to my surprise one morning coming back from the bakery with some Belfast baps for the breakfast. Suddenly, an RUC car pulled up and two burly custodians of the peace leapt out. In a split second, I assumed they didn't want a friendly chat and took to my heels, the baps and caps flying through the air as I disappeared down the entry next to Gallagher's, running through our neighbours' gardens and vaulting fences head first to flee my pursuers. It wouldn't be the last time I used that particular escape route over the coming years. To be honest, I wasn't sure why I ran but as I told a Gardai golf friend of mine many years later, when the RUC came to front doors where we lived, we usually fled out the back door. It was a historical thing, given that community 'Sgt friendly' they were not. I had survived the long arm of the law thus far, but it wouldn't be long until I found myself within their grasp just a few days later.

The following Friday, 3rd July '70, the army poured into the Lower Falls, hundreds of them in Saracen armoured cars sealing off a square mile of streets within a triangle between the Grosvenor Road, Falls, and Divis. The Tories had returned to power and this was an exercise to appease their unionist friends at Stormont. They began raiding houses mostly centred on the Leeson St. area. Large scale rioting soon spread around the area as evening moved into darkness. Once again, the guns came out and both wings of the IRA engaged soldiers in gun battles during the night and the army declared a curfew which was to last 48 hours. Imagine a curfew denying people the right to move in their own streets in a modern European city in 1970? We just managed to get outside the curfew area and continued rioting across the Grosvenor junction for several hours before heading back up the Whiterock through Ballymurphy where we met a young Gerry Adams. He told us that further rioting was futile and that there would be more advantageous opportunities in the future. As always, he had clarity of thought which would prove correct. Gerry Adams was, then, a young political activist, organiser, planner, thinker, and future leader. Before August '69, he was a barman just as I was down the city centre, and a few years before me, he was also an 11+ 'graduate' at St Mary's Grammar in Barrack St. In due course, we would be resident boarders at that esteemed college of higher education, Long Kesh.

The curfew would continue through Saturday into Sunday with violent clashes and the army uncovering arms caches throughout the lower Falls area. It appeared like a lesson was being taught to nationalists from the new Tory government, that they wouldn't tolerate continued opposition to the unionist junta at Stormont. The Falls curfew was the first major mistake the Tory Govt and Army made, one that would turn an already difficult situation into a lost cause. To compound matters, another six people were killed during the curfew, all shot by the army. After Ballymurphy, this was the beginning of the end of the 'Honeymoon' period.

On Saturday morning, 4th July, I was walking down the Falls to work as there were no buses; once again, they had made great barricades the previous night. As I passed the Falls Park, sort of reading the Irish News sports page as I went, I noticed an army checkpoint up ahead but didn't pay much attention when all of a sudden, half a dozen squaddies surrounded me and a big burly 'Trevor' (a colloquial nationalist term for RUC officers) grabbed me by the hair."You wee fcuker, get into the jeep."He landed me on my arse in the back of the jeep and headed to Andersonstown RUC station further back up the road. Once inside, things became a little clearer. 'Trevor' said that I was being charged with attacking New Barnsley RUC station the previous week. Apparently, he had spotted me from the upstairs window. They had then hidden under the bed rather than run away as we had presumed that day. He then whacked me around the head a few times saying that this nonsense was coming to an end, that the army was in complete control further down the Falls, that guns were being tossed out over walls and normality would soon prevail. Of course, he was being slightly disingenuous with his interpretation of events. I also thought to myself that if we had known he was hiding up the stairs in the RUC station the previous week, he mightn't have survived to adopt a superior attitude beyond that day; it was my first and last time inside the barracks which, in the modern era, has been demolished. A remembrance park was created in its place in honour of two stalwart local women who highlighted injustice in the community over the years. Van the Man sang, 'there will be days like this'. For us, they couldn't come quick enough and for Reginald Maudling things appeared even worse. Boarding a flight out of Belfast, he allegedly commented, "For God's sake, give me a large Scotch. What a bloody awful country."

The curfew ended on Sunday when thousands of women marched to the Lower Falls from all over Belfast and swept by the army checkpoints bringing milk and bread to the beleaguered mothers of the area. They covertly smuggled guns out of the area in prams as the army started to withdraw, but not before they drove a unionist government minister through the area to inspire a fit of pique and push the 'Croppies lie down' message home. The rest of the summer saw occasional riots and, for the first time, the name Crossmaglen came to prominence when two RUC men were blown up in a landmine explosion. Crossmaglen would become synonymous with the conflict over the years. In November, the IRA made a public statement of intent that things were changing in every aspect of life. Two local gangsters were shot dead in Ballymurphy after repeatedly being warned about anti-social behaviour. It sent a message out that behaviour which was against the community's interests wouldn't be tolerated, and that there was a new authority in town. These shootings were part of introducing a new way to community life as the conflict began. This was an example to all gangsters that the old ways wouldn't be accepted anymore. Interestingly as in all big cities there were hard men in tough working class areas, but as the conflict developed they were less inclined to get involved with the various groups, it exposed them for what they were in society, just bullies!

We hadn't a proper police force, so the IRA had to take over. For most of the conflict, the IRA auxiliaries acted as a form of 'police' utilizing kneecappings and punishment beatings. While not ideal, they had community support. Drugs were scarce within the community in the 70's unlike now where the place is awash with them and 'hoods' (young crooks) have a free hand without fear of punishment. It was a drain on resources and a distraction. Brendan O'Callaghan, an IRA volunteer and friend, was killed by the army as he went into the Whitefort Inn to take a 'hood' out for punishment in later years.

Policing the community placed a heavy responsibility on the IRA and exposed volunteers to unnecessary danger. It was also a distraction from their main efforts to attack the army and RUC. Christmas 1970 came with its usual flourish. I had been invited to a party by some girls who frequented the bar. I agreed to go but it was at the top of the Ravenhill near Paisley's church so I was a bit apprehensive, but this vision of beauty assured me I'd be safe and said if I wanted to bring someone it was no problem. So Micky Kearney and I headed over, walking down by the big man's church, home of the silent collection, and arrived safely at the party. It turned out to be a bit of a damp squib, she was pissed off I had brought Micky, we were pissed off that there wasn't enough drink to get pissed, and I never saw her again. Such are the vagaries of young love.

1971 — PRISONS, PRISON SHIPS, PRISON CAMPS.

In early 1971, I had left my job in the bar after getting phone threats from loyalists, might have been cranks but I didn't take any chances in the times that were in it. Belfast city centre was like a ghost town after 7pm and it was an eerie feeling walking dark streets to get a bus home. I applied to go to Sea School in Gravesend, Kent, where after six months I could have headed off to a career in the Merchant Navy, serving cocktails to retired millionaires as they sailed around the Med, it seemed quite idyllic but in the end, I decided throwing Molotov Cocktails at home was a more exciting option, it's one of those crossroads in life. If I had gone, my life might have been completely different but such are the little tangents which can change your life. We were descending into a spiral of violence which was soon going to have a major effect on all of us. Was there an alternative? I know not everyone embraced the armed struggle option. In fact, while it appeared that we were all involved in it, the reality was that it was a small cohort who chose such extreme methods. This was in the context of a population of 200,000 in West Belfast, but the numbers involved would rise into the thousands as time progressed.

The next significant event took place in early February 1971 when the first British soldier to be killed in Ireland since the end of the War of Independence in 1921, Gunner Robert Curtis, a 21-year-old not much older than ourselves, was shot during a gun battle in the New Lodge. He was the first soldier killed by the IRA since Sgt. C. Mears was shot just minutes before the Truce in 1921. Coincidentally, the army shot dead the first Provisional IRA volunteer on active service in the conflict, Jim Saunders, along with a civilian, Bernard Watts: they were killed in Ardoyne the same night. Loyalists attacked the funeral of Watts and pulled the tricolour off the coffin in the hearse on the West Circular which led to the Provos taking a different route to Milltown. It was still attacked by loyalists but the Volunteers were prepared with Hurley sticks and left the loyalists reeling. It was a sad reflection on society that the funeral would be attacked, but during the conflict the RUC and the army would attack republican funerals on many occasions.

In March, a mutually destructive feud developed between the two IRA factions with Charlie Hughes, a Provisional, killed. It would be the first of many. Not long after that, three young Scottish soldiers were lured to their deaths by women from a republican area. Considering the massive links between loyalists in Belfast and Glasgow, these killings struck a chord, as the soldiers were off duty aged 17, 18, and 23, respectively, it hit a raw nerve within loyalist communities. It was a particularly nasty development in the ongoing conflict and brought loyalists on to the streets in their thousands. That they were Scottish soldiers provided them empathy from loyalists who would have support from Scottish sources right through the conflict. Scottish regiments would be filled with loyalists, but like all soldiers, they were from working class areas and many Scottish Catholics would join as well. Indeed, on occasion, we had soldiers tell us they were Celtic supporters; they didn't realise it was the uniform we had a problem with.

In early May, another IRA volunteer, Billy Reid, was shot dead by British soldiers near the city centre. Local legend suggests that it was Reid who killed Gunner Curtis in his native New Lodge a few months previously. Reid gained legendary status with a song written about him which became a popular rebel ballad over the years. His brother 'Reddie' lived just three doors from us, and so a few of us went over to the New Lodge for the funeral which was a massive show of strength by the IRA. As they marched through Belfast to Milltown with a large colour party, there were shots fired over the cortege. Ironically, 'Reddie' was the guy who brought the news to me about young Gerard McAuley being killed in August '69, and now tragedy was at his own door.

Like lots of my mates, our continued involvement in rioting would lead to many of us being arrested and receiving a mandatory six months in Crumlin Road gaol. There were thousands lifted and the gaols were full: there were many youthful members of the Fianna, some guys who became quite notorious during the years ahead, Seany Meehan, brother Martin a legendary Ardoyne Provo leader, Hughie Torney who later became a leader of the INLA, and a young lad who would soon become a headline himself, Gerard Donaghy also 17. He would be murdered by the Paras five months later on Bloody Sunday during the Civil Rights march. Also there were young loyalists who became mainstays in the UVF and UDA. Inside, the divisions were as apparent as they were on the streets, but while we were there, events would take a major turn which eventually defined the conflict. The government in their wisdom, advised by Brian Faulkner and the Unionist Govt. decided to introduce a form of containment which had been used against nationalists and republicans since partition. Once again, internment was to be introduced; this was the beginning of the end for normality in society.

The lead up to internment had been bloody with a Sgt Willets blown up in Springfield Barracks as he took the full force of the blast to save others; two Catholics shot dead by the army in the Bogside, and two more soldiers killed in Belfast. It was like a race to oblivion. The Army, who had been warmly welcomed by some nationalists, had now reverted to type and were seen as joining the RUC as oppressors. Their modus operandi to uphold the unionist statelet, for the nationalist community, was the beginning of the end of any co-operation with the northern statelet. To many, this was no longer about civil rights: one man, one vote, housing equality, etc. It had moved on to the issue which created the northern state. The issue of Irish unity was propelled to the forefront in a way that it hadn't previously since partition in 1921. We weren't committed revolutionaries by any means, but we understood that Irish unity was an all-encompassing dream for nationalists. It would take years in gaol for us to understand why conflict was an essential requirement on the journey towards it. Communists in republican ranks in 1969 were scarce; most wouldn't know what a communist looked like if Lenin turned up under their beds! What those who became communists, Marxists, whatever failed to grasp was that you can't quote Mao or Trotsky and read pamphlets or throw red roses at people who were shooting you or burning your house down. Neither did Trotsky or Lenin when the time required militant action.

In early August, the army carried out a few dummy runs lifting around 50 men who were held for a few days and released. The word on the streets was that internment was to be introduced. At 3am on the morning of the 9th August '71, the scarcely secret plans were put into action and armoured cars and thousands of soldiers piled into nationalist areas all over the six counties. They kicked in doors and dragged off 340 men— all nationalists, no loyalists, no women. Many Provos who had prior intelligence or a premonition decided not to stay at home that night and escaped the initial arrests. Meanwhile, those arrested were hauled off to various camps for interrogation before being sent to Long Kesh, the old RAF base converted into a gaol which became the iconic symbol of the conflict!

The following days after internment were the bloodiest ever seen on Irish streets since the War of Independence? Both IRA groups engaged British soldiers in gun battles throughout Belfast and Derry, and thousands of nationalists were on the streets involved in street disturbances, rioting, burning, and throwing petrol bombs. Around many areas of Belfast, clashes took place with loyalists, and in Ballymurphy, the Paras murdered eleven civilians including a priest. The Paras went berserk, attacking civilians and shooting from the hip at anything that moved. Those murdered included young kids and older parents — not one was an IRA volunteer or carrying weapons. It was a precursor to Bloody Sunday, and if more attention had been paid to Ballymurphy we might never have experienced Bloody Sunday but the slaughter-fest was lost in the mayhem that erupted after internment. Not until recent times was it brought to public attention, having gone through the courts. Incredibly, the Secretary of State, Tory Karen Bradley, recently said that soldiers who murdered during the conflict shouldn't be classed as having 'committed crimes'. It's beyond comprehension that she wasn't sacked on the spot, but British understanding of the Irish situation has always been debatable.

Four days after the introduction of internment and a veritable 'uprising' by the community, a press conference was held in the middle of Ballymurphy. MP's, Councillors, priests, and a wee man with a cap were among them as the worlds media watched, fascinated by what was happening. On the streets, the Paras were still out in force. In the interrogation centres at Ballykinlar & Girdwood the internees were subjected to treatment similar to what the Army handed out during an uprising in Aden previously. A select group of internees were selected for special treatment: they were hooded, beaten, thrown out of helicopters which hovered close to the ground but terrifying to a blindfolded prisoner, sleep deprivation, and tortured in a sadistic nature. It again followed a pattern used by British forces fighting the Mau Mau in Kenya, and highlighted in a manual written by General Frank Kitson, 'Low Intensity Operations'. The severity of the treatment led to the European Courts describing it as torture after the Irish Government brought a case to court. On the streets, the IRA volunteers who evaded the operation kept up a continuous-yet-withering fire on the Paras, Marines et al. At the press conference, the wee man with the cap stood up and declared, "internment hadn't weakened the IRA, they were on the streets defending nationalist areas" as the Paras flooded the streets. The wee man with the cap was Joe Cahill, the Officer Commanding, Belfast Brigade, of the Provisional IRA. After the press conference, he slipped away into the shadows. On the streets, seventeen people were shot dead during the first week of internment: it was the most violent week in the history of the northern statelet.

Inside the gaols, the internees were moved to Long Kesh: over 300 men including fathers, sons, teachers and engineers, brickies and busmen, writers, poets, musicians, civil rights activists, and also a few IRA men. They were mostly guys from the '40s and '50s who had been interned then. The RUC intelligence files were slightly outdated and the new influx of young volunteers had stayed clear of the radar and were at the barricades with their M1 Carbines and old Thompson submachine guns that the guys from the '50s had dumped. It wouldn't be long, however, until the Cages would start filling up with a younger cohort and, unfortunately, I would be among them. During internment week, we were still in Crumlin road gaol and the atmosphere with the 'Screws' (the colloquial name given to Warders) was tetchy, to say the least. These upstanding citizens who were almost 100% loyalist, and the older ones among them who had been working since the '50s and had seen internment before, would inform us that this would soon end all the nonsense.

How wrong they were.

Most prison Warders, like the RUC, were Protestant and part of the front line to protect the statelet. Many, but not all, were sectarian bigots and we would have many encounters with them over the next few years. For many it was just a job but they were loyalists to the core and were unsympathetic to the cause of nationalism. In September, an escape attempt from Crumlin road was made as IRA prisoners on remand tried to climb over a perimeter wall, but it was foiled as a British patrol, by chance, was on the other side. But if, at first, you don't succeed?

Two other very significant events took place as well. The SDLP had proposed a campaign of civil disobedience which would include a rent and rates strike. It was an instant success and united the nationalist community in protest against the Stormont regime. The one problem with the rent and rates strike was that working class people just spent the 'rent money' and in later years were left paying back the money for a long time out of their benefits. As always, the wealthier put it in a bank account and had the money ready to pay back when Stormont came calling for it. Famously, Austin Currie as Minister in the Power Sharing Govt of '74 threatened farmers he would take their livestock in lieu or deduct it from benefits. The second and more sinister development was the restructuring of various loyalist paramilitary groups into the UDA. They became the biggest threat to nationalism and would continue a campaign of naked sectarian murder right through the conflict. It was a classic colonial strategy. The UDA, encouraged by British forces, would put pressure on the IRA, UDA volunteers like Brian Nelson would be British agents at the same time, and their activities would be covered up by an acquiescent RUC, UDR, and British Army. For all intents and purposes, they were all on the same side to preserve the Union.

Collusion was in full flow right through the conflict. Many RUC, UDR, and British Army members were either members of loyalist groups or had connections and passed information continuously — and not only in the six counties. IRA volunteers on the run in Letterkenny, Co Donegal, stayed in a house in town where, once, an aerial photo was taken by Special Branch in Donegal. The photo then found its way via RUC to the army in Derry and then on to the UDA. Just recently, the film *'Unquiet Graves'* exposed the extent of collusion with members of the UDR and RUC involved with loyalist paramilitaries in the murders of over 120 innocent nationalists in Armagh and Tyrone. The murder gang were known as the 'Glenanne' gang; they killed with impunity, and 20 years later not one individual has ever been charged.

After release from Crumlin road I reported back to the Fianna and we were in an accelerated mode at that stage. Working hand-in-hand with IRA volunteers involved arms training, transporting weapons, and reconnoitring future targets down the town, intelligence gathering, marching, and drilling. All of this would be put to good use almost immediately as 19-year-old Marty Forsythe, an IRA volunteer from Turf Lodge, was shot dead by the RUC Special Branch while planting a bomb at the Celebrity Club near the City Hall. The club had apparently been warned not to serve soldiers and RUC men but ignored the warnings. The unit entered the club holding two men at gunpoint as they planted the bomb. The two guys turned out to be off duty, armed RUC officers and shot Vol. Marty Forsythe dead on the street and a girl volunteer was also shot and paralysed for life. The getaway driver, on hearing the shots, drove off and another volunteer was caught soon after and spent many years in the Kesh. There is a possibility that the volunteers had entered a trap and the area staked out acting on info from an informer; Marty Forsythe was the first person to be killed in Turf Lodge during the conflict. At his wake, we provided the guard of honour outside his house where thousands of mourners passed through over the next few nights. On the day of the funeral, we made up a 14-strong Guard of Honour clad in black jackets, dark glasses, black gloves, and berets. Again, there were thousands at the funeral and as the cortege moved off, three volunteers stepped forward and fired a volley of shots and disappeared into the crowds. At this, the Paras who were positioned in the next street moved forward to block the cortege, hoping to arrest the Colour Party or firing party, but the crowd surged forward and hand-to-hand battles took place. In the guard of honour, we were standing to attention but aware that we were the target of the Paras. We couldn't break ranks so we defiantly stood our ground and, thankfully, the brave women and men of the area forced the Paras to withdraw and the cortege moved off slowly through the estate and down to Milltown cemetery. It would be the first of many similar journeys over the years.

After the funeral, we swapped our quasi-military uniform for ordinary clothes and moved back to the estate where rioting was taking place. Then, as dusk descended, the local IRA unit brought out the guns and a battle with British soldiers continued for hours. We had lost a fellow volunteer but there was a certain pride in that we were hitting back. We backed up the guys doing the shooting; it wouldn't be long until we were taking their places as internment swooped them up. Some of the older guys present that day who directed the funeral were arrested soon afterwards and took their place in the 'Kesh. Tommy Maguire, however, cut his stay in Crumlin road gaol short as in mid-November, 9 prisoners made good their escape in a carbon copy of the attempted September escape. Ropes were thrown over the wall from the outside football pitch and Tommy, 'Cleaky' Clarke; Christy Keenan et al made their way up and over the wall. It was the first great escape of the conflict and the 'Crumlin Kangaroos', as they were dubbed, turned up at a press conference in Dublin a few days later. A few weeks later, another escape took place. Well-known republicans Martin Meehan, 'Dutch' Doherty, and Hugh McCann hid in a manhole off the football pitch and escaped over the wall while the other prisoners prevented the screws getting a proper count until the boys were well away. The first the authorities knew about it was when bonfires were lit in their homeplace of Ardoyne causing great embarrassment. During the conflict, escapes became a major component of the struggle and brought morale-boosting celebrations among nationalists to the dismay of Stormont.

After the funeral of Marty Forsythe, virtually all of our Fianna slua (unit) made the transition into the burgeoning ranks of the Provisional IRA, as indeed some of our friends joined the Official IRA. Some of the guys didn't make the cut, but that was no problem. They were still friends, but we had to be realistic. What we were volunteering for wasn't the easy option, we weren't graduating from the minor ranks to senior football; we were making a commitment which there was probably only a few alternatives, with either gaol or death the most prominent. After several meetings with IRA leaders explaining the nature of what we were volunteering for, we were recruited as volunteers, taking an oath over the national flag. We were now committed to something with a serious health warning, but we freely entered this world of subterfuge and violence, imprisonment, and death. We mightn't have studied the famous 'Green Book', but we came across it later in the Cages when we had plenty of time to read it.

Of course, there was an element of excitement for 18-year-olds, but what lay ahead was way above anything we imagined. We would inflict violence on others and have violence inflicted on ourselves. We were stepping into a tradition which was a part of Irish history going back to 1798, and the IRB (Fenians) in the 1860s, Easter Week, the War of Independence, and civil war. There would be attempts to marginalise and demonise, and the epithet 'terrorist' would be thrown at us. We had to understand all this; it wasn't going to be a ‘walk in the park’. We were putting our lives and freedom on the line, but when we should have been preparing for 'A' Levels or Leaving Cert exams; we were instead on a journey which was going to define our lives for the foreseeable future. We had no delusions of grandeur, no thoughts of self-aggrandisement. We made a commitment to contribute our little bit to the armed struggle. We were no Che Guevara, but then you didn't need to be. To paraphrase Bobby Sands: “every person has a part to play in the struggle, no part is too great or too small, no one is too old or too young, we are not criminals but Irishmen, this is the crime we stand accused.”

In the following months, we were involved in the everyday activities of our unit in Turf Lodge hijacking vehicles, blocking roads, preparing attacks on crown forces, moving weapons, and observing potential targets whether military or economic. This was the everyday life of an IRA volunteer. It might seem exciting to others, maybe a bit mad to some, but a lot of the time it was pretty mundane: watching, observing, taking notes, dummy runs, and failed ops, as became a cliché later on, for every 20 IRA operations planned, maybe only one would reach fruition; urban guerrilla warfare was hard work, too. Being in the IRA wasn’t all that it seemed cracked up to be. It could be tedious at times, and hard work, but paradoxically never boring. Discipline was essential, however, and that was the difference between the Provos and other republican groups, and indeed loyalists over the years. If you didn't have a disciplined organisation it could morph into feuds as we saw with the INLA and UVF/UDA over the years.

A LIFE LESS ORDINARY

At this stage in the story, I have to say that my future involvement in events has to be told with some reservations. There are just some things that can't be talked about. As was illustrated by the Boston College fiasco post-conflict conducted by author and journalist Ed Maloney and ex-Long Kesh man Anthony McIntyre who gained a PhD at Queen’s after release and also morphed into a dissident! Combatants need to be prudent on how they talk about events during the conflict. This is just the reason the Bureau of Military History in the Republic didn't open the archives from the War of Independence until all participants had passed on. That's a reality even if we are almost 50 years on from those horrific days in the ’70s; there are just some things you can't talk about. In the Belfast of the ’70s to paraphrase a recent book by American author Patrick Radden Keefe, “whatever you say, say nothing.” While in recent times memoirs from combatants on all sides have been making an appearance, that idiom stood the test of time.

As I compile this tome of a part of my life as a young adult in ’70s Belfast, I am aware that the story might shock some present-day friends, possibly cause dismay to a few, and cause empathy in others. I will attempt to tell the story in as truthful a way as is possible considering the constraints I find myself in. It's a true story from a time when our young lives were in turmoil, and thank God we survived as many of my friends didn't live to tell the story.

In Lost Lives, the great tome of casualties of the conflict by David McKitterick et al, there are over 3500 names of victims: British soldiers, RUC men, UDR, innocent civilians, victims of sectarian violence, and IRA volunteers. I knew about 40 of them. They never got the chance to live life, and many volunteered with the same thoughts as myself. They weren't idealistic revolutionaries but young guys who found themselves in a world of conflict and became part of it; my story is their story. In part, it's to remember them and indeed every single one of the victims of the conflict, and indeed the many thousands who suffered yet survived; not all victims of conflict are physical.

From the introduction of internment in August ’71 until the end of December, the conflict took on a whole new ferocity. In the two years from August ’69 until August ’71, 80 people were killed, and in the five months after internment almost 150 were killed. They were IRA volunteers, British soldiers, RUC, UDR, loyalists, and innocent civilians. Internment, rather than solving the problem, had created a monster.

As young people we were facing a future of conflict and we were to play a part in it. Life was never meant to be like that, but then neither was it in Paris or Berlin in 1914 or 1940, or in Sarajevo in the 1990's or in Tripoli in 2010 or in Damascus in 2015. Internment was always the Unionist junta's weapon against republicans and nationalists as a whole. Right from partition, internment had been used in every decade from the '1920s-70's — democracies rarely use legislation like that, but then the six counties were never a real democracy. P.W.Botha in apartheid-era, South Africa, once observed that if he had that one Special Powers Act from Stormont, Section 23, he would never have had trouble with Mandela and friends. Do we ever get used to death in our lives? It's so natural, yet it's unnatural, especially when it happens in our youth to some of our youth, to our friends. We who have lived to 65+ and lived a lot of life remember someone who lost their life at 16, just a kid, really, although at that age we all thought we knew everything: that we were adult enough to work and date, play pool and act cool, not survive to have a wife, no kids to remember their life, blown to pieces on a Saturday night.

Wee Jimmy McCallum started work around the same time as me and big Hack; all three of us worked in city pubs. Hack and I worked down the city centre whilst Jimmy was in a pub on the Springfield, close to the future peace line. On a busy night the week before Christmas 1971, the UVF planted a no-warning bomb at this Catholic pub and Jimmy was killed. He was only 16, a friend from Turf Lodge. He was really the first victim that we knew personally, it was tragic. Our first instincts were to target young Protestant guys and take revenge. The sectarian DNA which was within us all from being born in Belfast exhibited itself in a moment of retaliation, but we didn't, of course. It wasn't the republican way, republicanism never embraced sectarianism, the United Irishmen like Wolfe Tone and Henry Joy McCracken founded on the Cave Hill in Belfast were Presbyterians and Tone espoused what became the republican ideal, 'to unite Protestant, Catholic and Dissenter under the common name of Irishmen in order to break the connection with England, the never failing source of all our political evils'! That's not to say that some people weren't sectarian just like, let's say, Celtic don't embrace sectarianism but a small percentage of the fanbase might, or perhaps Fine Gael didn't embrace fascism in the '30's but a section of their people did, or the Catholic Church didn't embrace sexual deviation but some of their clergy did. Certainly there was more sectarianism in Belfast than, say, South Armagh or Portadown rather than Derry, but those are the demographics that exist. Irish people as a whole didn't realise they were slightly racist until migrants started arriving on our shores during the Tiger from Africa and Eastern Europe.

It was with bitter feelings that we walked behind Jimmy's coffin, and behind grieving parents and siblings. This would become a regular occurrence in a nightmare world of sectarian bigotry: armed struggle, political divide, and a future without a future for so many. Wee Jimmy's funeral made its way to

Milltown. He wasn't involved in anything; he was an apprentice barman in his first job. The sobs of his mother were heartbreaking, and she wouldn't be the last by a long shot but it's always the mothers who most suffer with the loss of a child. I remember Jimmy like yesterday as I do the rest who were slain in our modern conflict. The sad walk down to Milltown cemetery would become a regular occurrence over the next decade.

In the middle of December, the IRA made a major statement of intent when every unit in the six counties was mobilised on the same day to bring the place to a standstill. Real bombs, dummy bombs, hijacked buses and cars, as well as barricades were planted from Belfast to Derry and from Strabane to South Armagh. Hundreds of incidents paralysed the entire 'occupied' area. The army, the UDR, and the RUC were stretched to the limit. It was a show of force by the Provos; the IRA had never embarked on such a show of force since 1920. It was a logistical challenge for the myriad units throughout the 6 counties but it sent a message of defiance to those in power at Stormont and Westminster. Four months after internment, the IRA was as strong as ever. The British Army would hit back, of course, and the number of arrests would increase dramatically. Interrogations, beatings, forced confessions, signed statements made under duress and off to court or if you kept your mouth shut, straight off to the internment camps.

A YOUTHFUL INTERNEE ON A PRISON SHIP!

On New Year's Eve 1971, I headed with some friends — all volunteers — over to Andytown to a disco. There, I spent the night chatting up a young lady, walked her home and then crucially walked back to our house at about 3am. I was only in bed for about half an hour when I heard an almighty crash down the stairs as the front door was battered in by soldiers of the Kings Own Scottish Borderers. Without waiting for my parents to open it, they kicked the door in and raced up the stairs leaving no time to think of escape out the back window or door, although it would have been fruitless as half a dozen of Scotland's finest specimens of soldiery were planted in the back garden. They had SLRs at the ready in case I had thoughts of leaving the party early. There was pandemonium in the house — my mum was crying, my sister shocked, my dad trying his best to confuse the soldier in charge. When asked who is "Patrick McMenamin", my dad quickly replied, "That's me." He was being hauled off by Private clod when the intelligence officer came in and shouted, "Not the old man you fool, it's the young one," and with that ruse foiled I was bundled into a Saracen armoured car and driven off in the middle of the night to Palace barracks, Hollywood, in the east of the city, and it wasn't to play golf with Rory's dad.

Hollywood was the home of the Paras and the main interrogation centre in Belfast, and is now the HQ for MI5. It had a fearsome reputation for stories of guys who had been beaten badly during interrogation. It was with trepidation that I entered the place, anticipating two days of a difficult nature ahead, sitting in a seat facing a white wall for hours on end, sensory deprivation to use a modern term, then regular sessions being interrogated by Special Branch, physically mistreated, and threatened with being handed over to loyalists. At one stage, I was let out to the toilet which was in an adjacent hut. As I walked over, I noticed the corrugated fence wasn't so high and contemplated escape over it but the Branch man was in tow. Several months later, another volunteer did exactly that and made his way to freedom. During the interrogation period, there was no sleep as they would bring you in for interrogation in the middle of the night. And looking at that damn wall with little dots in it—at times you thought you could see little green men climbing up the wall, illusions, disillusioned, depressed, frightened but defiant, keep your mouth shut for 48 hours and make it to the Kesh, Maidstone or Crumlin Road was the challenge. It wasn't easy, it was frightening for an 18-year-old but somehow I managed and was on my way to my next port of call, the prison ship Maidstone in Belfast Lough. After Palace Barracks, Hollywood, it was a welcome sight.

The Maidstone was a British submarine depot vessel built at John Brown's in Clydebank, then moored in retirement as a troop barracks in Belfast Lough. Ironically, it had spent part of WW2 in Malta, a place I would be domiciled in the future. I was transferred to the ship by Special Branch, then handcuffed and wedged between two burly interrogators. At the dockside, they unloaded their quarry to prison Warders and we 'walked the gangplank' up on to the ship. The head P.O waiting to check me in although, while it was in the area the Titanic was built, it definitely wasn't the Titanic hotel. The details were double-checked, the photo taken, and a letter was signed by the Right Honourable MP Brian Faulkner, Prime Minister of the dysfunctional statelet, stating that as a threat to society I was being Interned under Section 23 of the Special Powers Act. There I was, the son of parents from Tyrone and Donegal, following in the footsteps of republicans who had faced internment since partition. In every decade it had been used against the nationalist community. After the formalities, the screws brought me down to my new domicile under the decks where I was welcomed by some friendly faces and others that would become lifelong friends.

There were about 300 internees on the Maidstone and 700 Marines to guard us. We had just one small section at the stern, to use nautical terminology, and the soldiers had the other two thirds of the old boat. We didn't have any real contact with the soldiers; they were just there to remind us that if we decided to turn the boat into an armada heading for Donegal, they had 700 rifles at their disposal. The screws just went about their daily jobs, some of the older ones had seen this all before in the '50s, and some of the internees would remember them; they had been interned then as well. The sleeping quarters were quite confined and gave us an insight into what it must be like at sea for sailors. We were fairly cramped with bunks on top of each other, not much room to swing the proverbial cat. Upstairs, there were a few rooms for reading, writing, and meeting, and on deck, we could walk around the little triangle or just 'sunbathe' in the January sun. There were a few Turf Lodge guys on the Maidstone, most were 'Stickies' (Official IRA), our erstwhile enemies on the streets; but we had no problem mixing 'offshore'. Also on the boat were Gerry Adams, and Joe McDonnell who would die later on hunger strike, and seven other guys who had ambitions to test the security within the next few weeks.

Over the decades, even centuries, Irish republicans have had a positive approach to being in gaol. Going back to the Fenians, Frongoch in Wales, Kilmainham, the Curragh, and Crumlin road, the two main things on everyone's mind would be education and escape. When a volunteer enters any gaol, his position on the outside has ended but gradually his 'name' would give him a position if he wished. A tradition had grown up within the jails that education was important to understand why they were in gaol, but trying to escape from these places was paramount, as well as the logistical benefits for the IRA on the outside; escapes would be morale-boosting moments for the people during the War of Independence and the armed struggle of the '70s. Escape stories are legendary: the Manchester martyrs, Dev from Lincoln gaol, Seamus Murphy from Wakefield with Nicos Sampson who interestingly led the coup in Cyprus in '74 and Donal Donnelly from the Crum in 1960.

When IRA volunteers go into prison there is a duty to try and escape and return to active service in times of conflict. As prisoners walking around during their confinement, they are always looking for a weak spot in the security; it becomes second nature. Any little clink in the system is there to be exploited. So, the Maidstone was just one more challenge, there had been prison ships in the '20s and '40, the Al Rawdah being one. It had just been a few months since 9 had escaped from Crumlin road, and so escape was in the air. On the evening of the 17th January, seven of our comrades squeezed through a porthole and slid down a rope to the icy water and swam across the 300-400 yard wide Lough to freedom. Well, it wasn't just that simple: they were almost naked and had their bodies smeared in oil for protection against the January chill. One of them had difficulties swimming, and when they got to the other side they had to wait for an hour to hijack a bus and make their getaway from the shipyard area. None were sure if the puritanical loyalist bus driver was more shocked by the escape or the sight of seven naked terrorists on his bus.

Back on the boat, the plan was that we would keep walking about so as the screws wouldn't be able to make a proper count, which they were due to, do. It was vital when the boys were delayed that we kept disrupting the count which was successful both on and off the ship. The seven escapees made their way to the nearest republican area, the Markets, near city hall, and dived into a pub where people starting stripping and gave them clothes. The boys were able to get to West Belfast and hide for a few days before slipping over the border to a press conference which was seriously embarrassing to the authorities on both sides. It was heralded as the great escape and the boys were dubbed 'the Magnificent 7'. If it had happened in WW2, they would have made a film about it. Of the seven escapees, three were dead within a short time: Jim Bryson, Toddler Tolan, and Tucker Kane. The other four — Peter Rodgers, Martin Taylor, Tommy Gorman, and Sean Convery survived the conflict with varying degrees of experience. Rodgers got 40 years for killing a Garda, Seamus Quaid, and Tommy Gorman was recaptured and spent many years in gaol. As bonfires were lit in republican areas that evening, an army spokesman appeared on TV saying security hadn't been breached to the delight of the escapees having a beer in the relative freedom of Andersonstown. That was the third escape in as many months. The 'Crumlin

Kangaroos' involved 9 going over the wall: Meehan, Doherty, and McCann from the 'Crum as well — and now the 'Magnificent 7' from the Maidstone. No more than during the Tan war, it invigorated the volunteers and the community. It provided a massive propaganda boost worldwide. The stories of escapes from Colditz to British TV audiences had nothing on seven guys swimming to freedom across Belfast Lough. Whatever your views on the IRA, events like this were creating a certain mythology. It was the early 70's and Vietnam, the Sorbonne, Chile, and Palestine were creating world headlines. In Ireland, the Provos challenging British occupation of the six counties was right up there with them.

In the UK, there was a perception that the Irish Government were 'soft' on the IRA, especially when escapees would turn up at press conferences. Were they soft? It's doubtful. From '71 we had Section 31 introduced by Minister Gerry Collins; Portlaoise, Offences against the State Act, 'Heavy Gang' Garda Special Branch unit. The Irish Government put over 300m euro annually towards border security, Army patrols and checkpoints, special payments, overtime, prison warders, the highest wages in the state with security bonuses which they received up until the modern era. Republicans were demonised in the 80's in society. I don't recall any 'softly, softly,' approach; it definitely didn't happen in Donegal where the Special Branch and Irish Army made it difficult to operate along the border.

The following week, a civil rights march took place at Magilligan strand intending to march to the camp which had been converted into another internment centre. However, they were stopped by the Royal Green Jackets and more significantly, the Paras. The marchers, led by John Hume, were attacked in a frenzy of hysteria by soldiers as if they were wild dogs unleashed. Crucially, and once again, the RTÉ cameras were there to show it to a worldwide audience. This was critical as the following weekend would see a major march through Derry. We didn't know it then but events on that day would reverberate around the world and the conflict was destined to move to a different level. In the week leading up to the march, negotiations took place between the RUC, the army, the Church, civil rights leaders, and by proxy, the IRA.

Frank Lagan — a chief superintendent in the RUC, and one of the few Catholics to reach that rank — pleaded with government and army generals to allow the march to pass peacefully after assurances from the IRA that they would stay away. However, a decision was taken at the highest level that the army would initiate a major arrest operation on the day, sanctioned by Ted Heath — the British PM. According to Malachi O'Doherty in his book, 'Fifty Years On', on the morning of the march, Lagan made a personal plea to the army commander to let him go into the Bogside and negotiate with the march leaders. The army commander, General Ford, replied: "It's going to be dealt with." Ironically, O 'Doherty claims that Lagan was a young policeman on the Falls in 1964 and smashed the window of republican election HQ to pull down the tricolour which caused three days of rioting. Considering his later role in trying to avoid casualties and deaths on Bloody Sunday and Operation Motorman, it's worth considering his position within the RUC. Was he sympathetic to a change in society without wanting to reveal his thoughts in that ultra-unionist organisation? At that stage the conflict was reaching a pinnacle regarding ferocity. Two RUC men were killed in the Creggan during the week and major gun battles took place on the South Armagh border with thousands of live rounds fired by the IRA and British soldiers. Lagan, it is claimed again by O'Doherty, was in contact with nationalists and republicans in Derry on a regular basis. Lagan, an interesting character, passed in 2005 at age 90. Born just before partition, he had served the statelet through its paramilitary police force but sought a way to heal the differences.

On the day of the march, Sunday the 30th of January, it was a sunny day. The marchers set off from the Creggan to march down through the Bogside and head into Guildhall square. Derry was a nationalist city so there should have been no problem on the day but the presence of 1 Para was ominous. Their actions the previous week called into question their suitability to be let loose on Derry streets. Within a few hours, that suitability would forever be in question. The story of that day in January is so well known that there really is no need to go over it again. Needless to say, British paratroopers slaughtered 14 innocent civil rights marchers, all unarmed, on the streets of their native city, and the British state tried their best to deny the truth through the Widgery enquiry. It would take 40 years before Saville concluded that they were murdered and the British PM issued an apology to the families and the people of Derry. The issue of charging soldiers with murder, however, was watered down to just one soldier and no higher-ranking army personnel or politicians were ever charged. Recently even the charge against the one soldier charged was dropped and the British Government have set in motion plans to call an 'amnesty' for actions during the conflict, in reality it is to protect British soldiers from prosecution in the future.

'Sunday Bloody Sunday' would come to personify the 30-year conflict in the north. On the Maidstone, we watched with astonishment as the news came through. Many of us had friends who attended the march, including Madeleine, and there were nervous hours as we waited to hear if they were ok. On the day of the funerals, we organised a guard of honour on the ship in relays of teams of six. It was our small tribute to those murdered. The following week, we were transferred to the internment camp at Magilligan strand. A whole convoy of military vehicles brought about 100 of us from the Maidstone to the newly constructed cages in Magilligan overlooking the Foyle and across to Donegal. It might have been scenic but we were still deprived of our freedom, in gaol without trial, political prisoners. Britain was one of the few democratic states in the western world with political prisoners, a fact which our political allies in Sinn Féin would exploit to the hilt.

We were political prisoners, and I've often thought about it over the years. In 1968, we were young teenagers playing football on the streets, and then four years later we're on prison ships and in prison camps as political prisoners deemed a threat to the statelet. We were part of the mushrooming struggle against British rule. Over the decades, there would be 15,000 republican activists, and another 10,000 loyalists, mostly working-class kids, all caged during the conflict between 1971-2000, involved in something way over our heads. In August '69 armed loyalists and B-Specials attacking the Falls and Ardoyne. We became involved in something that would affect our lives gravely, some would die, most of us ended up in gaol. How do we analyse it? What would our lives have been like if the unionist council in Caledon had given the house to the Catholic family of six rather than the 19-year-old single Protestant girl? What if the RUC had let the civil rights march walk down Duke St. in Derry unobstructed in October '68? What if the Stormont government had banned the Apprentice Boys march in Derry in August 12th'69? What if the new Tory government hadn't sent the army in to enforce a curfew on the Lower Falls for three days in June '70? What if the government hadn't introduced internment in August '71? What if the Paras hadn't slaughtered 14 civilians in January '72?

What if...

But history doesn't work like that. When the shit hits the fan, it becomes an unstoppable tsunami; events take over with an onrushing stampede to anarchy. Would our lives have been different? Of course they would. It had been estimated in various reports that 90% of republicans who went to Long Kesh would never have seen the inside of a gaol cell were it not for the conflict. Some, of course, might have, as in any society, but a hell of a lot more would have become teachers, doctors, engineers, or lecturers. This can be assumed by the level of education which took place within the republican Cages, and it was within a history and tradition of resistance which gave a raison d'être to our actions.

Loyalists, on the other hand, hadn't that history to look back on. They were loyal to the state so it was confusing for them. They didn't embrace education to the same extent, although there were many who did. Their experience was of pumping iron, tattooed skinheads, and a sectarian culture which was reprehensible but part of their society which they brought into the Cages. But they were also working-class kids suffering from the same unemployment problems as those on the Falls Road. They lived in the same type of houses, two up-two down, outside toilet, with the same lack of achievement in academia. In fact, they had fewer chances than we had across the peace line. It has been shown that loyalist working class areas have suffered worse from the conflict than nationalist areas, an oxymoron in reality. Whatever way we analyse it, it was what it was: a quirk of fate. We were 15 at the start of the conflict, testosterone-fuelled youths looking for action. If it was a choice between taking your girlfriend to the cinema and throwing petrol bombs at a British Army foot patrol, well, the girl would have to wait to see Ryan O'Neal and Ali McGraw in Love Story.

Long Kesh was always in the headlines, right from day one, but more so for the first time in Feb '72 when the first escape took place. Francis McGuigan, a republican internee from Ardoyne, literally walked out of the camp dressed as a priest — a tactic used at different times over the years. The authorities didn't even know for 24 hours when, by that stage, McGuigan was in Dublin and ready to give evidence to the American Foreign Affairs Committee on events in Ireland. It was a massive propaganda victory for the IRA as Long Kesh was seen as escape-proof, but like Alcatraz and Robbin Island, the challenge was always accepted willingly by the inmates. Meanwhile, we got on with life in Magilligan as you do. There were outside drills in the morning, classes in the afternoon, history, politics and weapons (wooden weapons we made, of course), making handicrafts in the evening, hankies with republican designs, and rugs which we made from materials brought in by a local priest. He was a brilliant wee guy whose name escapes me, possibly Fr Shields, but he was very upbeat and supportive. We would donate some to him for fundraising for the parish; what the winners made of an AK47 silhouetted on an image of a hooded volunteer was another thing.

Making the handicrafts was a big part of an internee's life. The days were long and the ongoing problem with internment was that there was no release date. Some of the older guys had been interned in the '40s and '50s and might have been in for five or six years. It's soul-destroying not knowing when you would get out. At least when you were sentenced you had a release date and could work towards it; every day 24 hours, you were closer to freedom. We had old record players sent in and the Barleycorn's 'Men Behind the Wire' would be rattled out regularly along with 'Come Out You Black and Tans' and 'The Boys of the Old Brigade'. Nightly sing songs could occur at random, and there were always a few Joe Dolan types from the country, or Rolling Stones rockers from the city. And Top of the Pops would be popular once a week on the box with Pans People a treat along with T Rex, George Harrison, and Elton John et al. I always remember the number one single from that time in March '72, it was Harry Nilsson's 'Without You', the beautiful love song which had us all depressed and thinking of our girlfriends on the outside. Hard case revolutionaries have a tender side as well.

The next few months of incarceration were fairly mundane, to be honest. What kept us going was the ongoing war outside, but these few months saw one tragic event after another. The Official IRA went into meltdown after some devastating actions. The bombing of the Paras HQ at Aldershot in revenge for Bloody Sunday backfired as seven ancillary staff were killed, including a British Army Padre. Then, the Official IRA killed a young off-duty Derry guy from the Bogside who was home on leave from the Army. Killing an 18 year old local lad led to angry disputes with local women with the end result being the announcement of a permanent ceasefire which would take their armed wing out of the equation regards actions against the British Army at least? Beneath the surface, however, they held on to their weapons for all sorts of actions over the years while, politically, they morphed into Official Sinn Féin, the Workers Party, Democratic Left and eventually some made it into the Labour Party. Incredibly, they adopted a line on the national question which was almost unionist in thinking, and their hostility to the Provos would be long-lasting which led to many feuds. I had many good friends within the Official movement, a lot of them originally from the initial Fianna group in '69. Yet despite the differences over the years between the two groups, it never damaged our friendship.

The Provos, exclusively referred to as the IRA after the demise of the Officials. 'Provisional' was an early term used to define the new leadership and it stuck with the media. Provo became a short slang word, and 'PIRA'used by the British Army. There were a few horrific months of botched bombings, either claiming civilian lives or volunteers in 'own goals' — a term used by the army for volunteers killed by their own bomb. The Abercorn bar bombing left two dead and 130 injured, then four IRA volunteers were killed by their own bomb in the Lower Falls — one of them was Tony Lewis who was with us in the Fianna in the house on the Kashmir in August '69. The Donegall St. bombing left six dead and 100 injured, and then two old people were killed in a bomb attack outside Limavady RUC station. Three more volunteers were killed with their own bomb at Bawnmore, and then eight people were killed in a premature IRA bomb in the Short Strand, four volunteers included. It was a devastating series of events, all morale-sapping for us and horrific for the victims. When you think back on it, how we let guys with limited experience put the lives of civilians and our own lives at risk, putting our faith in them — it was baffling. I wouldn't say it was blind faith but we would have felt as though they knew what they were doing. It was a tough time, and conflict dehumanises us to the extent that we accept abnormal situations. The men in the trenches in WWI did as they did in WWII, in Pearl Harbour, at Hiroshima and Nagasaki, on Bloody Sunday and Bloody Friday; but it's not normal. It's not the way life is meant to be but through the centuries it has been thus. Ironically, a girl I knew in Donegal was, in a way, connected to the bomb at the

RUC station in Limavady. Netty was an Undergrad at the University of Ulster in Coleraine and had been thumbing a lift from Derry when two old guys stopped and gave her a lift. They had intended on dropping her off at the far side of town but she asked to be dropped near the bus station. The few minutes where she alighted and thanked the two old guys were crucial; as they drove off past the police station, the bomb went off and they were killed. Netty always felt mixed emotions about the incident, either guilt that her being dropped off delayed the men for those crucial moments, or relief that she had avoided being blown up with them. It was a perfect example of how you could be in the wrong place at the wrong time.

Years later in Long Kesh, I met up with a Scottish guy, Jock Hone, who had been charged with planting the bomb and was remorseful as a warning had been given but the road hadn't been blocked off — a tragedy for everyone. Netty told me she often thought about the two old guys and the devastation of their deaths. It wasn't intentional, never meant to be, but unfortunately in all conflicts tragedy occurs. I'm not excusing it, it was a tragedy, as were many things that happened over the 30 years, but the IRA volunteers didn't set out to kill those two old guys. How do we square that with the American Air Force dropping the bomb in Hiroshima? or the British in Dresden killing hundreds of thousands of innocent civilians, was that not out-and-out murder intentionally yet excused in the context of war? To use the cliché, the victor writes the history of conflict.

At the end of March as we whiled away the days in Magilligan making handicrafts, our thoughts would often drift across to Donegal just a few miles across the Foyle: the beautiful hills around Inishowen sparkling in the evening sunset; the small towns of Greencastle, Moville, and Redcastle; and further round to Culdaff, Malin Head, and Glengad on the peninsula. Inishowen is part of Donegal but it always felt as though it's in the hinterland of Derry, cut off by partition from its natural trading area. I, more than most, felt a bit homesick as my mum was from Donegal and I spent every summer there. Escape was always in the air, and with Donegal so close there was a feeling that something could be worked on. The camp leadership, whether to live a quiet life or to keep young internees under control, appeared to suggest that something big was to happen with the Derry Brigade going to take over the camp. This would always come up when any ideas of leaving the place without the permission of the Governor was put forward. One night, a few of the 'Sticks' cut the Cage wire and made their way through the camp before being apprehended near the perimeter fence. On the journey, one had looked into an officers hut and without looking up the Brit asked, "What do you want", to which the would-be escapee replied in his best Cockney accent, "Excuse me Sarge, wrong office." The soldiers who caught them didn't see the funny side of it, and with the boys caught entangled in the barbed wire they were unmercifully beaten with batons and lodged back in captivity before breakfast.

By the end of the month there were more things than escape on our minds as the first effects of the armed struggle kicked in. The unionist government at Stormont was suspended and power invested in Westminster. It brought great celebrations in nationalist areas. After 50 years of partition, the cracks began to appear in the 'apartheid' regime; Stormont was on its last legs. For us, early April would bring new surroundings for us. We were given a few hours to pack up our gear and then huddled together at the edge of the camp where a helicopter landed and we boarded quicker than Michael O'Leary could issue an online boarding pass. Two RUC men, two Brits, and the pilot lifted off in the helicopter with one of the soldiers sitting with his legs dangling out the door as it hovered over the north Derry countryside. For a few seconds, I think we all looked at each other wondering if we could possibly hijack it and fly to Donegal but we were neither Steve McQueen nor 'Sully', and so we sat back and relaxed as the chopper whisked us away to our next domicile just outside Lisburn, a place which was starting to acquire legendary status: Long Kesh. The move was completed over 24 hours with hundreds of internees being transferred to the barbed wire jungle, distributed between the various Cages. I think we were put in Cage 10 where I would return to several times over the next four years. We met many friends from the streets but there was a different atmosphere, a feeling that with Stormont gone things were moving in a certain direction; the release of internees, ceasefire maybe, talks between the IRA and the British Government? We hadn't long to wait until the gates of the 'Kesh saw internees being released on a daily basis. Families were reunited and a sense emerged that the conflict might be coming to an end, it was May '72 and pre first ceasefire. That, of course, would prove to be a forlorn dream. The gates of the 'Kesh would click open and closed for a long time to come — this would prove to be nothing more than a temporary hiatus.

In mid-April, the Paras killed the Official IRA's Joe McCann, in the Markets area, a small republican enclave near the city centre. McCann had become an iconic figure after internment week when a silhouetted photo of him carrying a rifle against a burning background was published. He lived in Turf Lodge, and for the 3 days of the wake and funeral, the Officials and Provos joined together to turn the place into a no-go area and launched waves of attacks on the army. His funeral from Turf Lodge, led by his Irish Wolfhound, demonstrated a massive show of strength. It would be the last time the two wings of the IRA would cooperate together, the bitterness between the two wings of the IRA was palpable, it was like the civil war split in 1922 or even the division between Fianna Fail and the Blaney's in Donegal, albeit without the guns in the hills! There were loads of internees from Turf Lodge in the cages. My big mate Paddy Smith, was in the Cage next to us and we used to talk across the wire every day. He was in the Officials as were many of my friends, but like many of them he was becoming more than a little disgruntled with the path their movement was taking. It was early days but the dynamics which would lead to another split and the founding of the INLA was already in the making. What made Hack go one way with the Officials, and I the other way with the Provos was fate, peer pressure, and family connections. We had both been Fianna boys before after the split and then progressed to each side of the republican divide. That he eventually morphed towards the IRSP probably put him closer to our side of the division, and like myself, he would spend many years in Long Kesh.

Back in the Cages, there was 'gate fever' in the air during the early weeks of May. Every day, a screw would appear and read out a list of names:

"Get your gear, you're going home."

On the 10th of May, I was chatting to 'Hack' across the wire when a screw appeared. "You're for off" he said, and so I said my goodbyes to 'Hack' and then others in our hut. I grabbed my stuff and was on my way to the front gate and the PDF mini bus home-free again. Hopefully, it would last, but the reality was that the life span for an IRA volunteer in '72 was about three months. Back in the 'Turf, the local band would arrive and play a few welcome home tunes as was the case for all internees, then a crate of Guinness appeared in the local club renamed after Marty Forsythe — the volunteer shot in the city centre six months previously. A few days of relaxation followed, and then I reported back to my unit. It was a no brainer, just the times we were living in. It might now feel like we had a death wish but it's just the way it was, swept up in the euphoria of it all. But we weren't like lambs to the slaughter; we knew exactly what we were doing. We were committed to the armed struggle; whatever lay ahead we went into it with our eyes fully opened. We lost many friends along the way, but do we regret it? The friends we lost, of course, but taking part in the struggle, no, it was our fate to become involved in our mid teens, if born anywhere else we would have been joining the local GAA club but c'est la vie!

THE LONG KESH YEARS

I was back on the streets and things had markedly deteriorated. Three days after release and back on active service, a weekend of murderous violence took place involving UDA/UVF, the IRA and the British Army. The incident to kick it all off was a bomb planted at Kelly's bar at the top of the Whiterock between Ballymurphy and Turf Lodge on 13th May '72. A no-warning bomb injured many, and John Moran, a part-time barman, was critically injured. John was the brother of a good friend, Tom, who would later spend many years in the H-Blocks. They lived in Turf Lodge close to the bombed pub. After the bombing, loyalists launched a massive gun attack on the general area from the Springmartin estate overlooking Ballymurphy.Two more civilians were killed during the shooting by loyalists and the British Army, a Fianna boy was shot dead in New Barnsley, and a soldier from the King's regiment was killed in Turf Lodge. A young Catholic was also the victim of a blatantly sectarian murder on the Shankill, and a Protestant youth was simultaneously killed by the army in Springmartin. Seven died over that weekend in May amid massive three-way gun battles. All IRA volunteers were involved in defending the area from loyalist gunmen and the army; it was as fierce a few days as we had seen. Thousands of live rounds had been fired during the gun battles, and for the army it was a situation they didn't want to be in, caught in the middle between the UDA/UVF and the IRA. Soon we would see that the British Army, RUC, UVF and UDA were essentially on the same side, the 'security forces' mixed with loyalist paramilitaries to keep them onside, recruiting them as informers and agents to engage in actions against nationalist areas, they all wanted to protect the union from republican 'terrorists', it didn't help that the Irish Govt threw their weight behind British Govt actions, the Provisional IRA led the struggle against British rule on their own!

John Moran died a week or so later and we went along to the wake. At the same time, we were planning an attack on the army near his house. We were preparing an ambush site at a large roundabout above his house when a large convoy of army Saracens, 'Pigs', armoured troop carriers, they came rumbling along, and as we lay flat on our stomachs, they drove around the roundabout a few times before driving off; it was a close encounter. We attended the funeral of John as a mark of respect to the family and especially our friend Tom, or 'Tonkas'. These occasions were becoming commonplace, and within a fortnight my childhood friend Norman Campbell would join the ever-increasing list of casualties. Of all the people I knew who were killed in the conflict, Norman was probably the saddest. He was just 19 and lived just up the street from me. We had known each other since moving to Turf Lodge in the early '60s. He was a good friend, a genuinely good guy, and he was probably one of the few who didn't get involved in the conflict. He never joined any of the various armed groups. He lived for his girlfriend and was to get married five weeks later. She was from the Shankill, and a Protestant, but they were soul mates. Norman was killed by loyalist gunmen on a building site where he worked on the Shankill. He was a hard worker, never missing a day at work, and even when he was younger he always made the best guiders (plank of wood, two bicycle wheels and ball bearings) that we played on. He was skilful, and a tradesman; it was oh so sad. Again, we went to the funeral and met his old mother who was distraught and never got over the death of her son. Norman was murdered by the UVF — the first of the group of four who sat on the wall in the Turf Lodge flats in '69 talking about the future. Micky Kearney and Kevi McCracken would follow him in the years to come

While there was virtual mayhem on the streets in the early summer of '72, behind the scenes, tentative talks were taking place between various groups such as the SDLP, the church, representatives of the British Government, and the IRA. John Hume met Willie Whitelaw, the first British Direct Rule secretary of state, and conditions for a first ceasefire were laid. Secret talks took place between British Government officials and the IRA leadership near the border and the IRA announced there would be a ceasefire from midnight on the 26th June 1972. In the 48 hours before the ceasefire, an undercover British Army unit, the MRF, shot four innocent civilians in Andersonstown and the IRA killed five British soldiers. It was as if both entered the suspension of hostilities from a position of strength. On the streets, it was welcomed equally by civilians, IRA volunteers, and British soldiers. After three years of conflict, there was a little chink of light at the end of the tunnel. As the news spread of an imminent ceasefire, people came onto the streets in party mode. There were water 'bombs' tossed about instead of nail bombs, soldiers driving through the estate were met with cheers and more water bombs; it was probably like Dublin in 1921. Even the dogs stopped barking at the soldiers; for the first time since they came here, the soldiers seemed to be enjoying themselves. IRA volunteers on standby in safe houses emerged into the streets to an enormous wave of emotion and relief that it was over. There would be no more shooting and dying, no more gaol; unfortunately, it was to be short-lived. If it had ended there and then it would have lasted the same length of time as the War of Independence, we weren't to know it was destined to become 'the long war'!

As in the case of the soldiers' deaths in the few days before the ceasefire, IRA activities continued unabated, and for the Turf Lodge unit, a final operation led to the arrest of six volunteers during a major armed robbery at Hughes Bakery just hours before the ceasefire: Jim Scullion, Sean Fryers,

Tommy Downey, Micky Flanagan & Gerry Cairns, all have passed in recent years, the final member of the group, Jimmy Dempsey is still with us but sadly his 17 year old son John, a Fianna boy, was killed the morning Joe McDonnell died on hunger strike a decade later. Like all IRA operations, it had been planned long before there was any mention of a ceasefire and coincidental that it was on the same day. With hindsight, it was probably a mistake to go ahead with it, losing six experienced volunteers on a fundraising operation when discretion might have been the better part of valour, but these things happen, I didn't know it then, but it wouldn't be long before I was meeting up with them again.

The first few days of the ceasefire were strange, to say the least. IRA volunteers were evidently on the streets, armed, and on occasion meeting up with British soldiers. A tense few minutes ensued as it was established that they weren't to enter the estate on patrol. All the while, they knew the volunteers were armed but took no action, and the parameters of the ceasefire were laid in a more solid fashion. In nationalist areas, the ceasefire was welcomed across the city. In loyalist areas the UDA and UVF were incensed and set up barricades, engaging in brutal sectarian killings in a bid to end negotiations between 'their' government and their bitterest enemies. Over a dozen Catholics were killed by loyalist paramilitaries in a sectarian blood fest during the few weeks of the ceasefire. Belfast became a scary place to be out at night.

On the 7th July, the first face-to-face talks between the IRA Army Council and the British Government since 1921 took place in an apartment in Cheyne Walk in Chelsea. William Whitelaw et al took the place of Lloyd George and Winston Churchill whilst Sean McStiofain, Daithi O'Conaill, and the late Martin McGuinness stood in for Collins and the plenipotentiaries on the Irish side. Also, Gerry Adams was released from Long Kesh for the discussions but the talks were doomed from the start. The IRA demanded British withdrawal while the British just wanted an end to violence, and so never the twain would meet for another 25 years. The ceasefire collapsed and 35 people were killed the following week after the breakdown of the ceasefire in Lenadoon and then, on one horrific day, Belfast was rocked by 22 bombs which left nine dead. Another bloody day was then added to the calendar: Bloody Friday. It was utter chaos. The Belfast Brigade set out to show the British Government that they could make the place unworkable but the logistics of placing so many bombs in downtown Belfast in a short period of time was just a disaster waiting to happen, from the high moral ground of Bloody Sunday six months earlier, the IRA took a major blow to its reputation as the revolutionary army defending the nationalist people. It took a major hit to its ability to go toe to toe on the streets with the British Army with the support of the people. Its core support would always be there but in the Republic especially, the people became disenchanted with developments north of the border. The years singing 'Sean South' were coming to an end in the disillusionment of real conflict rather than a misty-eyed emotional attachment to the fourth green field. It wasn't just that, people were used to singing all the songs in the Republic, and it was great when the War of Independence was 50 years ago but when the modern conflict started it was too close to home. Moreover, with a state moulded in the shape of Fianna Fáil and Fine Gael who had never done a thing about partition, their singing about 'The Dying Rebel' or 'Come Out you Black and Tans' didn't sit that comfortably, especially if there was a Garda in the family or you wanted a job in the civil service.

I headed down to Donegal for a few weeks as the ceasefire progressed and spent time at the uncle's Pub, the Mountain Bar, in Termon near Glenveagh Castle. A great wee rural pub which rarely, if ever, closed. The nights were always long with the sun rising as the last of the locals would be leaving. It was a great spot for the men returning from the bog after a day's work turning turf, footing, or taking the turf home. The tractors would pull in with a load of winter fuel onboard and several bottles of Double Diamond would be consumed and the craic would be mighty. The two uncles, John and Mick, were local legends who could kill a bottle of Bushmills a day. They never married, well, Mick did but that's another story, both led a bachelor life. They were handymen who could put their hands to anything, cars, washing machines, TVs, electrical work, plumbing, and welding. They were self-sufficient, surviving the decades of Bush (the whiskey, that is, not George) until their 80's when both died the same weekend. They had argued and fought all their lives, and couldn't live together but couldn't live apart. They were 'two tics' (lunatics) according to old John Lafferty who lived with them and did all the work on the farm and in the bog. He was a great old man who we treated like an uncle. I brought him to our wedding years later to spite the uncles who treated him almost in indentured servitude; I had great time for old Lafferty.

The few weeks in Donegal would be my last in freedom for a long time. It was a fun time, as Donegal is most of the time. I started to get to know many of the young guys locally: 'big Kevin' in the Lagoon, wee Eddie (RIP), John Doye, Dan Owen, Frank, Harry, Fred et al. They all became great friends over the years but unfortunately, there would be a slight hiatus before I really got to know them. As I was enjoying a few weeks of freedom in the 'Hills' that long hot summer, word was coming from Belfast that things weren't going to plan and the ceasefire was in danger of collapsing. The loyalists were putting pressure on the IRA to respond with their sectarian murder campaign and the British weren't playing ball in negotiations. There was a sense of inevitably about it all. Within weeks the British forced the issue comprehensively by sending in the tanks to nationalist areas to end no-go areas, especially in free

Derry. The biggest military engagement since Suez brought 27,000 troops, 22,000 British Army and 5000 UDR, rampaging through republican strongholds in West Belfast, South Armagh, and Derry. It had been fairly well highlighted by British generals and the IRA melted into the background as Operation Motorman added a new dimension to the conflict. Resistance to this massive show of strength by the British would have been foolhardy and thus the reaction on the streets was muted. Two were killed in Derry but a terrible incident took place in Claudy — a small village in South Derry — where nine people were killed in three car bomb attacks. As a mostly nationalist but mixed area, it was a sort of earlier version of Omagh 25 years later. Innocent civilians were slaughtered going about their business in the sleepy village. It obviously wasn't intended to happen but as in 'Bloody Friday', the logistics and warning systems were ill-prepared. Three weeks later, a similar tragedy took place at Newry customs post when a bomb went off prematurely and three IRA volunteers and five civilians were killed. It was another disastrous incident which damaged support for the IRA within their own community, but like many events at the time, there was so much happening that it got lost in the mists of time except by the grieving families of all involved.

In the middle of the month, I decided to head back to Belfast. The uncles were dismayed. "You'll not last a fortnight," John exclaimed. How right he was. I immediately reported back to the local unit, and things were crazy: daily riots, gun battles, and the city centre was being blown to pieces. Society was dismayed as what appeared to be some sort of solution to the conflict a few weeks previously was more than just a false dawn. The ferocity and the intensity of the conflict had moved to a different level, and the numbers of deaths had risen in every arena including British soldiers, IRA volunteers, loyalists, and civilians. In fact, 1972 would be the highest death toll of the whole conflict with almost 500 killed in that year alone. In Turf Lodge, the IRA unit were involved in attacks on army foot patrols day and night. It was a constant battle of wits. The volunteers knew their own backyard so well it gave a distinct advantage. They could skip over walls, veer through back gardens, down entries, at all times avoiding the army patrols who criss crossed the estate maybe 50 at a time, parallel, in a manner, to deny IRA volunteers room to manoeuvre between streets. What the army couldn't interrupt, however, was the capacity of ordinary people to give essential support to the volunteers by opening their doors as they escaped after a shooting, providing a change of clothes, offering washing facilities, or billets in safe houses where exhausted volunteers could grab some sleep. Little old ladies all through the area provided this logistical support to the volunteers, the fish in the water, who got by with the support of the people.

The British could never understand that these volunteers weren't terrorists to the people who lived in the nationalist areas. It was the Paras and the Marines who were seen as terrorists. No guerrilla army can survive without the support of the people, and so the IRA survived the 30 years of the conflict through massive support from their community. If you were walking down a street carrying a rifle, a wee woman would come out to her door and say: "there's an army foot patrol just around the corner." Or if you were racing away from attacking a patrol, a wee woman would peer over the hedge and shout, "in here son", no questions asked. The rifle would be dropped and escape would be made out the back door, across garden fences, and into a safe house a few streets away. The army patrol would get lost in the warren of houses, women banging bin lids, dogs barking and young guys lobbing petrol bombs. The soldiers must have felt that this was the tour of duty from hell.

All of this activity, of course, came with risks and while we weren't averse to taking them we tried to minimise them. But, sometimes your luck runs out and at the end of the month, mine did. On the 28th August in'72, after a meeting of the unit, a group of us attempted to set up an ambush at the street corner where we had noticed that Army patrols would take shelter against a fence. The regiment in the area at the time just happened to be '2 Para', full cousins of '1 Para' who went berserk in Derry seven months earlier. The reputation of 2 Para was no different; they usually shot first and asked questions later. They patrolled the area heavily, giving us little breathing space. Their tactics were different from other regiments who arrived in '72 who seemed intent on an easy life just getting through their four month tour of duty. The Paras had different ideas; they took the 'war' to us. When their patrols were attacked they would charge towards where they thought the shooting came from, whereas other regiments patrolled in heavily armoured cars, the Paras drove around in open jeeps and would leap out of them as shots rang out. We had a grudging respect for them; whatever area in Belfast they were based in, it was usually quieter than normal.

The only place where the Paras couldn't handle was South Armagh which became a major thorn in the Army's side, especially around Crossmaglen.They built their 'fort' adjacent to the local GAA pitch to give them protection; the locals became human shields. They did the same in Belfast building army 'forts' beside schools and GAA pitches like St Teresa's and Casement Park, totally illegal in humanitarian law, but great preparation for the army in Iraq and Afghanistan. The difference with South Armagh and Belfast was that in the city you couldn't prepare massive landmines. The danger to the civilian population was paramount whereas in South Armagh they could crater every road in the place to the extent that eventually the army couldn't move about on foot and had to fly into and out of the army bases by helicopter. South Armagh was, in effect, a de facto republic, a no-go area for British forces. Sec.of State Merlyn Rees coined the phrase 'Bandit Country' and Toby

Harnden published a book with the same title, but in reality, the British Army were the bandits among the ordinary decent country people. It was always an area onto itself down through the centuries, an area of smuggling and certain lawlessness. Throughout the conflict, Crossmaglen was an inspiration to republicans and to the IRA in particular.

At around 8:30 on the night, 28th August '72, we laid an IED (improvised explosive device) attached to the fence where the soldiers would haunch down, as we prepared to take cover behind a wall to observe the movements of the army patrols didn't a Para patrol appear. As we attempted to flee, others appeared with rifles pointed at us, bullet in the breech, and ordered us to lie down in the garden; the poachers were snookered by the gamekeepers.

We had other volunteers as lookouts in various positions but somehow they had missed the foot patrol — a moment of indiscipline and indecision caused some rancour among us over the years. It was carelessness from others which caused us our freedom. Just before the Paras arrived, another volunteer who was with us vaulted over the garden fence and walked down the street and into the Para patrol. He wasn't stopped and kept on walking and apparently his IRA 'career' ended that night. That close shave was enough for him and he settled into normal life, married a girl who used to play football with us in our teens, and years later their home would provide a safe house while a foot patrol of Marines chased us through a block of flats. Johnny Burns, a fellow volunteer, and I were made to lie face down in the garden, our shoes taken off in case we tried to make a run for it, amid kicks, punches, and being battered by butts of SLR rifles as the Paras unleashed a stream of expletives:"you murdering Irish bastards." As more and more soldiers appeared in jeeps and armoured cars, word soon spread that two volunteers had been caught by the Paras and hundreds of residents gathered. Soon, a riot developed as we lay crumpled in a heap. The rumour was that we had been knocked out by rifle butts but unfortunately, we were only too aware and trepidation set in as the Paras eventually threw us into an armoured car with about ten of them jumping in with us. We were face down on the floor of the Saracen with twenty sets of army regulation size 10 boots on our backs as they threatened to take us up the mountain and shoot us; it was frightening. As nervous tension prevailed, they drove us to the army base near Springmartin, a loyalist area. We were taken out of the armoured car with soldiers shouted to waiting loyalists: "We've got two more fenian bastards." They also threatened to throw us out to the loyalist crowd which would have only one ending.

Inside the base, other soldiers cheered as we were brought in and spread-eagled against a wall and searched. Our hands were checked for traces of explosives, then we were brought to separate rooms to be met by the I.O who I had met previously when held for a few days. He hit me a slap saying: "Thought you said you were finished with all this?" Considering we were caught red-handed, the interrogation was fairly straightforward. They had no need for violence to extract a confession as we were caught red handed. We refused to make a statement but, of course, that was irrelevant as they had the bomb we intended to inflict injury if not death on the Army patrol, our fingerprints all over it like a rash. Defeating scientific detection would still be a thing for the future; we were hoisted by our own petard.

Back in the estate, the Paras raided both our houses and turned the neat little terraced homes of my parents and Johnny's sister upside down hoping to find more incriminating evidence, as if they hadn't enough. We had been caught nearby my house and just around the corner from Johnny's, but my parents were unaware that it was their son who had been apprehended and was lying in a nearby garden. As you can imagine, my mum was distraught as was Johnny's sister, Ena, who would be plunged into even greater distress within a few months. It was a difficult time for all, including parents and siblings who were losing loved ones for a considerable period of time — and ourselves, of course, who had said farewell to personal freedom for years. Our local unit was deprived of two more volunteers as the attrition rate began to bite after Operation Motorman when the British Army re-entered 'Free Derry' and destroyed the 'no-go' areas in Belfast. Girlfriends, too, for whom the future had been compromised but at least there were no wives and children involved which would have made the future years of imprisonment more difficult to handle. On the plus side, considering the gung-ho killer instincts of the Paras within the previous year in Ballymurphy and Derry, we were still alive, but long years in Long Kesh lay ahead.

In the morning, we were brought to the courts and a charge sheet was presented to us with the relevant words being: 'Being in possession of a bomb and attempted murder'. As we were led into the dock by two Warders, we turned our backs to the Judge. Later that day, after hours in the holding cells at Townhall St barrack beside the Courts, we were handcuffed and loaded into police vans with several other guys who were headed in the same direction. We were driven through the city centre and on to the motorway to that place we had left just a few months earlier. Internment had been phased out (until the ceasefire collapsed), now the Cages were filling up again, both internees and remand political prisoners were held there while sentenced prisoners were held in Crumlin Road Gaol. We were bound for Long Kesh once again. The reality in that summer of '72 was that the average 'career' lifespan for an IRA volunteer was about three months, while an illegal guerrilla army the IRA was also operating openly on the streets with the support of the people, while an integral part of the peoples' part in civil disobedience it also led to a lack of security for IRA vols. and a certain 'laissez-faire' approach to operations and the numbers being 'lifted' reflected this. The attrition rates were difficult to sustain, not helped by our refusing to recognise the courts which, while initially a principled response to British courts, left us hamstrung with convictions almost guaranteed.

On arrival at Long Kesh, we were processed through the system and then brought to Cage 6, one of the republican remand cages. There, we met up with many friends and comrades from the streets. Tommy Gorman who had escaped off the Maidstone was in the next bunk to me after being recaptured recently, along with loads of Andytown, Ballymurphy and Ardoyne men, Derry 'muckers', loads of countrymen, Dublin and Donegal men. The effects of Bloody Friday and 'Motorman' resulted in a massive amount of volunteers filling the cages of Long Kesh; it would stay that way for the next 25 years. One of the first guys I met was big Jim Smith, a 'Stickie' who I visited just a week earlier with my mate Paddy, his brother. We laughed with incredulity that I was back in the place so soon; it wouldn't be long until Paddy was to join us. My parents came up to visit the next day. They were saddened by the situation but would always support me like all the families on the outside. That knowledge that our families and communities were behind us gave us great moral support. Madeleine also visited at the start but with the realisation that I was going to be imprisoned for a long time, our relationship petered out. That was the best solution. It was harder for those married, and while a majority of relationships would survive the years of imprisonment, many did not.

We settled into Cage life relatively quickly, I suppose, conditioned a bit by our previous stint as internees. There was a command structure within the Cage. We drilled and had lectures, and because we were remand prisoners we had regular visits, and there was the weekly journey to Belfast for the court appearance. "Mar bhaill de Óglaigh na hÉireann...as IRA volunteers we refuse to recognise this British court." After a few weeks in the Cages, a situation developed with the Screws that set the trend for many years afterwards. One evening near lock up time, they locked us in the huts at 9pm. This night, a row broke out over something fairly trivial, I can't recall what, but I think it was over a faulty boiler and no hot water. We refused to let the screws lock us up and they withdrew to the perimeter, and before we knew it the Cage was full of soldiers and we were frog-marched out of the huts, spread-eagled against the wire, hit by batons, and kicked as they emphasised their superiority over us. Then, after taking a headcount they made us run the gauntlet between two rows of baton-wielding soldiers. Some were beaten more than others. One guy who took a bad beating was Frankie Dodds from the Lower Falls. It was just pot luck. Some sadistic Brit took enjoyment out of battering a few defenceless Provos, it would have repercussions for Frankie in a few years. We would experience this many times over the years before exercising a form of revenge when we burned the camp in '74.

On the streets, things were getting seriously out of hand with everyday bombings on city-centre commercial property, along with IRA volunteers, loyalists, British soldiers, UDR men, RUC, and innocent civilians being killed daily, especially nationalists who were victims of sectarian murder gangs. Frank Corr lived at the bottom of our street. He was a top official in Antrim GAA, a hurling selector and referee, and in late July he was crossing the city to finish a job at a house when he was stopped at a UDA roadblock and abducted along with another man, James McGerty. They were beaten and tied by the hands and feet and put in the boot of his car, then shot in the head and the car set on fire. It was a horrendous sectarian murder, typical of what was happening regularly as loyalists responded to republican violence by killing innocent Catholics in an effort to get the nationalist community to put pressure on the IRA. It was an ill-thought-out policy on behalf of the UDA/UVF but it also satisfied the extreme sectarian bigotry of many loyalist paramilitaries who had an intense hatred of Catholics. It personified the sectarian nature of the six county statelet. It was a cesspit of disgusting bigotry which had led to the conflict in the first place. Gusty Spence murdered the first innocent Catholic in 1966; it would be the calling card of loyalist killers for the 25 years of conflict. Frank Corr's horrific death in '72 would personify the hundreds who would die just because of their faith. It was the most difficult area of the conflict. While the IRA took on the British Army, the loyalists just murdered Catholics during the long years of the conflict, many in the most horrific manner: stabbed, throats cut, hung, almost decapitated, and burned. The hatred of sectarian killers knew no bounds. The British tried to tell the world that it was a sectarian battle and they were keeping the peace, but the number of sectarian killings from republicans was minute in comparison to the number of Catholics killed by loyalists. Certainly, there were some: in '74, there was a spate of tit-for-tat attacks around the Ardoyne, and the killings in South Armagh in '75. Both cases were carried out to let loyalists know they wouldn't get away with killings without reprisal but it didn't sit right within republican circles and was never repeated.

On September 17th, a Para, Frank Bell, was shot in Ballymurphy and died a few days later. The Paras went berserk in the area for a few days and lifted loads of people and one of those arrested, Liam Holden, was battered so much during the interrogation that he signed a statement that he had shot the Para and he was charged with murder. The following April, he was sentenced to be hanged by the Lord Chief Justice just a few weeks after he had sentenced a loyalist killer to the same treatment. In the volatile situation on the streets, both loyalists and republicans upped the ante threatening to hang British soldiers from lamp posts on the streets if the men were hanged. It had been 30 years since the last IRA volunteer, Tom Williams, had been hanged, and this led to severe tension on the streets. The two men spent months in a condemned cell but then Willie Whitelaw, the secretary of state, fearing serious disorder ordered a reprieve and then took 'death in the manner authorised by law' off the statute books. It was not just a reprieve for the two men involved but for society as a whole. I got to know Liam Holden in the Cages over the years as he served his commuted life sentence. I have seen the depositions and his statement which started with, "I killed the Para." Liam Holden might have been hanged for something he didn't do. While he was a member of the Ballymurphy unit, he wasn't involved in the murder of that unfortunate Para; I was assured of that by other members of his unit. That was always the problem with capital punishment, that horrific ending to life; if you make a mistake you can't undo it.

A week later IRA, volunteer Jimmy Quigley was shot dead by the Paras in a day-long gun battle. Afterwards, a female volunteer in the Official IRA and a soldier was also killed. Jimmy had been in Crumlin Road with me for rioting and also interned. Two of his brothers, Frank and Tommy, were in the Cages with us and Tommy was gaoled later in England for bombing offences. Ironically, my dad and his dad, a photographer, were good friends. A few weeks later, another three volunteers were killed when a bomb they were making ignited and the house burned down. I had known one of them, John Donaghy, who was a young Fian with us. The curse of mistakes with explosives was claiming more lives than those killed by the army. It needed to be (and was) rectified as time went on and expertise increased. It was a difficult time; with hindsight, if I think back on it, there was a bit of blind faith in delivering a device prepared by someone else and not knowing the level of their expertise?

A few days later, perhaps the saddest death took place of four-year-old James Doherty who was shot by unknown gunmen. He was the wee son of Ena, sister of Johnny Burns, who had been lifted with me, the news was difficult for him and devastating for his parents. We used the situation to try for bail for the funeral but it was refused probably with a good foundation, we had no intention of going back. Over the years, there has been speculation on who shot young James. He was killed by a .38 bullet, not a type used by the army but that doesn't preclude them as they would have used non-official weapons in killings. The RUC suggested that it came from a republican weapon but that has never been proven. The IRA said no volunteers were in the street at the time. Years later, an ex-army guy made a statement that he had been with a group of undercover soldiers patrolling in the area looking for a republican on the run and one of the soldiers' guns went off accidentally and they sped off, but again, this has never been confirmed. It's a mystery that has left his parents lamenting the loss of life of their wee son, a life of heartbreak. Another extremely sad casualty of the conflict.

These deaths just highlighted how the growing conflict was affecting the whole community: innocent civilians, IRA volunteers, and British soldiers. In the same four month period, 28 Catholics were killed by the UDA/UVF, another nine Protestants were killed by loyalists, four Catholics were shot by the British Army, 17 IRA volunteers were killed, 37 soldiers were killed, seven UDR men, four UDA men, three Official IRA, two RUC men, three Protestants and a Catholic shot by the IRA, two loyalists shot by the army, three informers shot by the IRA, nine civilians killed in an IRA bomb at Claudy, seven killed in a bomb at Newry customs. 135 victims of the conflict from all sides. It was turning into a conflict of the ages seen in front of the eyes of the world on TV, fought out in the streets of a western democracy on the edge of Europe; a full scale guerrilla war, an armed struggle, sectarian warfare, paramilitaries, army, and the RUC. 1972 would prove to be the bloodiest year of the conflict with over 500 people killed that year alone in a small society of one and half million. Combined with the ever-increasing amount of non-fatal casualties, it was turning into an almighty blood bath. The dream of peace during the ceasefire in July and an amnesty for political prisoners by Christmas '72 was fading fast. The conflict was turning into a 'long war' — a phrase not yet in use. The turmoil, despair, tragedy, and sadness of conflict would run its course over the next 25 years. Put in context, the War of Independence lasted two years; the civil war one year; WWI lasted four years; WW2 five years; the Easter Rising lasted a week; the battle of the Somme lasted five months; the conflict in the six counties would span the generations.

One disturbing aspect of the whole conflict was the question of people killed as informers which needs to be looked at very carefully. To be honest, I never thought some 18-year-old volunteer would have much information to give away. Also, there was a difference between a guy who broke during interrogation and gave away 'gear' and names, and someone who was working for the RUC/army as a paid informer. In particular, the Scapaticci and Denis Donaldson cases highlighted something seriously wrong at the leadership level. Top level informers possibly had volunteers killed to protect themselves? Informing has been the bane of Irish revolutionary groups for 200 years. Denis Donaldson paid the price. Scap deserved to but didn't. Someone in the know delivered Gibraltar and Loughgall, in this country an informer has always been classed as the lowest form of human being, disgusting individuals?

Johnny and I settled into our life in the Cages along with hundreds of others, mostly republican. However, quite a lot of loyalists were starting to enter the Cages and as on the outside, we were divided but through time we would come to work together in the common interest — but that was a few years down the line. Most of our time on remand was spent in the Cages, although eventually before our trial, we would be transferred to Crumlin Road gaol. Long Kesh was in its early stages of development. The internees were held in the lower end of the camp, their numbers increasing daily as the army combed republican areas searching houses, roadblocks, army 'forts' set up at Casement Park, Fort Monagh, Whiterock, the Henry Taggart, and many others. There were hidden observation posts, other outposts on top of Divis and New Lodge flats. RUC stations became fortified military bases, Andersonstown, Springfield Road et al. West Belfast was being turned into an area with a high concentration of military forces, a virtual militarised zone, and the Ardoyne and Short Strand were similar, along with the Bogside, Creggan, and South Armagh. Every nationalist area in the six counties was under observation by the British Army. Almost every person, particularly young male, in these areas would be stopped by army patrols, questioned, and had their details logged. Houses searched would be photographed and the layout of the house documented, and so a dossier built up. The six counties would become the most militarized area in Western Europe, maybe even in the world in 1972. Only events like the Munich Olympics shootings or the PLO hijacking planes in Lebanon would knock Ireland off the front pages. In the last few months of ‘72, it became the most deadly, dangerous place on the planet. Possibly the saddest case of 1972 was the 'disappearance' of Jean McConville.Was she a high-placed informer? What information could a housewife and mother of nine really know? She was hardly an articulate highly placed informant, if anything she passed on street tit bits? Did the punishment fit the crime? It's very debateable. What it didn't deserve was to be removed from her family for 40 years.

Around Christmas in ‘72, a group of us remand prisoners were transferred to Crumlin Road gaol in preparation for our trial in the New Year. It was an old Victorian gaol which had welcomed republican prisoners in every decade since partition. Crumlin Road in 1942 witnessed the last IRA volunteer to be hanged in the six counties, Tom Williams. Williams was caught with Joe Cahill who would become Chief of Staff in the ’70s, and Dickie Cordner from Turf Lodge who I knew in later years. They were all sentenced to death but all reprieved except Williams. His memory is recalled in a Belfast republican ballad still in vogue today.

We settled into the 'Crum' — it was different from the Cages, obviously, which had open huts whereas the 'Crum' was a traditional gaol divided into four wings: A, B, C, and D with a circle from which the Screws controlled the place. We were placed in cells, with two to a cell measuring 6’ x 2’ with a fairly uncomfortable bed, a chamber pot, and a small grilled window. That would be our home for the next few months. We had a certain amount of freedom during the day in C-wing where we were domiciled and a few hours of exercise in the yard where we walked around anti-clockwise in the triangular space. Everyone on the wing was on remand awaiting their trial while over in A-wing, the sentenced prisoners were held — the numbers increasing every day. They had political status after a hunger strike led by Billy McKee in the summer had been granted during the negotiations leading up to the first ceasefire. We would all benefit from it over the following years but it caused consternation to the British Government. This would lead to the reversal of the decision in 1976 which led to the H-Blocks and the hunger strike of 1981, but that was all in the future.

January 1973 came in with a bang — literally —as the IRA blasted the city centre. There had been a temporary Christmas ceasefire but it was business as usual in the New Year. Inside the gaol, we continued with the usual activities: Lectures, drills, education, testing the security of the gaol, visits, writing letters and poems, and having problems with the Screws which led to the odd confrontation. This was prison life for republicans.

As well as the serious side of things, there was always a wicked sense of humour prevailing which, to be honest, helped morale, Belfast black humour at its best. Many stunts were performed which the 'victims' weren't overly impressed with but, in turn, they would inflict them on new suspects just arrived in the gaol. A few, I remember, were brilliant in the execution; escapes were usually the focus for any of the pranks. Martin Meehan from Ardoyne who had been caught again after escaping previously was a sort of iconic figure. He had already achieved legendary status for his activities in the Ardoyne and along the border when he was on the run. He was OC on the wing and would take part in the fun and games which lent an air of authenticity to events which threw the victims of the prank off guard.

A fairly routine skit was telling one of our comrades that he had been selected to go on an escape as he was considered important enough for the leadership outside to request his inclusion on the escape plan. The poor guy who was selected would be told that four would be on the escape and that they would be put inside laundry sacks; these would be left in the yard to be collected, and the orderlies and the driver would be in on the plan, and the bags would be loaded up and driven out of the gaol. So the guy would be well primed, told who to report to on the outside, given some money to get him across the Border where GHQ would be awaiting him, and after recuperation he would join a unit in South Armagh and the Cooley mountains to continue the struggle. When the day came, the guy would be put inside the laundry bag and carried out into the middle of the yard and left there while the rest of us would walk around the yard. Eventually, the guy (after maybe an hour sitting inside the bag suspecting that things hadn't gone to plan) eventually emerged out of the bag to the roars of laughter from the assembled ranks of volunteers. Indeed, even the Screws could be aware what was happening and enjoyed it as well. The poor guy, crestfallen, made his way across the yard back to his cell muttering several expletives but, to be honest, holding his hand up accepting that he was caught with his pants down.

Another brilliantly thought-out 'escape plan' which I was a victim of myself was really theatre at its best. It only worked on new arrivals and just after we arrived, six of us were told to be in a certain cell for a briefing on an escape plan. In the cell we were told that an escape was planned for that evening and we were selected. We had to blacken our faces with boot polish and were given strips of a blanket to protect our hands as we climbed over the perimeter wall which was covered in barbed wire. Meehan would then arrive in the cell to give a sense of authenticity and wish us all well. He explained the risks; we could be recaptured, or shot, but we were needed outside and what a great propaganda boost it would be! The plan was that all the Screws would be taken prisoner and held in other cells, and when the theme tune of Coronation St. was heard on television at the end of the programme at 8 pm, we were to dash out of the cell, down the stairs, and the circle (which had been taken over) would be open and we would have access to the perimeter — and freedom. We were excited, if somewhat sceptical, and if you think about it there was as much chance of escape from the heart of the gaol as there was England winning the World Cup. Nonetheless, as the Coronation St. tune boomed out of volume enhanced televisions, Meehan wished us good luck and like Paras leaping out of an aeroplane we charged out of the cell to be met by the whole Wing cheering, even the Screws; it was hilarious. What could you do but laugh? The Great Escape it was not. But events like this were great for morale and helped everyone face their incarceration. 'Doing time' wasn't easy for everyone, or indeed anyone; we were young guys as well, we had lost our liberty, we weren't hardened criminals for which gaol was a way of life. We did have a camaraderie which 'ordinary, decent prisoners' wouldn't have. We were involved in something much bigger than normal everyday life, and these little pranks helped us through the years of imprisonment.

As we awaited our trial date, we would meet up with some of the sentenced prisoners on occasion; the Turf Lodge guys who were caught on the day of the ceasefire had got ten years for their entrepreneurial skills at Barney Hughes Bakery. They were all in the A-Wing. One of them whispered to me one day: "Hurry up and get over here." It seemed an innocent enough comment but there was a hidden message: at that moment in time there was a plan to empty the whole of A-wing. A tunnel was in progress underneath the floor of the wing and also, on the outside, the IRA had taken over a house near the gaol and were digging from the outside with the plan for the tunnels to meet. The biggest escape in prison history was planned with up to 200 prisoners going to make their exit to the embarrassment of the authorities. Unfortunately, as the plan almost reached fruition the army, whether by chance or acting on information, came to the door of the house demanding entrance. Being in a sort of a middle-class area, the IRA volunteer who answered the door demanded a warrant and when the Brits went away, the volunteers scarpered leaving the army with an empty house to search and discover the 40ft tunnel underneath the gaol walls; the plan to empty A-wing was foiled. It would have been a spectacular escape but it wasn't to be. The following week, the 200 political prisoners were transferred to Long Kesh and so began the use of the Cages for the mass of sentenced IRA prisoners; within a few weeks, we would be joining them.

On the 1st February, St Bridget's Day, we wouldn't be making Celtic crosses but making our way through the underground tunnel which connected the gaol with the Courthouse for our trial. This was the same tunnel thousands of republican prisoners had walked through over the year's right back to the Fenians. Some would be facing the gallows; Tom Williams was hanged, Joe Cahill survived for another day, others like Jim Bryson would make a one-way journey as he escaped from the Courthouse, sadly to die on the streets a year later. It would be a fairly short and not-so-sweet journey, as, like always, we refused to recognise the British court choosing instead to make our objections as gaeilge, In hindsight, refusing to recognise the courts was a self-defeating prophesy; so many volunteers were only charged with membership, and by refusing to recognise the court they were sent down. Eventually, the leadership changed that tactic; essentially, it was just a tactic not a principle. The judge enquired of the Screws if we understood the lingua franca which they affirmed we did. They handed us papers relating to our case which we threw at the judge who threatened to gaol us for contempt of court before we even faced the charges pertaining to our case. We sat down in protest and the Screws manhandled us into an upright position to face the unionist judge. The Paras who arrested us trooped in and perjured themselves with all sorts of lies which weren't really needed as it was a prima facie case. The judge, a castle catholic of course, wasn't impressed by our efforts to take revenge for Bloody Sunday when the self-same Paras murdered innocent civilians. On a personal level they had also arrested Johnny and me!

The judge sentenced us to six years in prison for 'possession of a bomb with intent to inflict injury on members of a British Army patrol'. It wasn't exactly going to be 'bread and water' but we were to spend the best part of our young lives in the Cages of Long Kesh. We 'thanked' the judge for his slavish subservience to the British state implying he was a British lackey; flustered and outraged he instructed, 'take them away'! The Screws dragged us down below to the cells to await the return journey to the Kesh.We waved to our distraught families as we were led away. They understood us even if the judge didn't. They would be a great support over the coming years; in many ways, it was more difficult for them.

Readers might find it difficult to read that we had placed a bomb to take the lives of British soldiers? We didn't do it lightly but there was a conflict in our country and they were foreign soldiers on our streets, the British murdered many innocent civilians in Derry and Dresden, in WW2 millions of Germans were engaged in conflict as were British, all through that same quirk of fate as ourselves, being born in a country at war. Saying that, I abhorred fascism and Nazism; as with Franco and Mussolini, Hitler was evil, as was Thatcher!

We were to be domiciled in Long Kesh and nothing we could do about it. Our families had to travel up and down to the prison bringing food parcels, clothes, and news. Their weekly routine was interrupted by our imprisonment. It was the families of the prisoners who were the strongest in the whole situation; they never let us down. Most of our parents are passed on now but we will never forget how they stood by us in times of need. Sitting in the holding cell, waiting for transport to our domicile for the foreseeable future, Johnny and I contemplated what lay ahead of us: six years. It mightn't seem much now when you're 68 but when you're 18 it seems like a hell of a long time. We wondered what lay ahead and considered that the conflict would be over by the time we were released. How we would manage the long dreary years ahead wasn't a priority, just getting through the next three months was about as far ahead as we would consider. The big plus, of course, was that we would be among friends. We were political prisoners so gaol for us wasn't the normal. The establishment was just happy to get us off the streets so what we did in the Cages didn't bother them too much. Lock us up and don't let us escape, that satisfied the government. We had complete control within the Cages; life as a political prisoner might have been denied freedom like any other prisoner but we were on a different wavelength. Our strength was our conviction that we were political prisoners involved in a political struggle. We had political status during the whole period of our confinement, although after our release the new regime would be put in place which led to the blanket protest, the dirty protest, and eventually, the hunger strikes; but that was all in the future.

We held contempt for the prison warders who were, to a man; usually loyalists there for the big pay check to be earned. We despised them, usually uneducated, many with a bigoted approach to life. We had utter contempt for them, and they for us, I presume. But our principled stance was on a different plane to their financial greed. I've never hated any man in this world but my disgust for these 'Screws' exceeded mere contempt. In my opinion they were despicable, highlighted in later years in the H-Blocks when they abused republicans over 4 years of protest. Their behaviour inside the gaol led to over 30 of them being executed on the outside. Their tough regime within the H-Blocks didn't protect them when they closed the gates behind them to go off-duty. Our feelings towards them were nothing to do with what religion they were, but purely that they were agents of the state and continued an anti republican agenda in the prisons. They didn't say 'boo' when we had political status but when the shoe was on the other foot after they built the H-Blocks, their behaviour was horrendous; brutalising, inhuman, sadistic. I've never hated anyone in my life but I make an exception for these people. Their disgusting sectarian behaviour towards the hunger strikers and their families during that horrific time led to their demise, the IRA tried to create a situation where they wouldn't feel safe anywhere outside the prison gates, similar to RUC and UDR personnel when they left the safety of their fortified barracks, it was an integral part of the armed struggle. While conflict brings sadness to everyone, because of their actions against defenceless prisoners, can we say they didn't deserve their fate?

Johnny and I had just settled into our new surroundings in Cage 18 in the 'Kesh, part of new construction at the top end of the camp: also 15,16,17,20, and 21 were IRA cages; 14 and 19 were loyalist and 22 the Official IRA Cage; 9-13 were a mix of loyalist and republican Cages; while 1-8 held the internees. At the end of '72, almost 1000 were interned, and when internment was being phased out in '75, nearly 2000 in total had been interned: 1900 republicans and 100 loyalists. At the same time, there were over 1200 sentenced political prisoners in the cages. In a small statelet of one and a half million, it was a substantial cohort of the population. Cage 18, like all the Cages, had an eclectic group: city men and country guys; our Cage had a lot of men from Ardoyne; the New Lodge and Short Strand; Derry men; Armagh men; Crossmaglen, Strabane, Dublin, Donegal, and Tyrone; and just three of us from Turf Lodge, Johnny, Hughie Doran, and I. Hughie was a little older than us and he was the first guy lifted from our area. He lived around the corner from my parents, he was a quiet guy — sound and dependable. The Cages were made up of three full-size huts: two holding 30 prisoners each and one used as a canteen, and another smaller hut holding 16, a toilet, a shower block, and a library/reading/study area. The Cage, as the name suggests, was completely made up of 12ft wire fences topped with barbed wire. The outside rectangular yard was big enough to walk or jog around and play a bit of football. The 'Screws' more or less stayed in their hut at the entrance to the Cage with a double lock gate. Every 50 yards or so were watchtowers manned by armed British soldiers overlooking the Cages observing everything.

The normal everyday life consisted of getting up early, eating breakfast, drilling for an hour, that is marching in military formation across the yard. After lunch we had lectures in the afternoon, then a bit of free time in the evening. Occasionally, there would be a film shown and we got to play a match once a week on the big pitch in the centre of the camp. As time went on, night classes were organised with teachers coming in, and plenty of time existed for reading with loads of books sent in to build up an extensive library. The days would also include making handicrafts, hankies, rugs, Harps, Celtic crosses, miniature Thompson submachine guns, and plaques; everything was geared towards keeping morale to a high level. We set up our own education classes: Irish language, Irish history, political education, European and world history, and politics here, the UK, and the US. It was intense stuff, and add in many of us taking 'O' and 'A' Level courses through the Open University, we were political animals dedicated to changing society and our time in Long Kesh was going to be put to good use.

We weren't long in Cage 18 when word came in about a serious incident in the New Lodge area with six guys killed by the British Army and loyalists between the 3rd and 4th February. Three of the men were IRA volunteers, two were shot by the UDA early in the evening, and what followed later was a massive three-way gun battle between the UDA, IRA, and the British Army in which four more were killed by the army. This included Tony 'TC' Campbell, an IRA volunteer who I went to school with, a genuinely friendly wee guy. He and the three civilians were shot by army snipers possibly from the top of flats which they had occupied; none of the six were armed. It was another horrific assault on the community, similar to Derry and Ballymurphy. No soldiers were ever charged. TC Campbell had left school the same time as I did in June '69. Less than four years later he was dead. School friends, street friends, neighbours, IRA comrades, were all being killed as the conflict escalated. It was a difficult time within the Cages when we heard of someone we knew losing their life. In a strange sort of way, my mum used to say that even though we were in gaol we were safe, in a sense. Whereas on the streets some of us could have been victims ourselves. I suppose she was expressing a mother's fears. Unfortunately for many mothers, the sad reality of conflict would cross their door. They were dark, dark times. The euphoria of the early civil rights days. The mass-resistance of the nationalist community against the Stormont regime. The early rioting, stone-throwing, and petrol bombing had morphed into full-scale urban guerrilla warfare.

Belfast became a scary place, especially at night as loyalist killer gangs roamed the darkened streets in the mid 70's to pick up innocent Catholics and murder them. It wasn't safe to be in town having a drink and then walking home. Many a poor guy was picked up by gangs like the Shankill Butchers as they crossed Millfield and had their throats cut. In some cases, it was a relief to be shot as they tortured their victims. The UDA and UVF were made up of many psychopathic, sectarian killers. The Shankill Butchers were, as the name suggests, based in the Shankill Road area, the notorious loyalist heart of Belfast, it's hard to believe that any community could shelter such psychopaths but that's the way it was at the time. They might have had a political ideal to preserve the Union but their actions sometimes defied description. Their collusion with British forces, the RUC, and the UDR made life for nationalists a nightmare at times. Bodies were grotesquely mutilated by knife-wielding thugs and dumped in entries; that wasn't war but sectarian bigots unleashed and supported by elements within the crown forces. Their activities were covered up as John Stalker, the English policeman, would find out when he attempted to investigate the RUC years later.

In early March, a plebiscite was held which was seen as a 'border poll' but nationalists boycotted it leaving a massive vote to stay in the Union from the mainly unionist electorate. It didn't tell us anything we didn't already know. There was a built-in Protestant majority as partition was meant to preserve; it would be 50 years before a referendum on unity would again be on the agenda. On the same day as the referendum, the conflict came to England in time-honoured tradition. Bombs exploded at the Old Bailey as the IRA copied the activities of their predecessors in the IRB (Fenians) in the 1860s. The target was a symbol of British justice which never extended to matters concerning Ireland. These would be the first bombs in the UK during the conflict and they would be a major weapon in the IRA's arsenal over the years. The reality was that one bomb in London was worth 100 in Belfast. The thinking behind it was that this was the only way Westminster would listen and embrace Irish affairs. The active service unit which planted the bombs were all caught boarding planes back to Dublin — a rather naive move, given the circumstances — and received heavy gaol sentences. They included the Price sisters who would take part in a protracted hunger strike when they were force-fed for 200 days, and Gerry Kelly who would become a senior republican politician in later years. In later times post-ceasefire and the Good Friday Agreement, the Price sisters along with Brendan 'The Dark' Hughes et al opposed the direction that Sinn Féin was going in. It was a dissident republican line rejected by mainstream republicans and the general public. They were a minority grouping who failed to accept that there was a time for war, and a time for negotiations and peace. In saying that, the Price sisters were brave women. They suffered over 200 days of force feeding in an English gaol; they were as dedicated as they come and followed in the footsteps of their father, Albert, who was gaoled in England during the bombing campaign in a previous campaign before WWII.

When the bombs went off in London there was great satisfaction within the Cages. We recognised this was a natural progression in 'war' and as there were no casualties, it was a perfect operation. Irish nationalists had bombed England from the IRB in 1860's to 1920 and during WW2; it was a classic tactic to bring the 'war' to England. There was never any intention to harm ordinary people in these actions but to pressurise the British Government. As the campaign increased over the years however, and civilian casualties mounted, it became difficult and Irish people living in the UK suffered. Killing innocent civilians was never on the agenda despite British propaganda stating the contrary. I remember being in the Cages after the Birmingham bombs. Some said it was a job well done, but they were quickly told they were wrong. We didn't set out to kill innocent civilians; the majority in Long Kesh would have been sickened by the 21 deaths in the Midlands city.

At the beginning of September during an IRA feud with the Officials, a three-way gun battle took place with the army joining in and two volunteers were shot: Paddy Mulvenna died on the spot, while Jim Bryson would survive for a few weeks but on the 22nd of September, he passed away. Mulvenna's dad, also Paddy, was in our Cage in the 'Kesh; it was a sad time for him. Jim Bryson, as mentioned earlier, had escaped off the Maidstone and was then recaptured. He was in C-Wing with us when he escaped again from the Courthouse and continued on active service along the border before returning to Belfast where he was killed in that three-way gun battle. It has never been confirmed whether the army or the Official IRA killed him. He was a flamboyant character who embraced the conflict with gusto. Fearing nothing, he helped create an aura of invincibility for Ballymurphy in the early years. He also acquired a status like Joe McCann, Francis Hughes, and Brendan 'The Dark' Hughes, fearless volunteers who took untold risks in their commitment to the republican struggle. I knew 'the Dark' from the Cages but sadly he was like many volunteers who found it hard to accept that the struggle had to move forward and embrace struggle in a different political way. Delores Price was the same. Jim Bryson was in the same mould as 'the Dark'. I'm sure the same was true back in the day. I'm sure Tom Barry wasn't overjoyed at the announcement of the truce in 1921, as indeed many volunteers weren't happy with the truce of 1972?

It wasn't all doom and gloom in the Cages. John Francis Green escaped dressed up as a priest after swapping places with his brother. This was a regular escape ploy. In fact, I had discussed it with a Scottish cousin who looked like me. He was up for it, although many years later we laughed about it suggesting that I would have had the better half of the deal. In the early days, they would just throw you back in the Cages and ban the visitor from visiting, whereas as the years moved on they started charging both prisoner and visitor, and gaol sentences would follow. As a result, it wasn't as appealing for the visitor. A sad incident happened in the same month. On the 9th of September, I had been playing table tennis with Frankie Dodds before lunchtime when he felt a bit out of sorts and was taken to the doctor within the Camp and then on to Lagan Valley hospital on the outside. Word came back within a few hours that Frankie had died; it was devastating stuff. Frankie had received a bad beating in an early riot when we were first in the Cages and was always suffering pains in his legs and feet thereafter. Whether that was the cause or not is conjecture, but it was a real shock to me after our table tennis session. You just never know.

In the Cages, we got on with our daily routine: drilling, making handicrafts, language classes, and lectures. And every so often there would be a confrontation with the 'Screws' and the army would be brought in. One night as the Brits circled the Cages in preparation to search the huts, John Noonan from Dublin recognised one of the soldiers; it was a mate of his from Dublin serving with the Marine Commandos. It was a blow for John who could hardly believe what he was seeing. This lad had left Dublin to go to London for work and ended up in the army at the same time when John headed north to join the IRA. It was one of life's unexpected encounters that they would both meet up in Long Kesh on opposite sides. John mentioned the incident in a book he wrote in later years: "What will I do next?"

Education, as always, was a big thing for us with all sorts of classes. Those of us with a gra as gaeilge formed a virtual 'Gaeltacht' hut where the requirement was to speak whatever amount of Irish you had. It was total immersion in the language; no TV, just Radió na Gaeltachta for music and news. There were ranganna in all grades with the awarding of the fáinne as you progressed with your knowledge of the language. The Gaeltacht hut was an integral part of every Cage; it was progressive in its thinking. I moved into the hut at the end of '73 and got a good grounding in the language and enjoyed the experience immensely. Like on the outside, playing Gaelic games and speaking the language was more than just that in the six counties, it was part of who we were, part of our culture, essentially. We were Irish and not British despite Westminster controlling the six counties and us being identified as UK citizens. As in the revolutionary period between'14 and'23, the armed struggle was complemented by the literary revival, by language, music, and the GAA. It was not ethno-nationalist which had right wing connotations, it was just part of what we were, what we are. We felt that we were continuing the struggle which, in our opinion, was abandoned by the Treaty of 1921.

During the winter of '73, I enrolled in an 'A' Level course with the Open University: English Language and Literature, my love from secondary school. I was enjoying it and combining it with a lot of serious reading I was doing. It was essentially the beginning of my real education and it was something I would embrace during the rest of my time as a political prisoner, indeed, for the rest of my life. I enjoyed reading Shakespeare, Joyce, Wilde and G.B. Shaw, but like all things in the 'Kesh, education would be subjected to overall conditions and every so often there would be some trouble and the authorities would stop all education projects. They would refuse to allow books to be brought in and generally let us stew; thus, the Open University course went by the wayside before the 'third semester' was out. That was the organised education project by the establishment, of course, but we actually spent much more time on our own education efforts by writing and reading prose, poetry, drama, and language. It was a wonderful time in a sense, part of the whole experience as my granddaughter Tiarnach would say when buying expensive popcorn in the Eye cinema, 'it's all about the experience Granddad'! But in our 'experience' it also helped to put some structure into the daily routine. Some guys didn't get involved but they might have made the most beautiful wooden harps. They were skilful with their hands; whatever did it for you was fine.

When we first arrived in the Cages, we were raw young teenagers caught up in something extraordinary. It's not natural to be involved in clandestine organisations, learning to use weapons, committing yourself to a life of struggle and danger, watching over your shoulder, hiding in secret billets, planning attacks on soldiers and police which could involve death, organising bombing missions, gathering intelligence, or attending training camps in Donegal. The constant awareness that the next day could be your last, either of freedom or of life itself, that's not really the way life, is meant to pan out for teenagers, but for a period in the early '70s it was for us. Thousands of us, all disaffected nationalist youths in the six counties who embraced armed struggle with open arms. It was neither exotic nor exciting but it was for a long time our way of life. When we then landed in Long Kesh it became a place to re-evaluate why we were there in the first place, why we had initially taken these steps. Now was the time to understand what exactly the reasoning was for our rationale. Why were we so committed to a cause in which we were only the latest participants in the centuries since Wolfe Tone, Napper Tandy, and Henry Joy McCracken met on the Cavehill to announce the formation of the United Irishmen? Their vision, too, was to break the connection with England, the root cause of all our evils.

Political education was a vital component of our time in the Cages. We would have regular lectures on Irish history, the Plantation of Ulster, the Penal Laws, the Act of Union, Emancipation, the Land League, the GAA, Home Rule, on language and literary revival, and of course physical force republicanism. There were lectures on the United Irishmen, Robert Emmet, Young Irelanders, IRB-Fenians, Ribbonmen, 1916, the War of Independence, Civil War, and the border campaign. There were also lectures on WWI, WW2, as well as the Spanish civil war, Vietnam, Palestine, Cuba, Chile-Allende, Cyprus-Makarios, the French Revolution, the American War of Independence, India and Gandhi, Russian Revolution, Lenin and Trotsky, China and Mao, an eclectic mixture of armed struggles, independence movements, and global conflicts. We were eager to learn why we had taken the steps to follow in the path of fellow revolutionaries across the world. It was essential that we understood why we were fighting, to know the raison d'être for our actions. Of course, that has always been the way in Frongoch, Kilmainham, Curragh, Crumlin Road, Maidstone, Al Rawdah etc. Republicanism was an all-embracing philosophy which we embraced.

We were eager to learn because it reinforced our reactive actions on the streets. It enabled us to realise that we were involved in something much bigger than everyday life, and now we had the confidence to debate and explain our actions. We reinforced our lectures by reading anything and everything we could get our hands on, mostly political biographies, revolutionary struggles, and most importantly, the lessons from Irish history and how the deceit and treachery of those who signed the Treaty in 1921 created the conditions for us to become involved in the same struggle 50 years later. It was a lesson we hoped would prevent our children and grandchildren from experiencing the same outcome. We also read about our erstwhile enemies, the British Government. We read about their previous conflicts in Afghanistan, Palestine, Suez, and Aden; how they approached counter insurgency. We read about British politics and what made them tick. We tried to get inside the heads of Tory and Labour leaders, to understand their rationale for remaining in Ireland. They were an interesting combination of European democrats and old colonial sentimentalists.

The latter half of 1973 witnessed a lot of political talks between the various parties and Willie Whitelaw. There was a vacuum in political life as events on the streets dominated life. With Stormont suspended and a lot of unemployed politicos feeling side-lined by the activities of working-class armed groups, both republican and loyalist, they were desperate to get some form of talking shop up and running so as to hide their irrelevancy at the time. It was a difficult period; setting the cost of council rents or the price of bus fares wasn't exactly a priority when the IRA were making car parks of city centres all over the six counties. Soldiers were dying and returning to the UK in a Union Jack-draped coffin, and public opinion as always in England wasn't really bothered about events in Ireland unless their town was visited by a funeral of a soldier. An IRA bomb in central London, on the other hand, could focus minds for the city executives concerned about profits. Ireland was troublesome but what to do about it was beyond the comprehension of British politicians, probably to be honest the majority of them would rather be shot of the place. To fill the vacuum, Whitelaw had the parties in talks about talks with a view to forming some sort of power-sharing executive between the unionists, the SDLP, and the Alliance. At that stage, Sinn Féin concentrated most of their efforts on supporting the armed struggle and, indeed, weren't involved in mainstream politics as witnessed by non-participation in the Border poll, never mind in Westminster or in Stormont elections. They didn't even take part in council elections. However, all that would change after the hunger strikes, but a lot of water and blood would flow under the bridge before that. At the time, there was a feeling that we would drive the Brits into the sea by armed struggle. Obviously, it wasn't practical or militarily possible, but politics are an extension of war just as much as war is an extension of politics as we would find out in the '90s.

In November that year, an agreement was made to form the new executive. Brian Faulkner who had signed my internment papers was to be Chief Executive and Gerry Fitt, second in command, was an interesting character representing Republican Labour in the early years. He got us our new house in Turf Lodge in '62 and my dad used to taxi him. He gained massive publicity during the civil rights march in Derry which was attacked by the RUC. When the SDLP was formed he was more on the socialist/labour wing whereas John Hume was on the nationalist wing but they worked well together. In later years, he would gain the epithet 'Gerry Fitt is a Brit' as Gerry Adams would take his Westminster seat in West Belfast. He further earned the wrath of West Belfast nationalists by supporting Thatcher during the hunger strikes, an amazing turnaround which earned him a life peerage, the only nationalist/republican ever to sit in the House of Lords: Lord Fitt of Bell's Hill. The following month, the Sunningdale Agreement was signed. For the first time since partition, the Irish Government would be involved in affairs and it would prove to be a bridge too far for loyalism.

While the political parties were trying to regain some form of control over the situation on the streets of Belfast, Derry, and the country lanes around South Armagh, the conflict was ending its fifth year of everyday bombings, shootings, armed robberies, kidnappings, and sectarian killings. While it's flippant to say that people were getting used to the situation, there was a feeling that nothing was going to change very soon. We were in for a period of conflict equally as long as Vietnam; the 'Long War' was in gestation. While men in suits were doing what politicos do outside the doors of perceived power, the IRA were flexing their considerable muscles with ingenuity as they pulled off another incredible escape — this time, right in the heart of Dublin. With a hijacked helicopter, they landed in the gaol yard at Mountjoy and flew away with three IRA leaders: JB O'Hagan, Kevin Mallon, and former Chief of Staff, Seamus Twomey. It was an audacious escape which led to great embarrassment within the Fine Gael government and even greater hilarity within republican circles as the Wolfe Tones released the 'Helicopter Song' which reached top of the charts despite being banned by RTÉ. The chorus reverberated around the lounge bars the length of the country:

"Up like a bird and over the city,
'three men are missing,' I heard the warder cry.
'Sure, it must have been a bird that flew into the prison
Or one of these new ministers,' said the warder from Mountjoy."

As with all escapes, it was a massive morale-boosting operation by the Provisionals, and a major embarrassment to the Irish Government. Despite a huge security operation, the three escapees were spirited away and, after hiding low for a few months, took their places within the higher echelons of the IRA again. Twomey, a former OC of the Belfast Brigade and a tough, chain-smoking former bookie, oversaw the next few years of the campaign until he was recaptured in 1977. Mallon was recaptured within a few months but blasted his way out of Portlaoise with 18 others in '74. O'Hagan was recaptured about a year later. One consequence of the escape was the transfer of all IRA prisoners to the high-security Portlaoise prison. At least 20,000 Irish Army soldiers and Gardai scoured the country for the escapees but to no avail. The ordinary people of the country sheltered the escapees and the bird had flown the coop. Escapes were always massive propaganda coups for the IRA and when times were difficult they gave a boost to morale. It was always thus in Crumlin Road, the Curragh, Mountjoy, Portlaoise, Magilligan, Maidstone, and Long Kesh.When a successful escape took place it was celebrated with gusto in the Cages and the homemade poitín was put to good use. Many's a sore head would result in the morning after some of our comrades evaded tight security and returned to the 'war'. Those of us left behind would redouble our efforts to detect any weakness in the system and maybe it would be our turn next.

Former Tyrone IRA leader Brendan Hughes (the other Brendan Hughes), recently published a book about the escape, 'Up Like A Bird'. Hughes was the main organiser of the escape and the book makes fascinating reading about the spectacular freeing of the 3 IRA leaders, also a future escape when 19 IRA prisoners used explosives to break out of Portlaoise, Hughes hands were all over both escapes, unfortunately for him he fell foul of the IRA leadership in later years and was lucky to survive the conflict.

Two more successful escapes took place before the end of the year: Brendan 'The Dark' Hughes was concealed in a mattress in a refuse lorry and spirited away to freedom despite being half-suffocated on the way. Forty-eight hours later, Jimmy Burns once again availed of a well-used path to freedom by swapping clothes with his visitor and calmly walked out of the place. He jumped on the PDF bus (Prisoners Dependents Fund) and made his way to West Belfast before the alert was raised. Jimmy was a brother of Johnny who had been arrested with me and the next time we would see him was the night we were released while he was still on the run from the 'Kesh. We met him in a social club in Andersonstown and had a few drinks while outside, British Army patrols were walking through the estate. If his freedom was in danger of being compromised, Jimmy would have been spirited away, but he survived for several years before he was recaptured and returned to the H-Blocks.

Russell clan with Mum front right c1930

Kilmacrennan Fife & Drum Band including Grandad Russell, c1921

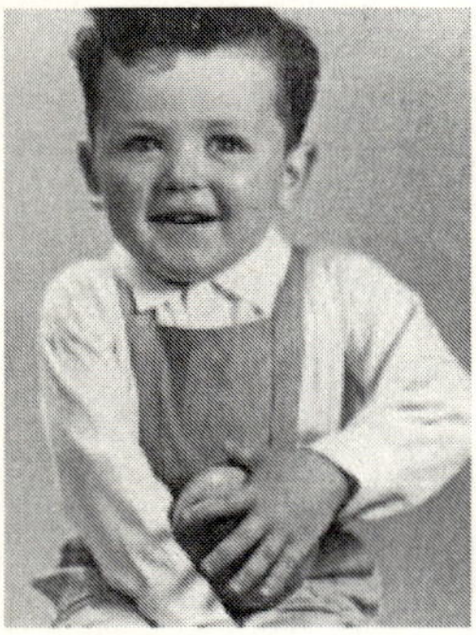

Baby Patrick Joseph 1954

Uncle Mick shoeing a horse at the forge in Doon, Termon
with Grandad supervising, c1950

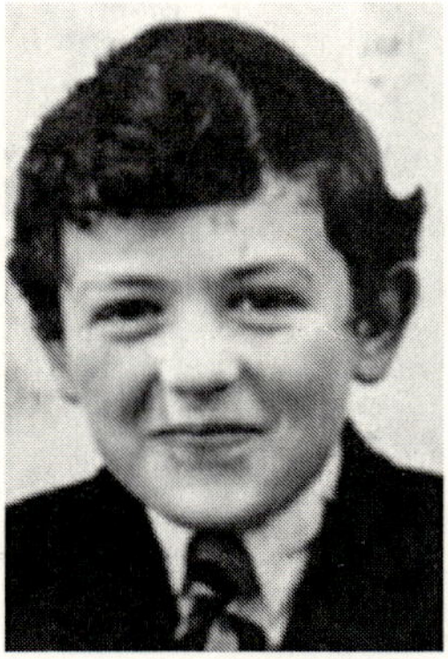

1st year at St Mary's Grammar, 1965

Mum & Dad arriving in Belfast, c1947

25th May 1967 the day Celtic won the European Cup in Lisbon,
myself with Paddy Moran, Jimmy Bell & Kieran Blake

Famous Celtic tea towel with bullet hole, 1971.

Lurgy Celtic 1977

Kilmac Celtic 1987

Lurgy reunion 2012

Mary, Oisin & I in Seville,
UEFA Cup final 2003

Padraic & Donegal Ulster Minor champions 1996

Padraic (Paddy) with
the Liam Murray trophy.

Kevin & Donegal, National League champions 2007.

Kevin (Wappa) 2007

Myself Padraic & Kevin, Termon,
Intermediate champions 1999

Georgie Best with John & Mick
at the 'Mountain Bar', Termon, 1988

Grandchildren with 'Sam Maguire' 2012

Proud Dads, Padraic & Kevin with Cian (Finn Harps)
& Caolan (Derry City), 2020

Golfing heaven, Galway Bay Golf Resort!

Muckish Ramblers in Scotland, 1998

Kirchhoff Golf Society, Gran Canaria 2000

Bogies & Fogies Golf Society, Ballyliffen 2019

Back where it all started, Gran Canaria 2018

Kirchhoff golfer of the year 1999

Books & Golf, my life!

BA Graduation 2009

PGDE Graduation 2010

Masters Degree Graduation 2011

Family are precious, myself, Padraic, Clara & Kevin, 2002.

Life long friendship, 50 yrs, from the streets to the Cages, but maybe not the golf links! Gerry & I, 2021

Marty Forsythe's funeral with guard of honour, October 1971

Paras attack the funeral and mourners protect guard of honour & firing party. October 1971

Turf Lodge group, Cage 10, 1975; Lawrence, Tommy, Sean, Frankie, Sean F, Eamonn & Pat; Johnny, myself, Gerry & Oliver: Tommy, Sean F, Eamonn & Johnny sadly passed

Myself, Micky McMullan & Bill Bradley (RIP), Cage 18, 1974

Johnny Burns (RIP) & I, Cage 18, 1973

'Riverdance' Cage 10, Easter concert 1976; Charlie (RIP), Micky, Joe Doc & Fenso

Gaeltacht Hut, Cage 18, 1973; Madra Rua, Peter, Christy, Kevin, Alfie & Joe Doc; Charlie, Johnny, Tommy, Micky, Joey & Anthony: Madra Rua, Peter & Joey (RIP)

Easter concert Cage 10, 1976

Turf Lodge group, Cage 10, 1975; Hughie Doran on right lost an eye during riot in '74 and passed recently

Turf Lodgers Cage 10, 1975; Frankie, Pat, Oliver & myself; Lawrence, Gerry & a Derry 'mucker'

Cage 10 group 1975 after the burning

Myself, Joe Doc & Charlie Hoban (Dublin), Cage 18, 1973

Myself, Johnny & Hughie (both passed), Cage 18, 1974

Brits corral us against the wire apres burning & riot, October 1974. Cage 18

In the midst of battle, Long Kesh October 1974

Leather bags & wallets I made for Mum & Dad in Cage 18, 1974, also door handle found after riot

Easter concert Cage 10, 1976, reciting Roisin Dubh!

Joe Doc, Joey, Johnny, Charlie, Tommy & Daithi, Cage 18, 1973

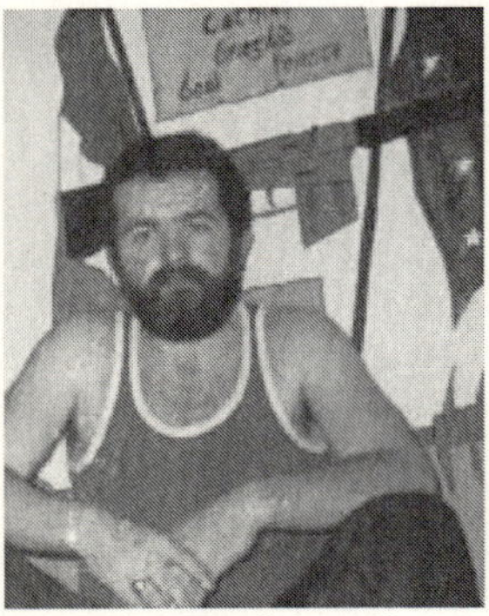

'my little armalite' mural!!

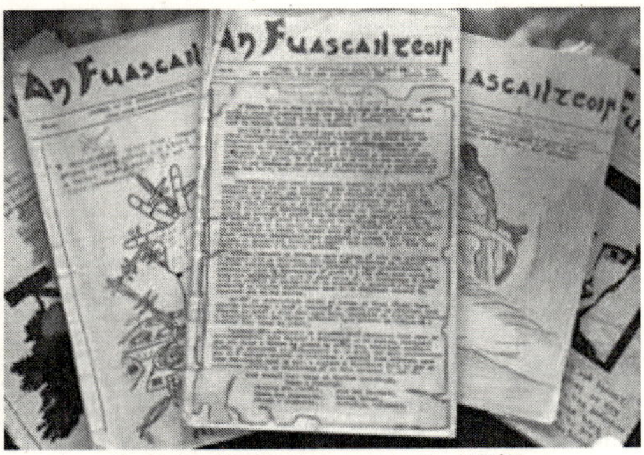

'An Fuaiscaillteoir', Cage paper I edited '75/'76

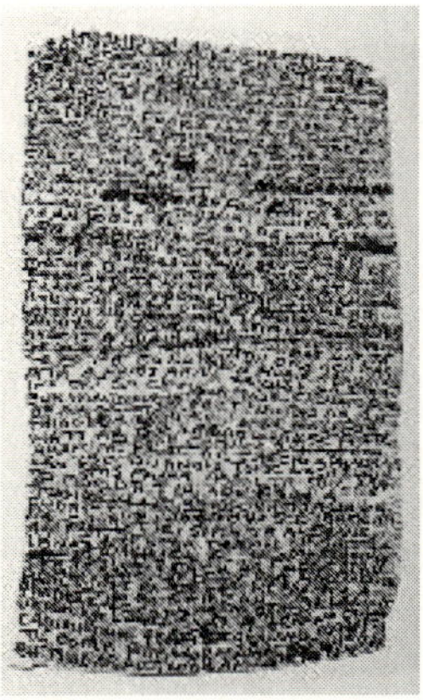

'Comm' smuggled out of H Block 7 by Kevi, 1980

Maire Comerford, Cumann na mBan

A message from Maire Comerford to me after my release in '76

Bernadette leads Bobby Sands' funeral, May 1981

Bernadette at Joe McDonnell's funeral just before the Brits attacked it in Andersonstown, 1981

Kevi's funeral, Turf Lodge, March '88; myself, Ivor Bell, Gerry Adams, Scappaticci, Bernadette & Siobhan

Kevi & I in Donegal, Xmas '87, 3 months before he was killed by the Army

Paddy (Hack), Micky & I after Ruairi O'Bradaigh's funeral, Roscommon, June 2013

Martin Monaghan & Brian Lacey meet up 40 yrs after Martin escaped from Magilligan Camp!

Micky Kearney & Hugh Torney, shot dead in INLA internecine feuds in '87 & '96

Moving in literary circles, Dromoland Castle 2020

With Michael Oatley, former Head of MI 6 at NUI Galway 2012

THE LONG KESH YEARS – PART 2

Life on the outside, of course, had to go as normal as possible. My parents were both hard-working country people who never missed a day at work; as they say, they kept the home fires burning. My dad was driving a big lorry for Maccaste based just next to Milltown cemetery, but unbeknownst to me he was still driving a taxi at weekends, one of the most dangerous jobs you could have. Many a Catholic taxi driver was murdered by the UVF/UDA during the conflict; they were easy targets. They would call a Catholic taxi firm and order the taxi and then wait for the guy to arrive and then either shoot him on the spot, or worse, take him away to be tortured to satisfy their sectarian bloodlust. My dad, being of the older generation, was driving taxis in the 1950s when there were only a handful of city centre firms. He thought, like many an innocent victim that he would be safe, that nobody would touch him, but the reality was that in 1970s era Belfast, any Catholic was a target for the loyalist murder gangs.

My dad had a few narrow escapes; once, four guys hailed him to drive out the 'seven mile straight' just outside Belfast but as he waited for his fare one came around the driver side and tried to get him out of the car, he slammed the door shut, locked it and sped off. Another time as he was driving through Springmartin taking republicans back to Ardoyne after the Easter parade at Milltown, a crowd suddenly blocked their way but he managed to manoeuvre the taxi around over footpaths to avoid the would-be attackers who threw a breeze block through the back window in frustration. Another time, he was driving a leading loyalist, Duke Elliot, whom he actually knew (and was later assassinated by loyalists); Elliot said to my dad: "Just be careful, Patsy, we know your son is in Long Kesh." For years, he was also banned from driving into the shipyard area or anywhere with security risk because of me being in the 'Kesh, but at least he survived. I only found out when I was released that he was still driving up and down the Shankill and East Belfast. He was just an honest worker, who thought he should be ok, but many people lost their lives thinking like that; times had changed from the Belfast he knew in the1950s.

1974 was to be a momentous year in the conflict; the new power sharing executive was set up, but loyalists couldn't handle the reality that the Irish Government would have a say in affairs in the six counties. It was anathema to them and it would be expressed in their resistance to the executive. In the Cages, we were monitoring the situation with trepidation. The loyalists' threat to make the statelet unworkable made us targets if they attempted to take over the camp, so for the next few months we prepared for a loyalist backlash.

We were on constant alert: men on night duty watching every movement; we made up masks and batons; and we encouraged community resistance to the Ulster Workers Council who were preparing a virtual coup d'état, a workers general strike to bring down the government. It would have been a brilliant workers' response to government inadequacy if the leaders weren't fascist in nature, but the workers strike — while resembling the general strike in the UK in 1926 was a sectarian reaction to a new dimension in Irish affairs and the power of workers was lost on the loyalist paramilitaries who provided the street power which made the strike a success and brought down the Executive.

The first few months of 1974 were focused on the new power sharing Executive. It was to be a unique experiment for the six counties and especially for unionists who were used to a one-party statelet since partition. It was difficult for them to understand that this had to be the way for the future. Bigoted, sectarian government by unionists was finished for all of time; some unionists understood that, but many didn't and the input from the government of the Republic would drive them over the wall. They just weren't ready for such challenging developments and events in May '74 would show that while the rest of the world had moved on, loyalism was still stuck in 1690. In saying that, the IRA was also intent on making sure the new assembly didn't succeed and the campaign continued full blast (excuse the pun) as they bombed city centres throughout the six counties and in England. Between the Ulster Workers Council and the Provisionals, there was probably no chance that the executive of Faulkner and Fitt was ever going to last. In later years, after the Good Friday Agreement, Seamus Mallon would deride republicans that the agreement was 'Sunningdale for slow learners', but the reality was that in 1974 unionism was still in a position of strength. Whereas 25 years later, their power base had diminished and nationalism and republicanism were able to debate from a position of much greater strength; and whether people like it or not, the reality was that the IRA campaign had provided that change in position. While, in effect, the IRA did not achieve the objective of British withdrawal or Irish unity, they certainly pushed the door ajar. The IRA campaign of 1919-21 wasn't fought for a 26-county free state, as it turned out. What was accepted was a lot less than the volunteers fought for, but to quote Michael Collins, "it gives us freedom, not the ultimate freedom but the freedom to achieve it". Hence the aspirations of every Provisional IRA volunteer who took up arms between 1970-2000.While they were not completely satisfied, it was seen as a "stepping stone" to unity. Anti-Sinn Féin republicans represent nobody — only themselves. The vast majority of nationalists/republicans had embraced the ongoing political process. Armed struggle was only one form of resistance that had moved on to a different phase — only those with a negative viewpoint couldn't see that. Hindsight is a wonderful thing; we can never know what position Bobby Sands would have adopted regarding the Good Friday Agreement. Similarly, we don't know what James Connolly or Liam Mellowes would have thought of the new 'free state' after the treaty.

We can only guess.

By March '74, a UK General election took place which saw Labour back in power and Harold Wilson as Prime Minister. In the six counties, 11 seats were won by parties opposed to the Sunningdale agreement; things didn't bode well for the future. In the middle of May, the Ulster Workers Council began a general strike that would last two weeks. Despite an initial lack of support, the procrastination of the Labour government, the army, and the RUC left a vacuum that the loyalist paramilitaries took advantage off. They were able to block main roads and intimidate workers from going to their workplace. They also had workers in strategic positions in power stations and in electricity, gas, and petrol that virtually closed down the 6 Counties. The UVF/UDA had virtual control over huge swathes of the 'north' and the UWC became a quasi-government issuing passes to civil servants and power workers to enter their workplace. It was a total farce but the British Government lacked the backbone to tackle loyalism and preserve law and order which they so relentlessly did against republicans. To face up to a majority was less preferable than facing down a minority. During the strike, loyalists engaged in a major surge in activity killing innocent Catholics all over the place. They also turned their attention to the Republic where they targeted Dublin and Monaghan killing 33 and an unborn baby, the worst atrocity of the conflict along with Omagh 20 years later. It was mass slaughter carried out with British connivance in the undercover world. The activities of British agents during the conflict have always been denied but it remains as one of the main reasons why the British won't accept a 'truth commission'. Even the very small amount of soldiers charged with murder in recent times has caused severe problems within the establishment and army circles. Denis Hutchins died recently before his trial for killing an innocent civilian, Hutchins trial, a former soldier, was causing uproar in British circles.

It was a difficult time in nationalist areas but while there was no attempt to attack these areas, there was still a severe shortage of food and essential services. Communities gathered together to provide services and the IRA were in defensive mode during the two weeks of the strike. In republican areas, there was a sort of WW2 response with fires lit under massive grills to cook, and water was delivered in large containers; a spirit of resistance ensued, but it was tough. During this period, Belfast Brigade leader Brendan 'The Dark'

Hughes was captured in the posh Malone area where he had been based to avoid capture after escaping from the 'Kesh in a bin lorry. In a search of the house, plans were found for the defence of nationalist areas in the event of attack during the strike. The plans included a scorched earth plan to repel loyalists. It was never confirmed if the plan was genuine, or a fertile mind or British use of fake news but it created massive publicity. It was a bit like Lannigan's Ball at the time in the 'Kesh: "I stepped in and you stepped out again." No sooner had 'the Dark' been recaptured when Ivor Bell, another Belfast leader, escaped from the 'Kesh by swapping with another prisoner who was being paroled to get married. Unfortunately, his freedom would only last a fortnight. In later years, Bell would fall foul with the leadership and, along with others, there was potential for a split within the movement, but like most he eventually toed the 'party line'. The conspiracy theorists had a field day about this but thankfully it never happened; only a relatively small and insignificant group broke away, but again that was in the future.

In Long Kesh, we had also prepared for any eventuality. Our biggest fear was that armed loyalists would overrun the camp and join with the loyalists already there to attack us. We had a 24 hour 'red alert' system in place where volunteers stayed up all night observing in case anything happened. We also prepared with batons, shields, gas masks of a sort, and we stayed on constant alert in case of attack. Our 'defence' systems were never needed that May but within six months they would be put to good use. It wasn't so much that we were worried about the loyalists within the Cages attacking us, but that loyalists would try and take over the camp bloc and, like what happened in Shatila and Sabra, would slaughter republicans in their thousands. Of course, in that situation the loyalists within the camp would have joined in the killings. It would have been a bloodbath as we were well prepared, but they would have had access to lethal weapons.

The strike came to a head at the end of May after Harold Wilson referred to the loyalists as 'spongers' and Faulkner and the mainstream unionists resigned, thus calling an end to the power-sharing executive. It led to massive celebrations among loyalists: farmers had blocked the road up to Stormont; and Massey Fergusons and Slurry spreaders amassed under Carson's statue as news spread of the collapse of the executive. On the Newtownards road, in the heart of East Belfast loyalism, and on the Shankill in the heart of West Belfast loyalism, there were street parties galore. UDA and UVF paramilitaries were feted as were the UWC members. The army who, by their inaction, had given encouragement to the strikers were conspicuous by their absence, and the RUC and UDR even shared wry smiles with their communities. The evil of power-sharing and the influence of the Republic had been defeated; loyalists celebrated as if it were 1690 all over again.

In the Cages, life moved on as it always did with drilling, lectures, escape plans, exercising by walking and running around the cage, playing volleyball, table tennis, and having quizzes. The three R's, 'reading, riting, and rithmetic', alluded to in Augustine's 'Confessions' in 400 AD were back in vogue. Perhaps, maths not so much, although some with Algebra & Geometry heads would study it for 'A' Levels. Reading and writing was practiced in abundance; we had a substantial library and it exposed us to great writers like Tolstoy and Tone, Joyce and Beckett, Dickens and Virginia Woolf, Connolly and Marx. We were reading to pass time but also educating ourselves as we went along trying to comprehend various philosophies. We become literate in a non judgemental way as to how the world works, why socialism and communism fails and why capitalism works for so many; there were so many questions and so few answers. The reading hut was like the library at University: hours and hours spent perusing through biographies and autobiographies; various war histories; guerrilla struggles throughout the world. We read about Ho Chi Minh, Chairman Mao, Fidel and Che, Liam Lynch and Tom Barry, indeed, even Moshe Dayan — the Israeli commander —who studied the self-same histories. They were inspiring and fascinating accounts of resistance to foreign control. We mightn't have been in the same league as the VC, Red Army, Cubans or the original IRA, but it helped us understand how British colonialism worked the world over.

Writing also became a big pass time. Firstly, letter writing was the big communicator at the time long before emails and Whats App; the old way of keeping in touch was in vogue. Ok, it had to pass the censor's eyes but we could always smuggle a few in and out during visits. You didn't want some nosey censor enjoying himself while reading your thoughts of love to a wife or girlfriend, never mind much more important messages that we didn't want them to see. For young guys, of course, communication with the opposite sex would be an important matter and a whole system evolved in response. We swapped names of girls we knew on the outside and so a Derry man might be writing to a girl from Ballymurphy, or an Ardoyne man might be writing to a girl from South Armagh. This would also lead to visits and probably many a relationship flourished in those dark days, as I know only too well! The letters were a bit of fun and looked forward to eagerly. Cards, Monopoly, and Scrabble were other activities which could pass a long, dark winter's night; charades, I don't remember, but I'm sure some did. Plays were written and performed, budding thespians would encourage many to tread the boards, although in gaol language 'tread the boards' could also mean a week in solitary confinement.

We started a Cage news sheet in '74 and I started writing for it. I also learned to type on an old black typewriter and became quite proficient, so much so that many years later when I first started using computers I could fly along whilst word processing as my more computer literate classmates were plodding along with one finger. We had a Camp paper and then some Cages had their own version; they would be typed up and a few copies were made and handed around the huts. The content would usually be focused on 'the struggle'; history, education, Vietnam, Palestine, etc.We would also have lighter reading with a bit of slagging, sports news, and a few cartoons. It was enjoyable putting it together and it was one of my main interests that continued my love for writing which I have to this day. The summer of '74 saw protracted protests within the Cages, not that it was unusual; there was always some sort of protest. But that summer it intensified with a refusal to take visits, refusing to eat prison food, and a lack of cooperation with the Warders; we didn't take visits for six months. Many of us shaved our heads as it was a scorching hot summer. Then, we upped the ante by refusing to let the Warders into the cages and then we started to throw the food containers over the Cage fence. We had upped the ante but the governor responded by sending the army in on occasion and they would wreck the huts and smash up handicrafts we had made; tensions were rising and would reach a crescendo in the autumn. During that summer, relations with the loyalist prisoners reached a high point with the camp council comprised of our OC, Davie Morley; the UVF Commander, Gusty Spence; Jimmy Craig, the UDA Commander and the Official IRA leader. They would meet once a month facilitated by the authorities who recognised their leadership of the various groups. The meetings would consolidate relationships between people who had been trying to kill each other on the outside, and now they were reacting to a common enemy, the Prison authorities.

The UDA/UVF gave guarantees that they would support us if things came to a head. It was difficult for them as their leadership on the outside was still consumed by sectarianism and the people in their communities even worse. The leadership in Long Kesh were more radical thinkers, however, and didn't renege on their word to support us in the struggle against Governor Truesdale, the Warders, and the army who were intent on removing our strength of unity throughout the camp. This also included the internees at the bottom of the camp. To illustrate what I mean by the various groups giving support to each other, we started hanging banners on the wire with political slogans. We were in Cage 18 and next to us in 19 were the UVF prisoners. They hung a banner on the wire with a graphic green hand and red hand clasping each other with the words: "united we stand, divided we fall." It was a form of working-class unity against the common enemy; if only we could have achieved that on the outside, society would have been a better place. There was a different dynamic within the Cages; we were all prisoners, all working class foot soldiers and we all had a common enemy, the prison governor and the establishment.

In the 1930s, working-class loyalists with a social conscience marched to Wolfe Tone's grave at Bodenstown but were attacked by rural republicans and it never developed any further. The interaction between republicans and loyalists during these months in 1974 would fizzle out as outside interference would demand that loyalist prisoners stop fraternizing with the 'enemy' inside the Kesh. It was a sad fact of life in the divided society but there would be one major battle before the relationship came to an end. During that long hot summer, I got to know William 'Plum' Smith, a UVF volunteer. He was in the next Cage and somehow we got talking to each other across the wire. I'm not sure how it started but he was learning Irish, so maybe it was through that? He was an interesting wee guy. We had both been lifted the same week in '72; he had shot an innocent Catholic near Unity flats. The guy was shot seven times but survived. In the early days in Crumlin road when we would clash verbally between 'C' and 'D' wings, I remember him shouting how the "fenian bastard" had fallen after he shot him. Plum was a victim of sectarian bigotry as much as the guy he shot. But Plum wasn't your average loyalist; he was a thinker, a socialist in thought. We had many great discussions across the wire chatting about everything related to the conflict. We talked about James Connolly and socialism, about why the UVF killed innocent Catholics. His answer was that they couldn't bomb 'their' town or kill British soldiers and their rationale was to make the nationalist community reject the IRA campaign through the pressure they exerted by sectarian killings. It was a flawed theory. We would both peel off as we walked our respective yards with friends and stand to chat for an hour or so. Many of our boys quizzed me about what we talked about, as I'm sure his mates did. It wasn't always conflict-related talk; like me, he was interested in football and labour/trade union affairs, and he had a real interest in the Irish language. He had acquired his fáinne and told me that on visits, some loyalist women had abused him for wearing 'a fenian badge.' Plum maintained that the language was as much theirs as ours in a time when Ulster-Scots wasn't even on the agenda. He was in the same Cage as Gusty Spence and became a protégé of his and a leader within the loyalist Cages, a role he would continue after release, becoming the main player within UVF circles and their command structure in later years. I really enjoyed talking to him, he was intelligent, articulate, and had as much disdain for the leaders of unionism as we did for the SDLP and Irish Government. He was a working-class loyalist youth living in the same areas as we did albeit across the peace line. They experienced the same problems as working-class communities everywhere did: a lack of employment, 3rd level education, a lack of investment in their communities, unhealthy eating habits, drink, drugs, and premature death. The Shankill was no different from the Falls in the matter of everyday living. Plum stayed a friend during our days in Long Kesh and a few months later, we would actually meet and shake hands during a 24 hour period of virtual 'freedom' as we stormed the 'Citadel'.

In early August '74, word came in that an IRA volunteer had been killed in the Lower Falls, shot dead by a soldier from an observation post possibly during actions against the Official IRA; the volunteer was Martin Skillen. He lived just five doors down the street from my parents. I didn't know him that well as he spent a lot of time down the Falls where I think his family originally came from, but I knew his brother, Willie, sister Geraldine, and his parents. He had joined the IRA in the Lower Falls instead of Turf Lodge and had been interned with me on the Maidstone and in the Cages in '72. Local folklore has it that he came up with the idea to fire at passing soldiers through an opened letterbox held open by another volunteer. Maybe, maybe not? I'm sure that in 1920, the IRA done similar things during the War of Independence in Dublin's narrow streets? Martin Skillen was another young member of our local community in Turf Lodge to lose his life during the conflict. Also, in August that year, we had the mass escape of 19 republican prisoners blasting their way out of Portlaoise prison. It can't be emphasised enough the morale boost these escapes gave us in the prisons and also to the armed struggle as a whole.

As well as escaping, of course, many were making their way into the gaols on a weekly basis, both internees and sentenced prisoners. Margaret Shannon from Turf Lodge was one of the first female internees, her brother Pat had been caught the night Marty Forsythe was killed in '71 and her Dad had been interned in the 50's, it illustrates the family connections which run through republicanism. Several other girl volunteers from the estate found their way to Armagh Gaol: Kate Fleming and two Deirdre's: Lennon and McCracken. They were all young blondes who grew up together but didn't spend all their time at discos. The three of them found their way to Armagh as sentenced political prisoners. Deirdre McCracken was caught with a rifle after a year on the run when she had previously been caught in possession of a rifle and escaped the low-security prison in Middleton near the border. She was back in Armagh gaol where Mairead Farrell was the OC. She would play a major part in my life for the next 15 years. After a few months in Armagh, some of the girls started writing to fellow political prisoners in the 'Kesh and one day I received a letter from the aforementioned Deirdre. Being from the same area, just a street away actually, it would have been impolite not to reply and I suppose the fact that she was a pretty young blonde helped as well. So, in the time-honoured tradition, we began a gaol 'relationship' of sorts, writing to each other for the next few years. It would have tangible results in the not-too-distant future which may or may not have been inevitable; for the moment it was just fun as I was writing others at the same time. My writing skills weren't just confined to polemics on British rule in Ireland.

As the winter of '74 set in, so did the IRA campaign in Britain? It was a natural direction to take, and not surprisingly, following in the footsteps of the Fenians, the IRB, in 1921 and 1940. The reality was that one single bomb attack in London was more beneficial in terms of publicity and propaganda than anything done in Belfast. On 5th October, bombs were left at two pubs in Guilford which were targeted because they were known as an off-duty soldiers' haunt. Five soldiers were killed and over 50 were badly injured. Because of the presence of so many soldiers, no warning was given, and although that wasn't normal, worse was to follow the next month. A manhunt of anti-Irish proportions took place over the next few weeks and four people were arrested at a squat in London: three Irish guys named Paul Hill, Paddy Armstrong, and Gerry Conlon; and a young English girl, Carole Richardson. Whatever they were, they definitely weren't an IRA active service unit and the police knew that from day one, but there was a political need to put someone, anyone, away for the atrocity and these young people would do the job. The four were arrested, abused, physically as well as psychologically, but it didn't take much to get them to sign confessions. They weren't hardened committed IRA volunteers, they were unemployed society dropouts smoking dope and living in a squat. They had as much knowledge on how to make a bomb as a politician knew of the contents of eating humble pie. The four were charged with the bombings even as they thought to themselves that it was all a bit mad. The judge would understand, they thought, but it was 1974 in London, right in the middle of an IRA bombing campaign and they were Irish. At their trial the next year, they were given life sentences with the judge lamenting that hanging wasn't on the agenda anymore or he would have ordered that final injustice. In due course, the reality that the Guildford Four were innocent would turn it into a cause célèbre, but these poor innocents would spend the next 15 years in British gaols and their lives destroyed before gaining freedom; it was a miscarriage of justice carried out by a xenophobic anti-Irish establishment.

Gerry Conlon, Paul Hill, and Paddy Armstrong were just three ordinary guys running about Belfast, not involved in anything except maybe a bit of rioting. Paul Hill was in the Fianna for a short period and spent some time in Turf Lodge staying with his Granny. Carole Richardson was the saddest casualty of the whole episode in which I include the victims of the bomb; she was only 17, English and a bit of a hippy who was involved in a 'counter-culture' movement. She was in a relationship with Paddy Armstrong when hell was unleashed on her as they were arrested; her life and the life of the other three became a nightmare which they endured for 15 years. She would die of cancer in 2013 without ever having received an apology. After release, Paul

Hill would marry Courtney Kennedy, daughter of the assassinated Bobby Kennedy. Paddy Armstrong also married, had kids, and settled into normal life in the Republic after release. I met up with him at the University in Galway recently after he gave a talk about his experience; his eyes told everything about what he went through. Gerry Conlon became the most vocal after his release by campaigning against injustice in the system. He had his own demons, namely drink and drugs, amid trying to comprehend what they went through, his Dad Giuseppe was also imprisoned with him and died in an English gaol, Gerry died in 2014. It was a sad, sad story and part of an overall conflict in which there was yet more to come.

The Guildford Four was only the start of a litany of miscarriages carried out by British injustice; among them was Giuseppe Conlon, the Maguire family, and the Birmingham 6. The British state responded to IRA attacks by putting innocent people in gaol for many years. It was a xenophobic anti-Irish response which reflected public opinion at the time. The people targeted were ordinary citizens, and few if any were republican supporters. Annie Maguire was a Tory and even had a photo of the Queen in her kitchen; they were all innocent, vulnerable people who didn't have the capacity to resist interrogation of the highest intensity, they were easy victims. The British police should hang their heads in shame for their part in this sorry episode, although they were capable of doing it to their own people too as they did in the tragedy at Hillsborough years later. Not all in the British judicial society bear culpability; Gareth Pierce, the solicitor, worked wonders to expose this slur on society. Her efforts, more than most, led to the eventual overturning of the verdicts and the freeing of innocent people, Gareth Pierce was a soldier for justice, sadly for the Birmingham 6 and Guildford 4 it was 15 years too late.

Inside Long Kesh, events were fast approaching a conclusion in a summer of discontent. Governor Truesdale and his senior Warders had decided on taking a tougher line with the men in the Cages. As it was, we had virtual control of the place, and this was no ordinary prison but a facility housing thousands of political prisoners, all the protagonists in the conflict on the streets. Each Cage held members of the various groups and had their own command structure. The Warders had no say in the running of the Cages; their prime duty was to prevent escapes. In any dispute, the prison officer in charge would negotiate with the O.C in the Cage, or the Governor with the camp OC of the Provisionals or the UVF commanding officer, Gusty Spence. As the protests intensified, the IRA on the outside upped the ante by killing the first prison Warder during the conflict. William McCurry had actually just retired after 23 years of service but that didn't prevent him from being targeted; he would be the first of many.

For the first few years of our imprisonment, Billy McKee was the IRA OC, a legendary figure within republican circles. He had been gaoled in the '40s and '50s and became the first Belfast Brigade OC after the split with the Official IRA in 1969. Famously, he led an IRA unit defending St. Matthew's chapel in Short Strand in June '70 when a handful of men kept thousands of loyalists at bay and saved the chapel. Quite symbolic in a sense for the 'new boys in town' as critics would condemn them as 'catholic reactionaries'? It was the first real appearance on the streets of the Provisional IRA and gave a new organisation great credibility in the early days of the conflict. In the spring of '71, McKee and Prionnsias McArt were named by a British commander as the leaders of the IRA in Belfast after a week of serious trouble and almost immediately, the two were arrested and charged with possession weapons, a political charge if ever there was one. McKee became the gaol OC and started to organise the prisoners along the usual lines for republican prisoners. A hunger strike began in the summer of '72 for political status. It upped the ante on the streets, and McKee was nearing death when the British gave in and granted 'Special Category' status, political in everything but name. All political prisoners benefitted in the next years, even the loyalists who didn't take part in the strike.

Billy McKee led a strict regime within Crumlin road and similarly when the prisoners were transferred to Long Kesh; it was an ethos he had inherited from his youth, and his republican values were part of the ethos of republicanism throughout the ages. It was strict without being overtly military in a fashion the loyalists adopted which followed a British Army standard of rigid discipline. Republicans, on the other hand, considered the values of revolutionary agitation and education to be of more importance. Billy McKee, for a man who lived with armed conflict most of his life, survived into his mid-nineties but sadly passed in June 2019. He had been at variance and would take issue with the Adams/McGuinness axis and with the modern electoral strategy of Sinn Féin. He was a great leader but maybe like old football managers in the modern era, he found it difficult with the massive influx of young IRA volunteers who were of the '69 variety of street resistance and were not steeped in the republican history. Young people who became republicans when the present conflict began were referred to as *'69'ers,* that is, they joined after August '69. Whereas those involved in republicanism previously were part of a small group of republican families and were isolated within the general population, the modern influx was part of the community.

That summer of '74, as well as the disputes with the prison establishment — there were also rumblings going on within the Cages. Many of the younger men were dissatisfied with the position adopted by McKee, that he was happy with keeping things calm and not pushing for greater escape efforts, etc.This led to a few volunteers being disciplined by the camp leadership.

Consequently, a rift developed within the Cages which led to a full-scale split with many volunteers being court martialled and suspended from the IRA. In Cage 18, like the rest of the Cages we split into two groups, and while it didn't lead to any physical disputes there was bad feeling. The focus of dissent in our cage was Joe McKee from the Lower Falls, and in Cage 16 it was Bobby Campbell from the New Lodge along with various others in different Cages. It's possible that this division might have been the beginning of eventual division on the outside in the form of the Adams/McGuinness faction removing the leadership of McKee, O'Bradaigh, and O'Conaill from the equation after the disastrous ceasefire in 1975 when the IRA came the closest to being defeated in the long years of the conflict. The reality was that the leadership were lured into a mix of British lies and duplicity; the British were never going to withdraw, and while they were telling the leadership this fantasy, they were building the H-Blocks!

Personally, I took the side of the anti-Billy McKee faction. I'm not sure if it was a rational decision or the impetuousness of youth but it was, with hindsight, the wrong decision. I had sworn an oath to the organisation and its ideals and should have stuck with that, but there was a precedent for us in the gaols and camps in the '20s and '40s where major splits developed in the camps. I suppose where you have thousands of men imprisoned with long hours, with days and years of discussion about principles, tactics, and the way forward, it can lead to disagreements. A little anecdote for me, personally, was that I was court martialled and brought in to face McKee and McAirt, the Camp leadership, to answer charges of insubordination. A good friend of mine gave evidence that he had heard me talking in support of those against the camp leadership. I was nervous and barely able to utter the words that I didn't know what I'd let myself in for. Billy McKee told me I was suspended from 'the Army' and that I wouldn't take part in any activities relating to 'the Army'. To make me understand the considerable consequences of my actions, he told me: "Volunteer, if this had happened on the outside you would have been shot dead."

As I left the small hut used as a 'court', my legs were shaking and for the first time, I was glad I wasn't on the outside! That I was in the company of half the Cage inmates gave us considerable leeway. There was no bitterness between both groups and within the year our suspensions were dropped and we were welcomed back into the fold. The reality, of course, was that we were members of a military organisation, a secret one at that, and had to conform to authority; discipline was everything. As part of a militant group unity was everything. Anything else bred disorganisation as seen within INLA and dissident groups in later years.

Volunteers took lives and gave their lives. This wasn't playing for your local

GAA team although, at times, that could appear like life and death. We were involved in a serious business and many of us wouldn't see the conflict out; this was life and death. The final outplaying of the sorry saga was a change in leadership within the camp with Davie Morley taking over as Camp O.C while Billy McKee prepared for release. Morley, like all transitions of power in any organisation, supported his predecessor, he was a McKee man, but things were changing within the camp. The 'boys of the old brigade' were gradually being phased out, both in Long Kesh and out on the streets, and a new phase of the 'long war' was in the early planning stages.

All this internal turmoil would soon be forgotten for the immediate future when events reached a boiling point on 15 October 1974, as a dispute in Cage 13 led to the Governor threatening to send the army in to control things. The Camp leadership had informed Truesdale that if he sent the army in again we would burn the place to the ground. It wasn't an empty threat; we had been preparing for such an outcome. Guys sent out personal belongings on visits just before the burning. In the preceding weeks we made up batons, shields, and gas masks of a sort to complement the stuff we had prepared previously during the UWC strike. We also used a semaphore system to send messages around the camp. It was a massive place, 22 Cages, the size of a small market town, so when we were confined to the Cages we used the semaphore system to issue orders to outlying Cages. 13 was the perfect example down at the lower end of the camp from us. As the army amassed outside the Cage, the OC gave the message to the volunteers on the roof of a hut: “Burn the place.” The news spread like 'wildfire' along the cages adjacent to 13, down to the internee cages at the bottom of the camp and, crucially, to the top end of the camp where we were between 15-22: the mass bulk of IRA prisoners.

From the get-go the Official IRA didn't take part but as agreed, the UVF/UDA, while not taking part, would give us logistical support. This would prove to be invaluable as they helped injured republicans during the battle the next day and also helped in negotiations to end the fighting on day two. The strange behaviour of the Official IRA was symptomatic of a malaise within that organisation. It had morphed from revolutionary idealism through a dolly mixture of guises and a stance on the six counties which was virtually unionist in thinking. Their behaviour throughout the conflict left a lot to be desired; they still retained an armed wing involved in gangsterism, and they had an undue influence on RTÉ coverage of the conflict through various high profile characters. But it’s no surprise that they became just a footnote in history.

The months of preparation were soon put into operation. First of all, we took over each Cage and the ‘screws’ were given free passage to leave their posts. No warder was attacked as they made their way to the camp perimeter. There were army sentries on top of the watch towers spread throughout the camp, and they were armed so no attempt was made to dislodge them. We were also under strict orders that nobody was to go near the perimeter to try and escape in case it gave the sentries the opportunity to fire on us. Whether it was the correct decision was debatable as there were thousands of us, and 38 escaped through the main gate a decade later, how could they have stopped thousands making a determined effort to overrun the camp? It's all hindsight. No one tried to escape that night. With the 'screws' gone, we raided their posts at the entrance to each cage and gathered up all the files they had on us including identification of each prisoner and various remarks about their clarification. With all 80 volunteers gathered in the centre of the Cage, volunteers went back into the huts and started the biggest bonfire that was ever seen in a wee country not short on bonfires. The old WW2 Nissan huts went up in flames in seconds and soon the camp lit up the night sky which could be seen from Belfast ten miles away. Each Cage had the same fate; the dry-inside of the huts with their newly added wooden cubicles made great kindling for the fire and as soon as it caught the evening breeze soon spread it. Soon, all huts in the Cage were burning vigorously; it was a sight to behold.

The iconic images of a 'p.o.w camp' in a modern democracy in the mid 70's magnificently burning to the ground brought a sense of massive achievement. Whatever the next day would bring, that night of the 15th of October, would remain with us for the rest of our lives as the night the iconic and obscene symbol of British rule in Ireland was torched to the ground. We exited the Cages in formation, each Cage unit staying within their ranks until we reached the large football fields in the middle of the camp. Here, we set up camp for the night while the warders had removed themselves to the camp perimeter. Meanwhile, the army stayed on the outside while reinforcements from Palace barracks in Hollywood raced across Belfast to the camp on the outskirts of Lisburn.Their main target that night was to seal off the camp to prevent escape; their attempt to gain back control of the camp would wait until morning.

On the football fields, we met up with old friends, some we hadn't seen for years. I spent a good part of the night with Tony Clarke and 'Fat' Campbell, both from Ballymurphy. Lots of the Turf Lodge guys were there too: Johnny Burns and Hughie Doran from 18 as well; Sean Fryers, Jim Scullion, Jimmy Dempsey, Tommy Downey, Micky Flanagan, and Gerry Cairns from 16 were there; Seany Seaton and Jimmy Gray were there from 20; and Tom Magill from 13 and his brother Sean, sons of a great, old, respected republican caught bombing England in the '40s. Cage 13 was where the order to burn came from, well; we're blaming Tom, at least. From the football field, sorties were made to the Screws' quarters, the hospital unit, and the dog compound which had Alsatians quartered. Most places were trashed except for the hospital area, although some medicines and bandages were taken for the future battle awaiting us. Thereafter, the dogs proved to be a problem and a decision was made to leave them alone and ironically let them roam free; unfortunately some were burned during the fires. During the night, we congregated all over the fields, campfires were lit, and we gathered around and waited. At first, we had expected a quick response from the army but then we realised that they weren't going to make an assault till morning. It would have been disastrous for them to confront thousands of prisoners under darkness and, in all likelihood; people would have been killed on all sides.

During the night, I walked over to 14 which was a UVF cage bordering the pitch and met Plum Smith and we chatted as usual about the whole situation. During our conversation, human nature took over and he said to me to use the toilets in their Cage which I willingly did but not without a little trepidation. Sitting on the loo in a loyalist Cage, I had thoughts that some of them could bust in at any minute and slit my throat as many of them had done to catholic victims on the streets. My fears were unfounded, however, and I returned safely to the field again. It's funny how our deep-felt fears were aroused even in a moment of generosity by an enemy. Plum told me that they were all for joining in the burning but the UVF leadership on the outside told them they couldn't take part as the loyalist communities wouldn't understand them supporting republicans while killing them on the streets. It was a quandary for the more advanced loyalists; how could they square the circle of supporting the union but also oppose those who had put them in Long Kesh in the first place?

There wasn't much sleep, if any, that night. It was a fairly clear night, no rain. A good night to camp out. The morning arrived as the early October sun rose over Lough Neagh. We had small transistor radios which had been smuggled in and we listened to the 7am news on Radio Ulster telling us that there had been some disturbances at Long Kesh. '...a few huts burned, but the army and Warders were back in full control and the prisoners back in their Cages....'! We received the 'fake news' with hilarity; the whole place had been burned to the ground. We were in situ in the football fields and there wasn't a Warder or soldier to be seen in the place. The Cages were crumpled up pieces of corrugated iron and ashes, and for twelve hours we had been in complete control of the camp. Governor Truesdale was like the Governor in Shawshank Redemption when Andy Dufresne flew the nest; he was in control of nothing but fresh air.

The morning of the 16th was a bright autumnal October day. All over the football field were thousands of republican prisoners standing and sitting around the dying embers of the overnight fires. They were unslept, unshaven, nervous, and expectant with adrenalin flowing and their mind working overtime with what lay ahead. Here we were in the middle of Long Kesh, the most secure prison in Europe, surrounded by watchtowers with armed soldiers and the perimeter surrounded by thousands more. Prison officers were planning with military authorities; the UDA, UVF, and Official IRA all observing events; there was tension in the air. This was going to be no ordinary day. In a corner of the pitch, the leadership of the republican prisoners in the camp were huddled together, planning on how we were to face the oncoming onslaught by heavily armed British soldiers. The planning involved basing ourselves on one of the pitches to maximise our strength of numbers. Whatever about chasing young rioters on the streets of West Belfast, preparing to charge into thousands of IRA volunteers was an entirely different matter? The young squaddies awaiting orders to advance on the pitch were probably as nervous as we were and the following few hours would bear that out. We prepared to face rampaging Paras and Marines for the next few hours. We had full control of the inside of the camp and took up positions inside the cages which were adjacent to the football fields; this provided a natural protective barrier. Then, all of a sudden around 10am, the gates further up the camp flew open and hundreds of soldiers came charging towards us firing CS Gas followed by Saracen armoured cars; it was definitely a frightening experience. The first problem for the soldiers was that many of them didn't have gas masks on and the wind changed direction. It blew back into their faces resulting in unexpected coughing and spluttering among the ranks of the soldiers as well as ourselves. The second problem for them was that we were relatively protected behind the wire of the Cages and they weren't prepared to enter the Cages at that stage. I clearly remember running alongside the wire in Cage 10 and a young soldier running parallel on the outside and he appeared more frightened than I was, probably a working-class kid from Glasgow. He didn't sign up for this in the recruiting office in Govan. We bombarded the soldiers with anything and everything we could get our hands on and with the Cages destroyed, there was plenty of ammunition: bricks and rocks, twisted corrugated iron, wooded slabs, all thrown at the squaddies who had never experienced this on the streets of Ballymurphy.This was the riot of all riots. At one stage, we noticed that the Brits had brought up a sort of cherry picker which was extended to gain a greater view of proceedings and they filmed everything that happened. This film must be locked away somewhere in the archives at military HQ or Kew Gardens. Eventually, the army brought in the armoured cars to smash their way into the Cages and we withdrew back on to the pitch and so still had the advantage of having a protective wire between us. At this stage, many hand-to-hand battles took place and the soldiers started firing rubber/plastic bullets, some of which hit Hughie Doran and Eddie Carmichael point-blank and smashed up their faces. Hughie would lose an eye in the confrontation. Soldiers would break through at certain points and fierce battles would take place. A few soldiers were caught by some of our men and for a few seconds they were in danger of being killed on the spot but some of our leaders ordered to let them go as the army would certainly extract full revenge on us.

The day dragged on with an ebb and flow between the Cages and fields. At one stage, I looked at my watch and it was 4pm, late October afternoon, almost 24 hours since we set out on the operation to burn the camp; it was surreal. It was twelve hours after they announced on live radio that everything was under control. We weren't street kids who rioted but experienced IRA volunteers who could stand toe-to-toe with elite British troops. I found it amazing that the all-encompassing riot was still in full flow and we were giving the soldiers as good as they gave us, indeed, at times, it felt like we were getting on top of things and you could see the soldiers reel under pressure, although they always had the advantage of having loaded SLR rifles to fall back on if need be.

Suddenly a British Army helicopter appeared over the pitch and flew low dropping rugby ball-shaped containers on us which contained hundreds of small gas pellets. They exploded on impact and the gas had an immediate effect, sending men spluttering and coughing all over the place. The helicopter swept over the field many times unloading their poisonous gas and causing mayhem. This wasn't the normal CS gas we were used to on the streets in the early days of the conflict. Back then, old women would leave out a bucket of vinegar laced water for us to douse our eyes with before returning to the rioting, but this gas had a debilitating effect if exposed to enough of it. Soldiers used this distraction to breach the Cage wire and encroach onto the pitch. At this stage, the leadership decided to split us between the two pitches. It was a decision which had far-reaching consequences as immediately after, the army brought up the armoured cars and broke through the wire thus separating us. Dividing our ranks was the crucial decision made that day and the army made full use of it. The boys who went to the second pitch were caught by a pincer movement of troops while the rest of us were able to withdraw to the top end of the camp and continue rioting with the soldiers. The guys caught in the lower pitch were overwhelmed and the soldiers, all fully masked, herded them up against the wire firing the CR gas at will. They fired plastic bullets point-blank and battered prisoners with batons. Our men tried to fight back but it was impossible, they were piled on top of each other, suffocating with the gas. Some just lashed out at the soldiers and were beaten unmercifully to the ground and kicked; some were battered till they were unconscious. Later, some would say it was like a dream, or more accurately, a nightmare. It was like a scene out of a futuristic Star Wars film with gas masked troops, almost ghostly like an out of body experience. Even though we were still rioting further up the camp, we avoided that cataclysmic moment, an almost deathly experience.

We had retreated to the top end of the camp back near where our Cages lay in ruins and the rioting continued with the soldiers. Cage 19 hadn't been burned and the loyalists continued to give us logistical support and much-needed water. Then, Gusty Spence appeared to talk with our camp staff but most had been captured on the pitch which left 'Big' Brendan McGeown from Turf Lodge as the highest-ranking IRA staff officer negotiating with Gusty who, in turn, negotiated with the army commander. Gusty told Brendan that further resistance was futile and could possibly result in deaths. He said we had made a magnificent protest which had garnered world headlines but now it was time to stop. Brendan and the remaining leaders along with Gusty then talked to the army commander and it was agreed that we would return to our original cages which we slowly did. We were like a defeated German peasant army returning 'home'. Once back in the Cages, the soldiers followed us in and made us line up spread-eagled facing the wire. We were kept in that position for hours on end as they identified us, some Cages suffered worse than others. We had a Scottish regiment and they were ok, to be honest. I even had a chat with one soldier who said he didn't understand us. He said he was a Catholic and a Celtic man, and I told him it was absolutely nothing to do with religion but the uniform and the government he represented that was the problem. Men in some of the other Cages weren't so lucky. Marine commandos were in cage 20 and they handed out bad beatings in reprisal for the day's events. Dingus Magee, if I recall, had his leg badly damaged by a soldier jumping on it. The Marines and Paras were always the most vindictive and sadistic; there was no love lost between us.

The 'uprising' of sorts was over, but it was the most amazing 24 hours of my time in Her Majesty's prisons. We had burned the place to the ground and fought the army for hours on end, and while battered, bruised, and led like lambs to the slaughter along the wire fence, we were still defiant and determined. Nonetheless, the events of those 24 hours would reverberate throughout the prison establishment and the British Government for years to come, culminating in the hunger strikes of 1981. But for the moment, we were left to stew in our burnt-out Cages. We didn't know what to expect; rumours were rife that they would move us to other prisons but that was unlikely as fellow republican prisoners in Crumlin Road, Magilligan, and the women in Armagh had protested as well, wrecked cells and causing damage. They burnt huts in Magilligan, held the Governor hostage in Armagh, and rioted in Crumlin road before being on the receiving end of beatings by Screws intent on revenge. The loyalists in Cage 19 told us there was talk on the TV that we would be moved to a prison in England or maybe a return to the Maidstone in Belfast Lough, but all proved unfounded and we were left to our own devices for the next six weeks or so in a burnt-out Cage with no facilities, we were bowed but undefeated!

The first night, we slept under the moon and then in daylight we started scavenging through the rubble to gather tin and rubble to build makeshift shelters; that was our 'home' for the next month or so. There were no toilets or washing facilities, and we slept in these wee shelters in our clothes and would wake in the morning with the rain running down into our boots. It was a surreal time but it was worth every minute of the discomfort just to see that our handiwork had delivered a scorched earth victory of sorts. Long Kesh was, for a period, on its knees. At the end of the few days, over 50 republican prisoners, 25 soldiers, and 14 prison Warders were injured during the rioting in the 'Kesh. Meanwhile, in Crumlin road gaol, 130 republican prisoners were injured as the Warders and army dished out heavy beatings. In Magilligan, many more were injured as the prisoners' burnt huts there. And in Armagh gaol, the female political prisoners kidnapped and held the Governor for 14 hours before a deal was struck to release him; it was an eventful few days. At the end of 1974, there were almost 2000 political prisoners in the gaols with over 100 serving 'life'. It was a political situation within political prisons with political prisoners, yet the British were still trying to deny it.

A few days later, the politicians started arriving in the camp including Gerry Fitt, John Hume, and Ian Paisley et al. We refused to let the SDLP delegation into our Cages but when Gusty Spence told our OC, Geordie O'Hara, that Paisley would like to visit our Cage, the next we knew, big Ian was walking into Cage 18 and his big bellowing voice thundered out to Geordie, a New Lodge Road man and IRA volunteer: "Hello, I'm Ian Paisley, how are you?" They shook hands, Geordie showed him around the shell of the Cage, and they talked about events over the last few days. It was an interesting moment as, at that time, unionists wouldn't talk to republicans in a fit but now big Ian was cavorting around the cages with confirmed IRA men. Paisley apparently went on television that night and said the conditions in the 'Kesh were absolutely appalling, not fit for human beings', and criticised the government for their handling of the situation in Long Kesh. Whatever the big man was, he was certainly an interesting character.

After a few days living in the cobbled together tin shacks in the midst of the rubble of the burnt Cages I made an interesting find? As we tidied up the remnants of what was left of the Cage huts to make the place more liveable didn't I come across a door handle from one of the huts, might have been ours, there it was lying in a pile of burnt out wood, corrugated iron, blocks and stones of all shapes, and sitting half covered was the handle, a bit of history in its own right, little did I know the significance of it, a door handle touched by hundreds of political prisoners as we entered the notorious Cages but also as we left for freedom. I lifted it and put it in my pocket and was carrying it about with me as we walked the Cage for the next 6 weeks until moved to a renovated Cage lower down the Camp and I smuggled it out on a visit. That's almost 50 years ago. This little piece of history has been in my possession ever since, within a leather bag I made for my Mum alongside a leather wallet I made for my Dad, all three having made the journey from the Cages to Belfast, Donegal and Galway in the years since. It's a unique momento from a time in our youth when life was precarious but thankfully we survived everything to live and embrace a better life.

The next few weeks passed by as we settled in for a cold winter. The authorities started rebuilding the lower end of the camp, and meanwhile at the internee end of the camp, IRA volunteers were busy digging a tunnel which was intended to emerge somewhere near the M1 motorway. After the euphoria of the burning, this would have been some morale booster but it wasn't to be. Tunnels were a cottage industry in Long Kesh; at any given time there would have been a tunnel on the go in one Cage or another. None really ever succeeded but sure, they were great for morale. Some guys were 'Tunnel Tigers'. They virtually lived underground digging through the earth. One guy in our cage, 'big'Pat McPolin had been a 'tunnel tiger' in England for years and he spent half his sentence down 'underground'. Years later when I heard the Canadian songstress Rita McNeill's lament, 'it's a working man I am, and I've been down underground', I would think of big Pat!

There was a certain danger in being underground, a fear of it caving in or even a claustrophobic difficulty for many, but for others their experience would have stood by them as they later built tunnels with McAlpine around the world. We could have done with more Donegal men in the Cages bar Micky Mullan, they were the original 'tunnel tigers' having spent their lives underground in Scotland over the decades.

The construction of a tunnel was tough work; obviously there were logistical problems to be overcome. The excavated clay had to be disposed of somewhere, usually in the space between the corrugated sheets of the huts or down the toilets but you had to be careful not to block them. Every so often, the Screws would raid the Cages and find a newly started tunnel or maybe stumble across one in the yard as it caved in. Nonetheless, they were great for morale even if you weren't going to get too far. One exception was the one in November '74, which had actually been started long before the burning and was almost a success. After the burning, the boys in that Cage began digging again and extended the tunnel under the perimeter wire and out towards the motorway. Unfortunately, as 30 prisoners tunnelled their way out, a routine army patrol come across some of the would-be escapees and Hugh Coney was shot dead. The cruel irony was that the British classed him as a terrorist, whereas if it was Colditz they would have serenaded them as heroes. It was a sad night to hear that Hugh Coney was killed but it also highlighted that the decision not to attempt to escape during the burning was the correct one. Otherwise, hundreds could have been killed that night. Over 30 escaped through the tunnel; most were recaptured quickly once the alarm was raised, but three volunteers made it all the way to the outskirts of the republican Twinbrook area where they were caught before they could reach safe houses. Meanwhile, the internees left behind in the Cage were attacked by British troops with gas and rubber bullets.

While the escape attempt ultimately wasn't successful, it was still a defiant blow to the system as prisoners once again defied the authorities and repeated attempts would be made in the near future. The escapes were a bit of a lottery; you won some and lost some. Like everything in life, a wee bit of luck was needed. Sometimes you benefitted from it and other times it was against you, but the benefits from a successful escape outweighed the lows of a failure. There was always the next time. On the streets, events continued as before. In the week beginning with the shooting of Hugh Coney in Long Kesh, two soldiers were killed in Crossmaglen, then two more in Tyrone. Another soldier was killed in a bomb in a pub in London while five Catholic and three Protestant civilians were killed in Belfast. At the same time, an IRA volunteer was killed while planting a bomb in Birmingham, an incident which would have far-reaching consequences for six innocent Irish migrants for the next 15 years. Another IRA volunteer shot dead by the army in Twinbrook was Gerard Fennell from Turf Lodge who had moved to London in the mid-sixties for six years but came home for a holiday in '72. He stayed and joined the IRA. His dad, Bob, was the manager of our football team in 1970 when young Che Guevara's cut down the goalposts. Naturally, Bob wasn't impressed. The army killed his son four years later. Gerard's brother, Marty, was our goalkeeper in the early days and another brother Liam was in the Cages with us. Life interspersed with the conflict would be the reality for many years to come. On the day of Gerard's funeral, I had the privilege of reading the oration for him in our Cage. I didn't really know him well but I thought of his dad and brother Marty; as I delivered the oration which I had composed myself. I tried to look at him as an ordinary guy rather than a revolutionary activist, another casualty of the British presence.

Another 'casualty' in the form of deprivation of freedom was the re-arrest of my 'old' mate Gerry Scullion, and a fellow volunteer, Micky Connors. They had the misfortune to walk into a British Army patrol along a street in Turf Lodge. There was a standoff and Gerry pointed his gun at Julian Ball who was the intelligence officer with the King's Own Scottish Borderers but was overpowered by several soldiers and both were arrested. In later years, they would probably have been shot dead. To his credit, Ball gave evidence at their trial in the 'No-Jury' courts and told the judge that if he had been born in Turf Lodge, he would probably have joined the IRA himself. Whatever the judge thought about this honest assessment, it didn't stop him gaoling the boys for several years and they were soon back with us in the Cages.

One bonus of their return in a sense was that they ended up in our Cage after the burning as we had moved down to the rebuilt Cage 10. For a short period Gerry and I would share our time in gaol before he was moved on to Cage 13. His brother Jim had been in Cage 16 when we were in 18 before the burning, also another brother Roy and a future brother in law Bisto interned in the lower end of the Camp, prison had taken its toll on many families. Years later after release Gerry and I would consider the various options open to us, needless to say valuing our freedom was uppermost in our minds but life took a treacherous path for quite some time. We have remained good friends in the 40+ years ever since, seen our children grow to adults themselves and the grandchildren come along, spent time together in the former British outpost of Malta where of all people we met a former prison officer and chewed the fat with him, ironically although being English he was called 'Kevin'! 50 years have passed since we first met in the early days of conflict, many of our former friends and comrades have passed on now, guys we spent many years in the Cages with, shared and risked our lives at times, good friends but mixed memories too!

LONG KESH - THE FINAL YEARS

At the end of November '74, one of the most tragic events of the whole conflict took place when an IRA bomb exploded in a pub in Birmingham, killing 21 innocent civilians and injuring 160. It was devastating for everyone involved, obviously those killed and their families but also the ASU involved, the IRA as a whole, Irish people in Britain, and the six innocent victims of the biggest miscarriage of justice in a modern democracy. A warning had been given to the police but like many other incidents, delays from both the IRA in delivering the warning, and the police responding led to the tragic deaths of over twenty innocent people just out for a weekend drink. It was horrific, and never the intention of republicans to inflict such carnage on ordinary working-class English people. In Long Kesh, the news brought a mixed reaction. Some thought it would make the British Government more amenable to discussions on the future relationship with Ireland, many more thought it was terrible and roundly condemned it, saying that was never in our agenda to kill innocent working-class people. We were a 'People's Army' committed to attacking a Government who had thousands of armed troops on our streets, unfortunately, all conflicts are tarnished by incidents which should never have happened. When the Brits dropped phosphorus bombs on Dresden, and people had to choose between burning or drowning, or the Yanks at Hiroshima and Nagasaki, I know it was war but there was Government intention to murder hundreds of thousands, to me the biggest terrorist act in history, but Governments at war don't have to explain themselves, as a working-class organisation we did and the Birmingham bombs were a sad day for all concerned. The immediate aftermath was the effect on ordinary Irish people living in Birmingham and throughout England, emigrants who had spent half their lives in the UK, they were sucked into the xenophobic aftermath of hatred, physical and verbal abuse prevailed, they had to keep their heads down for a long time after.

But the most significant response was the arrest of six men heading over to Belfast on the ferry for the funeral of James McDade, the IRA Vol who had been killed by his own bomb. The six were arrested at the ferry, perhaps initially due to their association with the funeral, but subsequently faced general interrogation about the pub bombs. These guys were easy targets for the police who needed arrests, and quickly. They soon became known worldwide as the Birmingham 6. Hugh Callaghan, Paddy Hill, Gerard Hunter, Richard McIlkenny, William Power and John Walker were all as innocent as native Americans at Wounded Knee, but would spend the next 16 years in

British gaols; another travesty of justice, similar to the treatments of the Guildford Four and the Maguire Seven, who were as wholly innocent as the victims of the bombs, the debris of the conflict. Sometimes I reflect, did these people suffer because of our activities? But I can't take this upon myself or others, it was horrific to spend that long in gaol completely innocent, but the reality is that the British Government and police were responsible for this display of anti-Irish hatred. For the victims of the bombings I have feelings of sorrow that they suffered because of the 'armed struggle' against British rule, but war has a corrupting effect on everyone involved, there is no such thing as a nice war, people get killed. Guerrilla war is a dirty war, with secret agents, informers, agents' provocateur, army intelligence officers and Special Branch colluding with loyalist paramilitaries, murder squads, all on the side of the state. But we can't wash our hands of actions which caused death and destruction, the 'Long War' has a legacy of long memories and long regrets.

As the year ended, secret talks took place between leaders of the Protestant churches and the IRA Army Council in Feakle, Co. Clare. These talks were a reaction to the ongoing conflict but were also motivated by a genuine desire to end the bloodletting. The talks were positive and led to a ceasefire at Christmas which would become semi-permanent in 1975. Unfortunately the Talks ended prematurely, with the arrival of heavily armed Gardai Quick Response Units. They were out of luck as a republican informant within the Gardai ranks had forwarded a warning, and DaithiO'Conaill, Billy McKee and Ruairi O'Bradaigh et al made an exit stage left through Tulla and Scarff, leaving a note for the Garda Superintendent saying they were just there for the Feakle traditional music festival. The meeting had a generally positive impact on events, and the IRA announced a Christmas Ceasefire that was extended for most 1975.With British Government co-operation, Sinn Fein 'Incident Centres' were set up all over the six counties and negotiations of sorts took place. There were suggestions that the British Government was considering withdrawing troops from Ireland, and loyalists and republicans held talks as well, it appeared to be positive time. But the reality for the IRA was that it was the closest they came to suffering defeat during the 25 years of conflict. It lured them into a false sense of impending victory in their campaign, which was about as far away from the truth as Cameron, Theresa May or Boris delivering a soft Brexit to the Tory 22 Club diehards.

1975 was a disastrous year for Republicans, the leadership had succumbed to ancient British duplicity, believing suggestions that they were on the verge of withdrawal. It was unfortunate, these men were republicans all their lives, had spent many years in gaol and their only interest in life was to break the English connection, as their inspiration Wolfe Tone had stated on the Cave Hill all those years ago. O'Conaill, O'Bradaigh and MacStiofain et al, were steeped in republicanism but their inept handling of affairs in 1975 led to their eventual demise in republican circles, and the rise of the Adams/McGuinness era. That the IRA survived the experience of 1975 was miraculous in itself, maybe the leadership thought after years of 'armed struggle', it was time to call a halt, no other period of resistance in history had ever gone on so long. We weren't to know then that it would be another 20 years before the guns went silent.

As well as talks between the IRA, British Government, Protestant clergy and loyalist paramilitaries, other talks within another tangent of Republicanism were not going so well. At the start of '75 the Official IRA imploded, and a new organisation entered the litany of acronyms, with the INLA prevailing. The Official IRA, which had morphed into the Workers Party, had totally disowned the 'armed struggle' concept to achieve Irish unity, and proclaimed themselves a Marxist revolutionary party which wanted to unite Protestant and Catholic workers before uniting Irish territory. Their intentions were laudable, but difficult to see how it would work in reality when working-class fascist loyalists were slaughtering working-class Catholics on the streets of Belfast, political theory is great but sometimes reality has to kick in. The Official IRA, in Belfast especially, was made up of many volunteers who were no different to us in the Provisional movement; they were street kids who wanted to take on British forces patrolling their streets in Turf Lodge, the Markets and the Lower Falls, all Official IRA strongholds. Another major split had taken place in their ranks, 5 years after the split which formed the Provisionals. As Brendan Behan would say, "the first motion on the agenda of any Irish organisation is the 'split'." As to settling differences in Irish republican groups, it was bloody. The Officials tried to cut the umbilical cord at birth; they launched massive military attacks on their would-be 'dissenters' and many were killed. I had many friends in the Official movement who joined the INLA; they were good guys who fought alongside us in the years on the streets and in the battles in the Cages. Many would have joined the Provos before their split. but there was a fear that if too many were admitted it could have an unbalancing affect on membership so many were turned down which probably led them to setting up their own organisation. During the same period the UVF/UDA were involved in a similar dispute which led to killings, it appeared that while the main protagonists of the conflict were on a ceasefire, the smaller groups were involved in internecine feuding, it wasn't an easy time. A friend of mine, Danny Loughran, was an early victim of the Official IRA/INLA feud, shot by the Officials at Divis Flats. He was also a member of the Irish Army, only 18, his Granny lived in Turf Lodge and I got to know him there, another death of a friend, sadly I was getting used to it. The 'Stickie/Erps' feud as it became known in Belfast was cruel, sadistic, uncompromising. It showed how former comrades from 1921 could kill each other in the Civil War, nothing goes as deep as former friends falling out. Before the month was out Liam McMillan was shot dead by the INLA, he was the OC of the Official IRA in Belfast and a life-long republican. Evidently the stakes were getting higher.

My big mate 'Hack's' brother Jim, was shot in the head by the 'Stickies'. He was for death but thankfully survived. His mother Annie was a great old republican, she went on TV and called on the two groups to end the feud or she would name those who shot her son. This would have been anathema to republicans to felon set but she was so disgusted watching republicans killing each other, and her appeal greatly helped in ending the feud. But the violence that year continued to worsen, it felt like the loyalists thought something was happening between the IRA and the British Government and were going out of their way to stop it, their archaic way, of course, was to murder innocent Catholics. Before the summer was out they would launch an attack to shock the world. They murdered members of the Miami Showband, with a bomb that killed some of their own members. The UVF Vols were also on the payroll of the British Government through the RUC, the same people involved in the Dublin/Monaghan bombings, the Glenanne Gang. It was a classic counterinsurgency strategy, there was overlapping of membership between the UVF/UDA and the British Army/UDR and RUC, police files would be handed over for the assassination of republicans. In every colonial situation in the world this had happened, and it continued throughout the conflict. In essence it's the real reason the British refuse to call a truth commission and want an amnesty for British soldiers, there is so much dirt there and they couldn't afford it to be reach the public domain?

Plans at the beginning of the year were calling for a Constitutional Convention which hoped to cut the feet from the IRA, and deliver power back to constitutional politicians. Elections would be in May and the Convention meeting in June. The Government also published the Gardiner Report which recommended the ending of political status 'special category', in the Cages of Long Kesh, a highly embarrassing problem for the British as it forced them to admit having political prisoners in a western democracy. The final working out of Gardiner's suggestions would be devastating in their outcome, but would only copper fasten the idea that the prisoners were political, in gaol because of participation in an armed struggle against the state, no fine-tuning of the system could deny that fact. In February the British, in their colonial way, issued another Government Paper which, allowing for the Convention; it was also the first time these words came into the lingua franca; 'H Blocks'! This new cellular structure was to be built-in Long Kesh, a British reaction to republican resistance. With the construction of the H Blocks a battleground was being set, the next phase of the 'war' would be fought in the prisons and it would be a battle to the death literally.

Escapes were still in vogue in '75; Patrick Campbell wearing a priest's garments virtually walked out of Long Kesh and was even hailed a lift with another priest by a 'kind' Warder. By this stage of the conflict there had been 56 escapes from Long Kesh, 29 from Crumlin road, eight from Magilligan and seven from the Maidstone; the north's prisons had a defence like Antrim in the championship! The year of 1975 was depressing, loyalist and republican feuds prevailed, and a new threat emerged with the rise of 'the hoods' in republican areas. This feral youth group had no respect for anyone; Provos, RUC, Army, they brought disgrace to their families and became a problem as the conflict continued. Essentially anti-social thugs, thieves and druggies, they acted as parasites on their own communities. They posed a problem for the IRA, but initially the only way to deal with it was through kneecappings, exile or even death. The first wave of these thugs were just wayward youths, but they gradually developed into serious gangsters, and many who moved became part of the gangland scene in Dublin. While the conflict continued in Belfast the IRA could control them, but post ceasefire they would become a major problem, parasites on society. Loyalist sectarian killings were another major problem, they were killing innocent Catholics at will, putting pressure on the IRA to retaliate. This would lead to certain actions which were totally against republican principles, but on the streets in north Belfast if your community was under severe attack it was difficult not to hit back. The final months of '75 culminated in a major feud between the Provos and the Official IRA, it appeared as if it was a massive attempt by the Belfast IRA to finally wipe out the Officials, who were weakened by their earlier feud with the INLA. This latest blood-letting was vicious and only damaged republicanism, the only winners were the Brits. There would be one more episode of internecine warfare, before it was agreed it was not in the interest of republicanism, no matter what branch you belonged to.

The IRA at this stage had decided that the ceasefire was leading them up the garden path, and while trying to uphold it in the six counties, they embarked on a major bombing campaign in London and surrounding areas. They took the fight to the English capital in a way not seen since the German Luftwaffe was dropping serious ordnance on Buckingham Palace. The ASU's were criss crossing London, prestige targets included restaurants where PM Ted Heath was dining and military targets, it sent shivers up the British establishment. But maybe the ASU became a bit cocky, and they were cornered one night in Balcome St, where after a five day siege they surrendered. They became known as the 'Balcome St 4' and entered legendary status, but served 20+ years for their efforts. In later years I got to meet up with two of them; Hugh Doherty who was from Donegal and Joe O Connell, two men who you'd think wouldn't blow up a balloon never mind half of London. They were ordinary guys who took the war to England, but two of the most gentle guys you'd ever meet. The conflict took twenty years of their lives, everyone is a victim of conflict.

The year might have been a disaster on the streets, but in the Cages of Long Kesh we had a changing situation which would have serious repercussions in the years ahead. After the burning of the camp, the authorities decided that it could never happen again and began building 30 foot walls throughout the camp, dividing different sections,. It was a building bonus for some big contractors, but some paid with their lives. Despite IRA warnings not to work for the Army, RUC or Prisons, those who chose to ignore it paid a heavy penalty. Money isn't everything in life, but some are so greedy they will do anything and in the six counties during the conflict, that came with a serious public health warning. After six weeks or so, living in the remnants of the Cages at the top end of the camp, we were suddenly moved down to the lower Cages, in our case Cage 10, which would be my final domicile in Long Kesh. Sad news reached the Cages at the end of January '75, when we heard that John 'Bap' Kelly and John Stone were blown up by their own bomb as they were transporting it to the Law Courts in Chichester St, just off the City Hall and where I used to work in Lavery's Bar. John Stone was on the Maidstone and John Kelly was in our Cage in the Kesh, a popular guy he was a great singer and organised concerts and sing songs. He was released in the summer of '74, and reported back to the IRA, but also continued his singing career and actually recorded a popular republican ballad in America, 'Say Hello to the Provos'. Unfortunately, his new found freedom wouldn't last six months, and he died along with Stone just before the IRA announced its' latest ceasefire.

As 1975 progressed with a ceasefire of sorts, in the Cages, we had begun a political process which would be far-reaching. We formed 'Community Councils' with Volunteers from the different areas, forming groups to discuss how we should address the problems in society, how we as a political party should become more relevant to the people who supported us in the military struggle and how we could translate that support into political support at the ballot box. It was still early days and electoral intervention hadn't really been on the agenda, but these early discussions would later play a large part in the political growth of Sinn Fein. Discussions would take place once a week in our own groups and then together in a forum of sorts, with various ideas swapped around. These ideas included; how to deliver a socialist perspective on life, how to integrate ourselves within the community, how to make the IRA relevant to a political agenda and to understand that to continue the struggle we would need more than a military edge. We discussed how to avoid defeat in the long term by the military side being isolated; the perfect example was if the local ASU or unit were captured there was a void, whereas if the Vols were rooted in the community and some were captured, others were there to fill their shoes. The first move towards the armalite and ballot box strategy began to take shape in the Cages in 1975. I was involved in the Cage education programme: History lectures, PRO work sending letters to papers etc, writing articles on politics, history and current affairs. I had learned to type on an old black typewriter and spent hours rattling out a black and white typed Cage news sheet, along with Daithi MacThomais, a Dublin guy who was Cage Education officer. We would produce the monthly news sheet entitled 'An Fuaiscailtor', the Liberator. Whilst the name was a nod to the great constitutional Irish nationalist Daniel O'Connell, who achieved Emancipation and fought for Repeal, the 'Liberation' we were seeking involved 'armed struggle' which he would have disagreed with in his day of the Young Irelanders and the Fenians. That year 1974, a lot of my time was taken up with the little paper, it was definitely therapeutic. I enjoyed the writing part and became so attached to the old typewriter it was like my right arm, so much so that when I was released the following year the local Sinn Fein chairman Gerry Kelly (not thee Gerry and sadly passed) arrived at my house with a big black typewriter and said, “I hear you've been doing great writing in the Kesh”. All I wanted was a holiday in Donegal, maybe a Bo Derek lookalike and a crate of Guinness.

The little paper would represent all aspects of gaol life, obviously anything happening in the Camp would be covered: current affairs on the outside, articles on republicanism, socialism, liberation struggles like Vietnam, Palestine, Angola, Mozambique, 'war' news from South Armagh and West Belfast, and an Irish language page with sports, quiz and crossword. It was a great experience editing it and continued my love for the syntax of the language and the written word. In our Cage after the time our Huts were divided up into cubicles and I shared one with Rab McCallum from Ardoyne for a long period. We would all try and be creative, and painted our cubicles with various mural type paintings. We painted the iconic red and black image of Che Guevara created by Irish artist Jim Fitzpatrick, and so we went to sleep every night with Che looking down on us. Handicrafts were the big thing while in gaol, the more skilful guys were great at making wooden harps, these must be in houses all over Ireland, magnificent pieces of woodcraft. Those less gifted, although just as creative, would make handbags, wallets, rugs, hankies with political messages and wooden plaques painted with political images. The really gifted painters among us would paint portraits of family members. Tony Bell from our Cage was a virtual Van Gogh, his paintings of dead Volunteers were a classic piece de resistance, and thankfully he held on to his left ear.

Our Irish language hut was a brilliant little 'commune.' It gave us total immersion in our native tongue, we embraced the language as if we were in the Gort a' Choirce or Gaoth Dobhair gaeltacht. "Cad e mar ata tu a chara?" "Ta bron orm, nil ach beagan gaeilge agamsa, ach bhe me ag folaim", "ce tu ag leadh Seamus O' Conghaile" "Nil, bhe me ag leadh Ulysses" We had classes morning, afternoon and evening; grammar, vocabulary, listening skills, role play, drama, seisun, ceol, scoraicht and Clannad, Chieftains. It was a wonderful experience and I loved it. A big regret of mine in life is that when we eventually moved to Donegal, we didn't continue the journey through Termon to Gaoth Dobhair, where I could have perfected my grasp of the language and the children would have been brought up fluent with that unique Donegal-Glasgow blas. The great interest in the language within the Cages would blossom in future years, as many newly released prisoners would help kick start the cultural revival and gaeilscoileanna would spring up all over the six counties, usually under the tutelage of ex Provos. Like in the early 20th century, it was part of the overall resistance to British control of a small part of our country.

The months of 1975 were long and slightly depressing, a ceasefire which appeared to be sapping our ability as a military force, feuds between the Officials/INLA, Officials/Provos, UDA/UVF, and sectarian killings. Also during the summer, after they had built the 30ft walls, Long Kesh felt more like a prison than ever, whereas the Cages felt more open. Then on the horizon, between the Internee Cages and the M1 Motorway, we began to see a massive building development. As it took shape it looked like strangely shaped cellular blocks in the form of an 'H'. We didn't know it then but this construction would determine the future development of the 'armed struggle', and political progression within Republicanism. As the building continued apace Governor Truesdale met with Davie Morley, Gusty Spence and the Official and INLA leaders in the Camp, he invited them to 'inspect' the new developments. He stated they would be state of the art cellular units: each man to his own cell, greater educational facilities, better visiting experience and even better communication with the 'Screws/Warders' who were being specially trained to a higher standard. It appeared too good to be true, and of course it was. Morley returned to the Cages and went around with the Governor's approval, to give his impression of the new facilities. He informed us that indeed the facilities were excellent, much better than we were domiciled in, but he felt that something wasn't right, that there was something coming down the line. He said that the British were past masters in duplicity, and we knew that fine well. It wouldn't be long before we found out what exactly was in store for us, and more so the thousands of prisoners who would take our places in the next decade.

For the time being we had to watch and wait as the building continued at a frantic pace. The IRA put the contractors on a 'hit list' and many desisted, but there always others to pick up the slack and dosh. Many would pay the ultimate price, but like the Warders, they could virtually live in Long Kesh and reap the financial rewards; loyalty to the Crown was important to many but loyalty to the half-crown was more to the liking of the greed merchants. Some of these people would sell their Granny, like the warders they were unscrupulous, usually but not always loyalist, when they were killed there would be the usual outcry that they were “only doing their job”, but it wasn't just a job in the six counties. They were all part of the system which preserved Partition, RUC, B Specials, UDR, Prison Warders, Judges, they perpetuated a system which was bigoted, sectarian, gerrymandered, and used sectarian murder gangs with security force involvement. They couldn't expect that there wouldn't be a reaction, but when the IRA hit back they cried wolf. Conflict is a two-ended sword, in the six counties it was three sided, with the involvement of the British Government and Army. The next step by the authorities was going to up the ante considerably, and lead to the most serious times during the conflict, which would include Prison Warders and Hunger Strikers deaths. The stakes were getting higher, for the British Government policy of Criminalisation and Ulsterisation were prioritised, and for the IRA 'the Long War' concept was evolving. Long Kesh would be centre stage in this period of conflict that would be devastating in the extreme.

It wasn't all doom and gloom within the Cages at that stage. At the end of '74 two groups of six were caught trying to escape. One group had an elaborate plan; they had made up fake Army uniforms and wooden SLR rifles used by the troops, and after cutting through the Cage wire in 16 they formed up as if they were soldiers patrolling the perimeter. But they hadn't got too far when an alert sentry spotted the ruse, threatened to shoot if they moved any further and raised the alarm. A posse of soldiers arrived to deposit the would-be adventurers back into the Cage from whence they had departed earlier. One of the would-be escapees was Larry Marley; he will appear in the story on a regular basis. He became a sort of perennial escapee, while others read or made handicrafts, Larry was totally focused in getting out of the place, he would have made parts for Andy Dufresne in Shawshank Redemption.

The twelve potential escapees eventually were brought to Newry Courthouse in March '75 to face charges for attempted escape from the Kesh. But while awaiting the trial they were all put in a single cell underneath the court and within minutes they had made a pyramid up to the glass ceiling window which they broke through, and quickly all ten had departed the holding cell and made their way to freedom. This event was embarrassing for the police, army and warders, there was a certain Irish irony that the prisoners escaped while awaiting trial for escaping previously. Ten of the lads made successfully escaped into nationalist areas of Newry, among them Larry Marley and Phil McMahon who died recently and father of Philly McMahon the five in a row Dublin GAA star. Three of the boys, Terry 'Cleaky' Clarke, John 'Duice' McMullan and Mal McCarry tried to be too smart for their own good and headed straight for the Border which was just five miles away. Unfortunately for the boys, a Farmers Union strike that day had whole place blocked and wouldn't let the hijacked car through. The boys didn't chance to tell them that they were escapees in case the farmers were loyalist, so they ditched the car and started walking for the border. It almost worked, but just as they made it to the border post armed soldiers arrived and their short-lived freedom was over for two of them, McCarry bolted through fields and made his escape. When the news came through, the last ones we wanted to be caught were the two boys, both characters, but instead of a cool pint and freedom in a pub in Dundalk, they were on their way back to the Kesh. Both Cleaky and Duice have passed away in recent years, Cleaky especially would spend many more years in the Kesh. For the other guys it was a matter of lying low for a few weeks, then quietly slipping across the border and another successful escape would make the headlines, much to the exasperation of the authorities.

As the year closed in, a rather disturbing factor emerged among the ranks of IRA Vols within the Camp confines. It has never been talked about much, but it was a devastating time for some Vols and overall a demoralising period for all concerned. It sort of summed up the year that was in it, with a debilitating ceasefire, sectarian slaughter, meaningless talks with the British Government, and a realisation that there would be no 'Victory '72, 73, 74 or '75, and no amnesty either as was the talk in the early days of the conflict. Instead, what followed during 1975 was an indictment of allowing individuals within an organisation to gain powerful positions, and make potentially dangerous decisions, that goes for Bankers, Hedge Fund merchants, Judiciary, Politico's as much as IRA vols. During the summer of '74, the IRA leadership in Belfast took a major hit with Brigade OC Brendan 'the Dark' Hughes arrested in the leafy Malone area, with major plans for aggressive defence in republican areas if under sustained attack from loyalists in a civil war situation.

During the next six months or so there was severe paranoia in the Cages as senior officers led a witch-hunt against Volunteers who were suspected of anti republican activities such as accusations that they were working for British intelligence, the RUC or loyalists. Many Volunteers were interrogated over a period of time, it was devastating stuff, brought on by paranoia from out on the streets. It was sickening to see some of your friends being put through this trauma, men who had given up a good part of their young lives in the struggle, only to be falsely accused of ridiculous nonsense by the people in power. It left a sour taste in the Cages and thankfully it came to an end within a short period. But for the Vols concerned, it must have left them with serious doubts of what they were involved in. In fact, in later years when it was revealed that some leading Volunteers were informers for many years and that some young Volunteers had been 'sacrificed' to protect these British agents. It created some doubt about the legacy of the whole project, and whether it was really worth all the killing and dying. But that's a topic for another day. One thing for sure it was a period during the conflict we shouldn't be proud off.

Back on the streets, or in the country lanes to be more precise, one of the more notorious killings of the conflict took place when the UVF posing as soldiers, well actually they weren't posing, as four members of the gang were in the UDR, stopped the Miami showband on the way home from a gig in Banbridge. Whatever the original plan was, it ended up with three members of the band murdered, and two of the UVF/UDR men killed, as the bomb exploded prematurely. It was devastating stuff as the popular band, who played in the north when others wouldn't, were slaughtered by the sectarian bigots. It also exposed collusion between British armed forces, the RUC and loyalist gangs which has been covered up even to the present day.

In September '75 in our estate, Turf Lodge, another young lad was shot dead by the British Army. Leo Norney was only 17, a young postman with plans to get married the following year. He had just got out of a Black Taxi which had been searched by soldiers of the Black Watch regiment a few minutes earlier, when shots were fired and Norney was killed by the Army, who then claimed he was a gunman. It was another travesty of justice; a young kid from West Belfast murdered by Scottish soldiers on the streets he grew up on. Leo Norney was only a kid, just left school and in his first job, killed by a bullet fired by another kid from Glasgow, but who had protection from the uniform he wore. No soldier was ever charged with killing Leo Norney, when people wonder why the IRA thrived in these areas you just have to look at incidents like this. It poses the questions: why did British soldiers get immunity and freedom to murder on our streets? Why was the body brought to the nearest Army camp and not to hospital? Why was his lifeless body beaten with rifles, if not to transfer lead traces? Why was his mother not told of his death for 16 hours, if not to allow the soldiers to concoct a story to limit their culpability? Leo Norney was another young person lost in the conflict, and another reason the conflict would continue.

Of course, it wasn't always the Army who did the killing in nationalist areas. In interface areas there was always the danger of attack from loyalists, and within republican circles, there were more feuds which resulted in many deaths. A few months later in Turf Lodge, the Official IRA (Stickies) killed young Paul Best, a Sinn Fein activist who was out doing community work during the latest feud between the Officials and Provisional's. He was an easy target for Official IRA gunmen who abducted him and shot him four times. Best was one of the first of a new wave of young Sinn Fein activists who would eventually become major players on the political scene after the Hunger strikes, unfortunately, he died three months later. Ironically the Incident centre he worked out of became the Sinn Fein HQ in Turf Lodge in later years, and a plaque on the centre commemorates his name along with Vols from the area who died in the conflict. The people who killed him became irrelevant as the years moved on and morphed into a caricature of their former selves. Republicans they may have been at one stage, but as the years progressed they descended into a world of drinking clubs, discussing the merits of Marxist Leninist theory in the post-Perestroika USSR!

Back in the Cages, the end days of '75 heralded a major change in direction by the British Government. Merlyn Rees the Secretary of State in the Labour Government announced the end of Internment without trial. They had been phasing it out over the previous months and in December the last 50 guys were released from Long Kesh. Phil McCullough was the last Internee ever to walk out of the prison and made a defiant statement on release, "I will always be a Republican, no amount of prison will change that." Internment in the '70s had lasted four years and four months, and had been used by the Stormont establishment in the 1920's, 30's, 40's, 50's and 60's. Thus in every decade since Partition, internment had been used against the nationalist community. Between '71-'75 almost 2000 republicans had been interned with only 100 loyalists. If ever there was evidence of an unreformable sectarian state, let these statistics stand testimony to the true nature of partition. At the same time building was continuing over in the new H Blocks, it became a major topic of discussion in the Cages, at a higher level between the OC's and the Governor, and on the outside between the Government and the IRA. Davie Morley, the OC in Long Kesh, was actually allowed temporary release for a few days to meet with the Army Council to discuss the new H Blocks. As a test of genuine British commitment, it was decided to ask to give Morley a weapon for his own protection while on the outside, an appeal granted by the authorities. Morley had a few days freedom but returned with the unequivocal message for Governor Truesdale and the British Government; that under no circumstances would republican prisoners conform as ordinary prisoners, no matter how spic and span the new cells were. It was a no brainer, there was going to be conflict over the H Blocks. The amount of conflict and the impact on society couldn't have been identified at that early stage, but by the middle of the following year it would be obvious we would be heading into a new Armageddon.

Meanwhile, life in the Cages continued as usual. It had been a long hot summer, we played football and volleyball within the Cage and weekly on the big pitch. Many people would use the confines of the Cage to go jogging around it, Peter McAuley from Ardoyne, a former amateur boxer, organised training and we had equipment sent in. Even though I never boxed, I did the training: circuit training on the punch bag, skipping, shadow boxing and medicine ball, it was a really good work out and kept us fit. I loved the skipping and indeed years later I introduced it to our football club during training, which wasn't appreciated by the players. Inside the Huts was like a cottage industry, Harps, leather wallets and handbags, miniature Thompson sub machine guns made and smuggled out, I have handbags and wallets that I made for my parents in perfect condition 40 years later, lovely mementos.

The weekly Lectures continued on every subject under the sun. In the 'Gaeltacht' hut Irish was the lingua franca, and enthusiastic gaeilgeoirs engaged in their native tongue with a slightly Long Kesh blas. As for myself, it was probably the most productive period of my time in the Cages, I was involved in education and public relations work, composing endless letters to the papers and media outlets on the outside. Any issue worth highlighting would be typed up and smuggled out to the Irish News, Irish Press, An Phoblacht, even the News Letter or the Irish Independent, but the chance of them printing anything was as likely as the DUP accepting same-sex marriage. It was slow and laborious work as I laboured long into the night, typing on the old black typewriter. With no PC, iPhones, WhatsApp or Gmail in those far off days, it wasn't as simple as word processing 1000 words and at sending it around the world with the touch of a button, but I enjoyed it, it was a labour of love. Our Cage paper, 'An Fuaisceoilteoir', had an Irish language page, sports page, quiz, I edited it and smuggled out a copy of each edition and have over a dozen of the originals preserved for posterity, as they say, all in surprisingly great condition as they were stored like former President Mary McAleese described WW1 medals, "hidden in a shoebox in the attic" for the last 45 years. NUI Galway, where I completed my Masters many years later, want to digitise them and make them accessible for future students in the archives and Special Collections section of the University, it would be nice for them to be preserved in academia, a part of history.

Visits were a big part of our life in the Kesh, the weekly connection with the outside world was a welcome half-hour break from the regular daily routine. Parents, wives, girlfriends, mates, relations, would all visit over the years. They brought news from the streets, kept us au fait with outside events and filled us in on family events; who was getting married, separated, births, deaths, 21st and 50th birthdays. The visits were a lifeline back to our community, that we had been separated from for many years. Once my aunt and cousins from Clydebank came up to visit me, with the Uncle from the pub in Donegal. It was great to see them, but by the end of the visit they were all crying, days like that were difficult. The visits were also a conduit for smuggling things in and out, the IRA leadership would have 'Comms', passed between visitors and prisoners. These were tiny handwritten notes folded and hidden in the mouth or other more intimate body parts, and they acted as a lifeline between the military leadership and the prisoners. On a less intense form of smuggling, 'An Phoblacht' would be smuggled in; small cameras and radios, vodka syringed into oranges or in balloons, probably for the Loyalists, drugs, porn and muscle supplements, they had a different perception of political imprisonment having never experienced it before.

Relationships flourished and floundered over the years, it was a difficult time for married couples. For the guy, he was locked away for years and couldn't do anything about it. For the wife on the outside, she had to bring up the kids on her own, but she also needed to have a life, and some would succumb to the distractions of life. C'est la vie, and marriages break down. However most marriages survived, and the women were strong and waited for their men. But society was changing and challenging; in the early years the IRA would punish men who preyed on prisoners wives, but as time moved on and society became less principled, let's say, it became difficult, and the last thing the IRA wanted was to become embroiled in family matters. On the other hand many relationships began in the Kesh and Armagh and have survived the test of time; girls going up to visit guys and vice versa in Armagh. Some of these relationships became the bedrock of republican communities, despite the epithet given by the media that these people were 'terrorists', in reality, they were some of the most decent, honest, principled people you could meet. They might have been young and idealistic, but they held values dear to the families and communities they came from, and to be honest I feel privileged to have spent those long years in their company.

During 1975 several more escape attempts caught the imagination of the public, one successful one was from Magilligan Camp near Derry, where I was interned in the early days of the conflict. It was used to hold sentenced prisoners, mostly from the north-west, and after the burning of the Kesh a lot of the Derry prisoners and guys from west of the Bann were transferred to Magilligan. One of these transferred was Martin Monaghan, a good friend of mine. He had moved to the Camp overlooking the Donegal hills to finish out the remaining few years of his sentence. But events took a turn when some of his fellow prisoners noticed that he resembled an English teacher who would come in once a week to deliver lectures. The more he lectured on Macbeth and Virginia Woolf, the more Martin and comrades took an interest in his appearance and a plan started formulating in their seditious minds. This plan involved Martin taking his leave from the northern side of Lough Foyle, swapping it for the southern shores of Lough Foyle, escaping from a British controlled prison, across a British claimed stretch of Irish water. Donegal was in Martin's thoughts while the teacher waxed lyrically on James Joyce.

The plan was worked on for several weeks. They would hold the teacher when he came in for his lecture, he and Martin would swap clothes and they would switch places. Martin was a virtual double of him, so the plan was for Martin to exit the Cage at the end of the lecture disguised as the lecturer. The other Vols would tie-up the actual teacher and hold him for several hours, giving Martin enough time to get through the Camp, exit it, make his way to Derry and then across the border, before the alarm was raised. It worked almost to plan. Unfortunately on the day of the planned escape, another lecturer came into the Camp with the intended target, so he had to be told of the plan, with the warning that if he opened his mouth he would be shot dead on the outside, which certainly concentrates your mind. Martin and the other teacher exited the Cages without a problem, and made their way through the various checks, 14 in all, before they reached the main gate. The other teacher actually started giving out stink to the Screws for holding him up, Martin thought he was trying to give him away and had to inform him that the earlier threat wasn't an idle one. Eventually, both exited the prison and Martin made his way to Derry and headed towards the Bogside where he was to rendezvous with other IRA Vols. Unfortunately he forgot the name of the street, though he remembered the name of the woman of the house. Walking around 'Free Derry' looking for the house, he suddenly came across a British Army foot patrol and just made a beeline for the nearest house, where a young girl let him in. Amazingly the woman Martin was to meet up with was her Aunt, and she contacted her and told her Martin was in her house. Minutes later an IRA unit came, picked up Martin and took him across the Border to Buncrana, where there were several celebratory pints and a phone call to the BBC telling them that a prisoner had escaped from Magilligan!

Inside the gaol the Vols released the teacher from his ordeal, and he made his way home to relate his story to his family. Martin would stay on the run, and reside in Donegal for the last 35 years, before he received a Pardon from no less than the Queen herself after the Good Friday Agreement. Interestingly he would make his way to the US for a period while still ‘on the run’ and was feted by the Irish American community who didn’t see an Irish political prisoner escaping from a British gaol a crime in their eyes.

I would meet up with him again in later years. Thirty years later the teacher guy was giving a talk in Letterkenny library. Martin and his son went up to the library on the night, sat at the back as he delivered the lecture, and at the end, Martin walked up and said, “Hello Brian, how are you keeping, it's been a few years since we met.”Brian looked at the stranger in front of him for a minute and then exclaimed, "Martin, I don't believe it, how are you, it's great to see you." They became great friends after that and eventually wrote a book together about that day back in 1975, when Martin swapped places with Brian to embrace the freedom of the hills in Donegal.

Another fellow prisoner who moved to Magilligan at that time was wee Tony Patton from Strabane, he was very friendly with Micky Linehan in our Cage and his path to the Kesh was quite interesting. Hailing from a golfing family in Strabane which in itself would be quite unusual, the local golf club in which Tony's Dad was Captain would, let's say, be a major handicap to Tony's future career in life! I hadn't seen Tony for almost 40 years, until one day I was golfing with an ex priest at Cregmore, and he asked me did I know a guy from Tyrone called Patton who played there. Immediately Tony came into my mind and several weeks later we met up on the 1st tee at Galway Bay for an inter-club match. To be honest, I didn't recognise him, or he I, but by process of elimination, as I knew the other two guys, I knew it had to be Tony. I had the advantage on him and said, "I think we know each other". But he was completely baffled, I suppose 40 years previously we both had black curly hair and mad beards, now we were two old men in the twilight of our golfing careers, having swapped our Armalites for Ping Irons. As we walked the fairways I jogged his memory and eventually the penny dropped. Needless to say we have remained great friends ever since, as all ex Cages men are. Every year we spend a week playing in the Donegal Links Classic along with an eclectic group of ex Gardai, Bankers, an Artist, Musician, Teachers, Priests, a 3 times All Ireland winner, Rally driver, Businessmen, two Englishmen, a Scot and a few 'nordies', life had taken its course in the intervening years but we're in a good place now.

Christmas 1975 was an emotional time for all of us, as we recognised that our time in the Kesh was coming to an end. A massive number would be released during '76, the first wave of prisoners of the conflict had served their time. There was a feeling of nostalgia, that we had come through something which wasn't normal, not in the way life was meant to be. But we had survived, and defeated any attempt not to recognise us as what we were: political prisoners in an age-old conflict. There were thoughts for the future; what would it be like when we hit the streets. The conflict was in full flow again, would we re-join the ranks of the IRA, or had we a different plan after release. There were many imponderables; we were older, wiser, self-educated, the future would be a different place. Of course, we didn't really know what lay ahead, it's over 40 years now, the majority of the lads I spent those years in Long Kesh with I've never seen again. We're all in our 60's now and have lived a lot of life, but for many life panned out on a different tangent. Many of the boys in the Cages would be dead in a short time: Jim Mulvenna,

Henry Corbett, Danny Lennon, Joey Surgenor, Frankie Fitzsimons, Bobby Sands, Kieran Doherty, Anthony McKiernan, Brendan Davidson and Denis Donaldson were all either shot by the British Army or loyalists, died on Hunger strike, or were shot as informers. They were horrendous times, every one of those guys I knew so well, and spent my youth with in the Cages. They would never get the chance to experience life as it should be lived. That Christmas as we enjoyed a little drop of 'uiscebeatha', while Micky Linehan et al rattled out a few ballads on the guitar, there was a feeling of emptiness, loneliness felt acute. We all knew that special experience in our young lives was coming to an end, the poitin went down well and the 'Boys of the Old Brigade' were killed several times over in a musical sense. Great comradeship comes at a price, "Happy Christmas my arse, I'd rather be dead."

1976 was heralded in with two of the most horrific killing sprees of the whole conflict. On the 4th January, six innocent Catholics from two border families were murdered by the UDA/UVF; the Reavey and O'Dowd families lost three siblings each. It was a disgusting example of a sectarian bloodbath, and what happened in South Armagh would have consequences which reverberated around the community in the six counties. This wasn't Belfast, or isolated Catholic families and loyalist paramilitaries couldn't act here with impunity. The very next day the IRA murdered ten Protestant civilians in retaliation. Again it was horrible sectarian slaughter; no republican can defend sectarianism, it isn't within our DNA, but a message had been sent out to loyalism; south Armagh wasn't Belfast and their actions would cause a reaction. While I could never condone what happened, the reality was that there were no further sectarian killings in South Armagh again. The bigger problem was the existence of a murder gang based at Glenanne; this included paramilitaries, UDR and RUC, all colluding throughout the armed forces. They killed over 100 Catholic civilians during the conflict and never faced justice, as recently revealed in a book and film by the BBC's Anne Cadwallader, under the cover of darkness; on lonely country roads they carried out their deadly work to terrify the nationalist population, a classic counter insurgency tactic.

In our Cage, we were in creative and literary mode. We organised a play as Gaeilge, it was fun rehearsing our lines and acting for a 'captive' audience. We produced an old Irish play, 'Labhar tar Bearla Anseo' by Tristan Bernard and translated by the playwright Leon O'Broin, who was involved in the War of Independence before becoming a Civil servant in the new Free State. I had a small part in the play as 'Freas', and a few lines, "Ta ceann thios ag an staisiunm, an dtig liom a dhath a dheanamh duit." It was fun playing to 'sell-out' crowds every night during our little drama festival in Cage 10, sadly half the cast have passed on. Anton O Cathain, and Peter Stewart, while Micky Linehan, Daithi Boyd and Joe Doc are still going strong. Micky had the acting bug in his veins as his brother would become a household name in later years as 'May McFettridge', a great comedian, as indeed Micky was in the Cages; Joe Doc would attain 'celebrity' status in the '80s after escaping from Crumlin road gaol. He headed stateside where he was jailed for a decade as he fought deportation, and became a cause celebre in New York.

Our 'gaelteacht' hut was a hive of activity, language classes, ceoil, poetry, drama, it was total immersion in the language and we loved it. Charlie and Johnny, two Dubs, Anthony, Kevin and Frankie from Armagh, Christy and Joey from the Strand, Joe Doc, Tommy Mc and MadraRua from the New Lodge, Alfie, Kevin, Daithi, and Peter from different parts of Belfast, an eclectic a group as you'd ever meet. There was never an argument in all the years, we complimented each other; readers, writers, jokers, messers, serious heads, posers, extroverts and introverts, all great guys and sadly more than half have passed away at this stage in life.

As well as learning the language we had regular sing songs and learnt many popular tunes as gaeilge as well:'rince Philib a cheoil', 'teidhir abhaile riu', 'fear a bhata', 'Na buachilli den sean bhriogaid', 'Cad e sin den te sin', 'Gleanntain ghlas Ghaoth Dobhair', 'Bheir mi O, Nil se na la', 'Oro se do bheatha bhaile', 'Leanaigi siar go Ceatharlach', 'Siun ni Dhuibhi' and also poetry: 'Roisin Dubh', 'Teach an Phiarsaigh', 'O leabhair an teanga gaeilge liom', 'Mise Raifteri', 'Preab san ol', and of course 'An T-amhran Naisuinta' and 'Forogra na Poblachta'. One of my favourites was actually as bearla, 'the Gaelic Tongue' written by a Protestant rector, Rev P. Mullins; "It is fading, it is fading, like the leaves upon the trees, it is dying, it is dying, like the wailing ocean breeze". Composed in the 1890's he lamented the language being lost for future generations. He would be proud to know that in the 21st century the language is still alive, the lingua franca in Gaoth Dobhair and Connemara; gaeilscoileanna all over the country; TG4, Radio na Gaeltachta and the recognition of Irish as an official language within the EU. The recent conflict brought a major revival in the language in the six counties, much of it led by ex-political prisoners from Long Kesh who began their language experience in the Cages and H Blocks.

I also spent quite a lot of time producing the Cage paper, the first edition of '76 was dedicated to Frank Stagg who had died on Hunger strike; the second focused on the Celts, with a 'K' not the football club; The following issue was on Hunger strikers throughout the 20th century; the next had a look at modern communism, long before Perestroika, had a graphic image of an Armalite and a description of an AR15, sister of the AK47 which was challenging the British Army's SLR's for the balance of power on the streets; The April issue especially focused on the Irish language and its part in the 'struggle'; and the final issue that I had the pleasure to type up was an Easter special, with the Proclamation as gaeilge on the front page. It was just 60 years then from Easter Week and we reflected on those times and how far we had come with a poem by Pearse, the 'Wayfarer', and a message from the IRA leadership and a major article about James Connolly by yours truly, my writing skills being exposed to a selective readership.

Writing is a therapeutic experience, I've always loved the written word. At that time it was exciting and liberating trying to collect our thoughts on life, and our place in it, despite being behind the wire. Nowadays I word process as the sun sets over Galway Bay, with a glass of red wine to stimulate the grey matter. I still love writing, but I remember those far off days in the mid 70's, the boys who shared my life, many who are dead now. Some were killed in the conflict, many died too early of natural causes, and many more have suffered from the effects of CR gas which was fired at us that day in October '74. Apparently, research shows over 150 who were affected by the gas dropped from the helicopter have died prematurely. Was it because of the effects of the CR Gas? Is it coincidental? Was the use of CR gas legal? Were we used as guinea pigs? Will we ever get the truth? It's very unlikely, documents related to that day in 1974, as indeed to all controversial events in the conflict are locked away for another 50 years and which point everyone involved will be dead. The British Government refuses to release these documents, they refuse a Truth Commission, as it is they who have the most to lose, not republicans.

Our last few months of captivity were spent contemplating what we would do when we got out of the place. The Ceasefire of '75 was well and truly broken, and we had to make decisions which would affect our future lives. Many a time walking around the Cage, I thought of the guys I had been domiciled with the past five years, they had become like family and now we would be going on our separate ways, God knows where we would ever meet up again. I'm getting ahead of myself, but flicking through old photos taken that summer in Cage 10, the lads look out at me, Joey and Frankie blown up by their own bomb at the gasworks, just 6 months after release. Joe Doc part of the M60 ASU who killed SAS man Westmacott and was caught after a siege, then escaped with seven others from Crumlin Road. He became a gaol hero to New Yorkers, while Thatcher tried to bring him back for a decade. Hughie Doran, who lost an eye the day after the burning when hit by a plastic bullet, died just a few years ago, Anthony McKiernan shot as an informer, that's hard to believe. Bill Bradley spent 20 years in New York as well, and died just recently. Micky Linehan and Fenso in photos Irish dancing, Pat Shannon caught after Marty Forsythe was shot dead, just met him at Hughie Doran's funeral after 40 years. A photo of me reciting 'Roisin Dubh' as big Frankie Cox looks on, another man passed on. Micky McMullan, the first man to get recommended 30 years for a soldiers death, my old mate, he served 19 years before Good Friday released him early, an all-round good guy. Daithi Saunders posing in a photo with me with a dummy rifle used for training, Daithi passed recently; he was a celebrity when caught in '72 driving a bomb into Belfast city centre, the Brits tied a rope to his leg and made him defuse it! Johnny Burns who was lifted with me, Sean Fryers, Eamonn Maguire and Gerry Cairns all gone way too young, all Turf Lodge men; Johnny, Eamonn and Gerry sadly passed since I began writing this at the start of the COVID pandemic.

Tommy Gorman who escaped off the Maidstone, John Noonan, a Dub where he became a leader on release and stood for the European elections and wrote a book in later years, 'What will I do Next', Tony Bradley 'the Cat' also gone, old Paddy Mulvenna whose son was killed in Ballymurphy, Billy 'Fuzz' from Ardoyne, Tony Clarke and Sean McLaughlin from Ballymurphy, Rab McCallum and Rob O Hanlon (gone) and two Mallons from Ardoyne. Kins Rooney, Kevin Sullivan and Paddy Gilliland from Andytown, Bob Haughey from Lurgan also passed, more Turf Lodgers: Frankie Ormond, Oliver Burns, Lawrence Donnelly and my old mate and life-long friend Gerry Scullion, a thinker and a socialist. Geordie and Hughie O'Hara (gone) from the New Lodge, Christy Keenan from Short Strand, Matt Kelly and 'Blue' Kelly; Jim Mulvenna shot dead a year later by the SAS, Brendan 'big Ruby' Davison shot dead by the UVF posing as RUC men, his brother Terry, Henry Corbett shot dead by the UVF a few years later in Bawnmore. Peter Stewart shot but survived during an INLA feud when two were killed at Rosnaree hotel near Drogheda, he died in recent years; Daithi MacTomais a Dub who married Susie Weir's daughter after release and passed recently; Johnny Johnston another Dub who landed back in Portlaoise for many years; Jimmy McGeown from Lurgan also passed; Jim Byrne from Portadown; Syd Elliot from A/Town gone; Leo Morgan and Jim McGivern from the New Lodge, Jim also passed; Squire Maguire from the Lower Falls, so many, I've probably left out many friends from the Cages, everyone had a story to tell as the years passed by, now many of them have passed on. I haven't seen most of them for over 40 years, our lives took off on a tangent, but for those years in the 70's we were together as one unit, imprisoned as political prisoners, we had a bond that couldn't be broken. Ironically since I started writing this tome I've been contacted by three of the Dublin guys who had come across an article I had posted on my Blog, 'OnlyOurRiversRunFree'. I hadn't seen any of them since we were released back in '76; Johnny Johnston, Charlie Hoban and Noel Sillery, it was great to hear from them and they weren't slow to remind me of the Dubs five in a row! Recently I met up with Johnny and his Belfast wife of 45 years, we hadn't met since release all those years ago, we spent an afternoon reminiscing about old times and those that were gone, it was great to see him.

The last few months dragged slowly, as they would as you count down the days to release. I read 'Bury My Heart at Wounded Knee' by Dee Brown, the quintessential story of the ethnic cleansing of the native Americans in the 1800's, with the final slaughter at Wounded Knee creek in 1890. It's probably the best book I've ever read and that runs into thousands. I actually read it again at University in 2010 and recently suggested it for our Book Club. In the midst of their extermination, I always think of the Choctaw Indians sending money to help victims of the Famine in the 1840's, indigenous people who suffered like us, they were on our side of history.

Many of the boys were finishing off handicrafts for family before release, Harps plaques, wallets, leather bags, I made two for my mum and aunt in Donegal, I still have them along with wallets, recently included in a book on interesting objects in the last century presented at Collins Barracks, now the National Museum. The last few months I was heavily involved with political propaganda, to counteract British claims that we were terrorists or criminals and that this was not a political struggle. They were working hard on a new policy of Ulsterisation,which would see the RUC take primacy over the Army to give the impression to the world that it was a policing problem not an anti-colonial struggle. The building of the new H Blocks was part of it, as was the phasing out of political status for prisoners, and the classification of new prisoners as ordinary criminals. This all necessitated a rigorous response, and I was involved with other P.R.O.'s in the different Cages, working with Richard McAuley, the republican camp PRO, to flood the papers with statements slamming the new policy as ill-founded and heading for disaster. McAuley on release became Gerry Adams ' aide de camp' of sorts, always at the bearded one's side on his travels around the world. He would have the final say on access to the future Louth TD, and press the flesh of anyone worth talking to. He would also furnish detailed statements on the republican agenda and provided great detail for the many books that Gerry Adams published, throughout the later years of the conflict right into the peace process. I was also engaging with our local Sinn Fein Cumann in Turf Lodge, although at that stage they really were a paperweight in the political stakes, more a support group for the military wing rather than a political organisation on their own right. However my connections with 'our' Gerry Kelly- 'Bishop Tutu' would lead to a challenge on release, he had the big black typewriter waiting for me.

For the past year or so I had a young lady visit me from Short Strand, Patricia; Joey Surgenor had given me her name and we started writing to each other, and then arranged visits. She was a really pleasant person to meet, and we got on quite well. She came from an old republican family in the Strand, the Granny apparently was a great old woman, staunch to the hilt, she had old stories from the pogroms in the 1920's after the birth of the northern statelet. A republican of great integrity, she was very proud of her grandson who was in the Cages with us, he was an intellectual guy, well versed in socialist politics. After release he quickly moved through the ranks of the IRA, and then later in Sinn Fein. His family and the community saw him as a respectable citizen who breathed republicanism, and he was going places within republican circles, but things soured in later years. I always felt for the old Granny, what he did must have turned a knife in her stomach; her grandson was Denis Donaldson, he will return to the story in later years.

In the middle of February, Frank Stagg died on Hunger strike in England. Both Governments in the UK and in the Republic were determined to stave off the same type of show of strength seen at Michael Gaughan's funeral. The Fine Gael Government redirected his flight to Shannon, where they hijacked the coffin and brought it straight to Mayo, where a grave had been prepared. His emaciated body was buried, and the grave cemented over amid massive Gardai presence, but it wasn't to be the end of the story. A few months later the IRA dug up the coffin during the night, and reburied Stagg in the Republican plot, another massive publicity coup. A few weeks later on March 1st, the British Government announced the ending of political status. This meant in future, all prisoners would be treated the same; those caught planting bombs or carrying weapons would be treated the same as shoplifters and rapists. It was obvious to all that this was nonsensical, obvious to all except the British, they just couldn't get their heads around Irish history. Ironically the date selected to abolish was the same date that Bobby Sands would embark on his fast to the death after five years of protest. While Merlyn Rees was announcing the changes in the Commons, he was utterly unaware that he was opening a can of worms, and that his decision would create mayhem in the years to come.

Just before Rees made the statement in the Commons, we were given the statement from the British Government in the Cages. The OC read it out to us on parade in the long Hut. Ironically the IRA had the statement before the Westminster MP's, that also would set a pattern in the years to come. In the Cages we debated the implications for us; initially, it didn't appear a problem, as all prisoners already in the Cages would retain political status until release. But as time went on, the implications for those arrested after the 1st March became clear; upon sentencing they would be sent to the new H Blocks without political status. The Camp leadership told Governor Truesdale it was unacceptable, and the IRA leadership on the outside told the British Government that all means possible would be used to break the new regime in the H Blocks. The writing was on the wall, the next five years would see the most difficult times in prison history; Long Kesh and the Cages would morph into the Maze and the H Blocks, it was a recipe for disaster. As the 1st of March deadline for ending political status arrived, the IRA issued a warning that "all

Prison officers and their families were legitimate targets." Within six weeks, two warders were killed, one based at Magilligan, the other at Crumlin road. Evidently the stakes were getting higher.

The weeks were closing in on my time in Long Kesh, my release date was the 10th of May. I would complete the six-year sentence with remission on exactly the same date as I was released from Internment in 1972, how ironic. All through that early summer of '76 many of the boys were being released. It was a sort of oxymoron; we were always glad when someone was released, but at the same time there was a sadness that guys we had spent so long with were gone. The reality was that I would never see many of the boys again. As gaol release fever hit us, we spent the time walking around the Cage, Joey 'the Snake', Micky Linehan, Micky 'Che' McMullan, MacTomais, Kevin 'the Druid', big Rab and Johnny, the guy I was 'lifted' with all those years previously. We chatted about life, about the future, plans and dreams, sometimes we felt like the guys in the 'Life of Brian', 'always look on the bright side of life', other times we felt like Georgie Best, 'where did it all go wrong! We were at a crossroads in life, we could return to normal life or the 'armed struggle' which might mean an eventual return to prison or the possibility of death.

All these things were swirling through our heads as we walked the yard around the Cage, although our immediate thoughts were of our impending freedom: getting pissed, meeting a petite blonde and heading to Donegal for the craic was foremost on the agenda. I wasn't to realise it then, but all these things would come to fruition for me, just not immediately. There was more 'war' to come and less R&R for the foreseeable future. At the end of April, an IRA bombing of the Conway Hotel had gone badly wrong. Mairead Farrell, who was later killed at Gibraltar, was arrested at the scene, while Sean McDermott and Kieran Doherty made off on foot and attempted to hijack a car at a nearby house. The owner said the car keys were upstairs and went to get them, but he was an RUC officer and pulled a gun and shot McDermott first, before firing after Doherty as he got away. Sean McDermott died a few hours later, and at his funeral near Turf Lodge 'big Doc' could be seen in photos watching on. Kieran Doherty would of course, die later on Hunger strike.

Easter 1976 was an emotional time with our Cage, as we probably realised that by the end of the summer, most of us would have exited our domicile for the past 5 years. There were some who would still be here for quite a considerable time, but most had sentences of ten years or less, so release was looming. Easter Sunday is a special day in the republican calendar; while the Christian world recall the guy with the beard (not Gerry Adams) dying for his faith and re-emerging on Easter Sunday, republicans and indeed most of the Irish nation, if 2016 was anything to go by, remember that Sunday in April as the beginning of the Easter Rising (well Easter Monday to be exact, due to Eoin

McNeill). Easter marks the time when the Volunteers took over the GPO and fought the British for almost a week, proclaiming the Irish Republic. While initially a military failure, the British executions of the leaders would set in motion a mood within the 'natives' that we had enough of foreign rule. Within five years of the Rising, the British were brought to the negotiating table and colonial rule was ended in most of the country, which would eventually become the Republic. They were heady days and the present generation commemorated them with gusto and pride just a few years ago in 2016.

In the decades since the Treaty, Easter Sunday was always celebrated and massive commemorations marked the 50th anniversary in 1966. But when the latest conflict kicked off during the 70's, it became less fashionable in the Republic, and, the Government didn't even commemorate the 75th anniversary in 1991. It was thought to be difficult to commemorate the IRA killing British soldiers in 1916-21, which apparently wasn't the same thing as the modern IRA killing British soldiers in 1991. Whilst the Government were reserved in their commemorations, Republicans held Easter parades in every county with the largest parades in the six counties, especially Belfast and Derry. Thousands would parade up the Falls from Beechmount to Milltown cemetery, similarly in the City Cemetery in Derry and Drumboe in Donegal. The Proclamation would be read and republicanism enhanced for another year of struggle, 'who dares to speak of Easter Week'. In Long Kesh, each Cage would have its own Easter Parade. We would have a Colour Party, flags were made up: the four Provinces, the national flag, the Starry Plough and the Fianna flag. The whole Cage, or as we were designated, 'C' Company, 4th Battalion, would turn out in their Sunday best and march behind the colour party. Then the Easter statement from the IRA leadership would be read out, followed by the Proclamation read aloud. It was heady stuff, as well as an act defiance towards the Screws and British soldiers up in the watch towers. It mightn't have been 'Tiocfaidh ar la' but we had our day in the sun.

After the parade was over in Easter '76, preparations were made for the concert that night. A lot of work went into it, and it was a brilliant night. We set up a stage and a sort of lounge bar environment, with the backdrop being the flags we carried earlier. The poitin makers had been hard at work the previous few weeks, and the Screws did their bit by not raiding, looking for the poitin still, and so we had a good supply of the 'cratur' and it definitely helped the evening flow. There was a special feeling that night, we definitely understood that this wouldn't happen again with this group of people. We didn't know at that stage, but by the end of the year Joey Surgenor, Frankie Fitz, Danny Lennon, Anthony Gallagher and Patrick Smyth would all be dead. But that night was about celebration and commemoration; we remembered the men of that Easter 60 years previously, readings from Pearse and Connolly.

Jim Gibney read the statement from the Army Council, Anthony McKiernan read the Proclamation, he too would be dead before long. I recited the poem 'Roisin Dubh', looking into my cup of poitin, Joey Surgenor sitting beside me, I almost blanked it as the nerves tingled but managed to deliver it: "Ah Roisin na biodh bron ort, fe'reirigh dhuit, ta na braithe teacht thar saile, is iad ag trial ar muir." Funny the words are still etched in my brain all these years later, a romantic old poem/song, Roisin a metaphor for Ireland and her woes, translated by Pearse, and later in the modern era by Thomas Kinsella who also wrote 'Bloody Sunday'. We then had a display of Irish dancing with Micky Linehan leading the troupe which included Fenso, Joe Doc and Charlie McKernan. Riverdance they weren't, but it brought the house down. Next up on stage, was a sort of Johnny Cash/ Elvis 1950's rock 'and roll group with Christy Keenan, Sean Fryers and Kins Rooney on guitar. It was brilliant stuff as they boomed out hits like 'In the Ghetto', 'Blue Suede Shoes', 'Jailhouse Rock', and 'Folsom Prison Blues', 'I shot a man in Reno just to see him die' and 'A Boy named Sue'. It was great stuff and like the prisoners in Folsom, we roared our appreciation. The night finished with 'Amhran na bhfainn', but as with all good shows it was the après party that sprung to life, with renditions of 'The Boys of the Old Brigade', 'Sean South from Garryowen', and the 'Lonely Woods of Upton'. There were some sore heads in the morning after the night we had. I recall that night so well, as I said earlier we all knew that after this our lives would be different, and we celebrated accordingly.

Before our official release dates in mid-May another 'great escape' took place from the Cages in the Kesh. This time nine INLA guys tried to tunnel under the perimeter fences, but came up short. They then had to cut through wire and climb a 20ft wall to make their way to freedom, hijacking cars on the M1 Motorway to get away. Two were caught pretty quickly, but the other seven made it across the border. For two of them it was their second escape, they had escaped from Crumlin road courthouse the previous year, clearly the 'spirit of freedom' was hard to quell. One of the escapees was Gerard Steenson who had created a reputation in recent years. He allegedly was heavily involved in the shooting of Billy McMillan, the Officials Belfast OC on the Falls as a 17 year-old during the birth of the INLA. He went on to play a major part in several feuds within the INLA in future years before his luck ran out and he was killed in Springhill, near Ballymurphy, in yet another feud. Internecine feuding sucked the lifeblood out of the nationalist communities, the only people who benefitted were the RUC and Army. The problems stemmed from the smaller armed groups having personalities with large egos taking control, and splits galore created feuds. The loyalist groups were continually feuding over essentially the same issues. However within Republicanism there was a history of armed resistance and organised secret societies, leading to the IRA's strict disciplinary code. Whereas within loyalism, there was no history and the groups were filled with part-time gangsters, sociopaths, some with psychopathic tendencies and sectarian bigots. It took little for power-hungry zealots to use guns against opponents for personal benefit, and as the conflict continued similar developments took place within the smaller splinter republican groups. It served no purpose, only increased the growing death toll and left communities in a state of despair.

Finally, the 10th of May arrived. I was up early in the morning as I would normally do, and prepared for my imminent release. I showered, shaved, had breakfast, packed up my earthly possessions and then walked around the Cage perimeter for an hour with a few of the boys. I then called into the other Huts to say a few goodbyes, and finally to the Gaelteacht Hut where the lads I had spent the past few years with were waiting: It was some eclectic mixture; sadly almost half passed now, we hugged and shook hands and they presented me a Tomas De Bhaldraithe Bearla/Gaeilge dictionary which they all signed, a wonderful book and keepsake which I still have to this day. Slowly I gathered up my stuff and made my leave of the Hut for the last time. I still had one last call to make to the next Hut, where my old buddy Micky McMullan was. As the rest of the boys gathered near the Cage gate, Micky decided to stay in his Hut. It wasn't easy for him, he was serving 30 years with no remission, he had to watch on, as one by one we were released, while he had nothing to look forward to but the inside of the Cages for another 25 years, it was a bleak thought. We hugged each other and maybe a tear was shed, I told him I would call in with his mother in Andytown, then it was time to go.

Micky would actually serve 19 years before being released as part of the Good Friday Agreement. We only met up once since his release in Free Derry in a folk village. The latest I heard he's running a bar in Latin America or somewhere else exotic; he'd like that, he always felt he was a bit of a Che Guevara. In the Cage yard I bid farewell to all the boys, it was emotional, they had all came out to say 'goodbye'. Johnny Burns my 'partner in crime back' in '72 accompanied me, the Screw in charge opened the gate to let us through. I gave one last glance back and swore to myself that I would never enter these gaol Cages and walls again. The Screw opened the second gate, ushered us through and we walked towards the administration area. I never looked back, whether by hook or by crook or just plain good luck, I would never see the inside of the place again, saying that, it wasn't for the want of trying. The next year would bring a sort of death wish in its wake, we didn't know what lay ahead of us and it's a good job we didn't.

BACK ON THE STREETS – FREEDOM OF SORTS

Just as we prepared to leave Long Kesh for the last time, there was a quirky incident, to say the least. My Dad, sister Bernadette and Johnny's sister Ena had arrived in the car park to welcome us out, my Dad took a few photos on his fancy camera he bought from a friend, Jimmy Quigley's Dad; Jimmy had been shot dead by the Army back in '72. As we chatted we noticed Dad missing, after half an hour or so he came walking back, we enquired, "Where were you?" He replied, "Special Branch arrested me for taking the photos, saying they might be a security risk." Apparently the Branch checked the photos, and finding nothing damaging to national security gave the camera back to my dad, and let him go. My poor dad, the most civil man you ever met, accused by the local Gestapo of being an international terrorist, if only they knew he was smuggling in An Phoblacht in his shoes for years!

We travelled back to Turf Lodge on the PDF bus with lots of visitors who gave us a great welcome. Back at home, the tricolour was proudly flying from the house and a crowd had gathered. Then my Mum appeared and we embraced, both shedding tears, the wee Donegal woman who made a life in Belfast. A hard-working country person just like my dad, but they were both staunch and defiant in their own way during the conflict. They supported me all the years in Long Kesh, played their part like so many ordinary families, kept men on the run or used the house for meetings, billets or stand bys, and hid weapons. That's just the way it was, the IRA could never have survived without the overwhelming support of ordinary people throughout the six counties, and indeed in the Republic. It mightn't suit the D4 media, British apologists or the Irish Government, but that's the way it was. You won't hear that in the overpowering studies of the conflict by professional political authors, but in every nationalist community from Crossmaglen to the Bogside, Turf Lodge to Tyrone, the story was the same. While the vanguard might have been the cutting edge of the armed volunteers, the real heroes were the wee women in the streets who kept the guns, wore blankets during the H Block protest, marched for the Hunger Strikers, and when time came, voted for the future. They never made a fuss, but they made a major contribution. Many are long gone now, but their memories prevail, drive through those same streets and people know. They understood and they delivered over and above, wonderful people in difficult times.

Not long after we arrived home, the local accordion band appeared outside the house, a community recognition for the volunteers who had been in Long Kesh. It was slightly embarrassing, but I recognised as they did that we were all in this together. It was a community effort, not everyone could volunteer to join the Republican Army, but everybody could play a part. That was the difference between a paid British soldier and an IRA volunteer; they were unacceptable in our community, whereas we were welcomed in every house in the area; they were foreign soldiers, paid killers, mercenaries, we were part of the community, there was no way they could defeat us. That evening we had one job to do first, a black taxi brought us over to a social club in Andytown and we met up with Jimmy Burns, Johnny's brother, who had escaped from the Kesh and was still on the run. We met for an hour or so and then headed back to Turf Lodge where a party had been organised and many friends called in: former comrades, ex-prisoners. We had a good night; several beers or ten, bodhrans, guitars and even bagpipes, there were a few sore heads in the morning. Among the guests at the party were a few who would gain certain notoriety over the years, Seanna Walsh and Evelyn Glenholmes to name a few. Seanna would return to the Cages for the best part of the next 20 years, and after being released as part of the Good Friday agreement, Seanna, representing the Republican dream, would announce on worldwide satellite TV that the IRA 'war' was over.

Evelyn Glenholmes, daughter of the guy who swore us into the IRA in the first place, back in the early '70s, would face extradition for bombing offences in London. But in a chaotic day in Dublin, she was released by the judge, only for Special Branch to try to re-arrest her. This led to a chase through the city centre streets, as Republicans tried to whisk her away on a motorbike, and the Gardaí fired shots and pursued her, eventually capturing her. It was all filmed and shown on the RTE news as the astonished city centre shoppers dived for cover. It ended up as a bit of a sham by the Gardaí, as the judge let Evelyn off again. Among others at the party was the guy in charge the night we were lifted. We had blamed him for allowing the Para foot patrol to spot us in the first place, when lookouts should have prevented it, but c'est la vie. These things happened, we went to school together, that night the only time I've met him in 50 years. The next day we went up to the 'Marty Forsythe' club, the local republican club named after the Vol shot dead in 1971. We were welcomed heartily, and the traditional crate of stout appeared. We hadn't a drink in years, bar the homemade 'hooch' in the Cages, and when we were presented with two crates of Guinness, let's say we enjoyed the afternoon. Johnny Burns and I had spent the last five years in Long Kesh, but this was the parting of the ways. Johnny went off on his own tangent, whilst I thought long and hard about what the future held. Before I made my decisions I would be heading to Donegal, there was something in those hills which would eventually drag me back.

I didn't know it then, but Donegal was going to play a big part in my life from there on. A week before I was released, a friend from Derry, James Anthony Gallagher, was also released. The following Monday he was on a Lough Swilly bus travelling out the Strand road, towards the border at Bridgend on the way to Buncrana, when the bus was stopped at the British Army checkpoint. A few soldiers got on to check faces, not collect fares, and as they alighted shots rang out from a soldier in a Sanger, and three people were shot. One of them was James Gallagher, who later died in hospital. Whether the soldier recognised him from mug shots or he just flipped isn't known, the soldier was heard shouting after the incident: "I'm cracking up, I'm cracking up." Anthony Gallagher had just one week of freedom, the soldier was never charged with either murder or manslaughter, but his military career ended, probably to the relief of most people in Derry. A few days later I made a trip up to Armagh gaol to visit the girl who was writing to me the past few years. She would turn out to be one of the sorrowful mysteries in later years, but for now I was smitten, maybe it was the blonde hair, whatever. For my troubles I was arrested outside the gaol by Special Branch and held for an hour or so, time would tell if she was worth the visit.

I headed to Donegal for a well-earned break; six summers spent in British prisons were just a bit too much to accept. It might not seem much now but six years when you are 24 is a hell of a long time, a quarter of your life. We might have been young and innocent, but those years in gaol in the '70s were something else. In Donegal I met up with loads of guys who would become good friends in the years ahead; 'Giggsy', Hugo, Harry, Fred, Frank et al. I also met up with Fred's sister, Margaret. One night we were in the Lagoon thinking of going to Falcarragh for a dance. A guy came in half pissed; another friend, Dan, suggested we take a lift with this guy but we declined as he was obviously drunk. Five minutes later after he left the pub he crashed into a car coming the other direction from Creeslough, killing himself and the two occupants of the other car. The next morning I was in the bog cutting turf with my uncle and we noticed cars coming to a house in the distance. One of those killed was a girl from the house, her twin sister was distraught, we easily could have been in that car!

After a few weeks in the 'Hills' I went back to Belfast and faced up to the reality. We met up with some leading republicans and decided on our future. To be honest, we weren't over-impressed with the way things were going in the area, and decided to hold our fire, excuse the pun. But events took a major turn, as many of the volunteers in the estate were lifted including Sean Seaton who had been in the Kesh with us. We had tried to persuade him to hold off, but he went straight back and ended up back in the Kesh in quick time. Another guy lifted was Jim McCarthy, he was stopped in a car along the Monagh road and pulled a revolver on the arresting soldier; there was a standoff, but he was eventually arrested, the next time I saw him he was escorting a Sinn Fein MEP in her duties to open a local festival almost 20 years later, the struggle had evolved!

The summer of 1976 was a long hot summer; Rocky Bilbao was in the movies, Steve Jobs formed Apple, the US Ambassador to Lebanon and the British Ambassador to Ireland were both assassinated and Chairman Mao died. The beaches in Marble Hill, Downings and Dunfanaghy were sweltering in 30 degree heat, the 6 counties emptied for the '12th' as the hills beckoned for nationalists. Arriving back in Belfast I met up with a few others just released from Long Kesh. One afternoon we walked up to the new ring road they were constructing on the edge of Turf Lodge and sat on top of massive stone piping which was going underground. Looking out over the city we contemplated our future; what we should do, what was the situation locally and could we make a difference? In the back of our minds, we all knew that making a decision to re-join the 'armed struggle' would most likely lead to further years in prison, or even the possibility of being killed. We didn't make the decision lightly; we thought of our parents, they were getting older, if we went to gaol again they would most likely be dead by the time we got out, as the Government had doubled all sentences, so where it used to be ten years now it would now be 20. We took all the variables into account and finally shook hands on it, the struggle continued and we were part of it, and so we decided to return to action. At first we didn't join up again carte blanche, we wanted to know what plans the leadership had for going forward. We met up with the local OC and told him our concerns, he explained how things were and what our part would be.

We suggested that the four of us be kept aside from the local unit and form a special ASU to carry out selective attacks on prestige targets, but Belfast Brigade already had a unit like that. We were concerned that by staying locally we would be identified quickly by British intelligence and set up for arrest and we wanted to stay as anonymous as possible. This wasn't '71 and the IRA on the streets openly, the 'war' was developing into a more technically sophisticated operation, and small four man units operating independently were the order of the day. But as it happened fate would step in to play its part, a week later as I mentioned Jim McCarthy and almost the whole IRA unit were arrested in one fell swoop and charged with serious offences. This by chance left a gap in the structure, which we stepped into. We, who had been street kids at the start of the conflict were now in a position of leadership and responsibility for the younger guys who we found flocking to join up, in no time we had built up the unit to its previous strength, smaller groups imperative, security vital, info on a need to know basis, cell structure, it was going to be a busy few months.

In the H Blocks the first prisoners arrested after March 1st were processed through the court's system and sentenced to long periods in gaol. But this time they were not going to be treated as political prisoners but 'ordinary decent criminals' as the prison system would like to describe them. Kieran Nugent was the first republican prisoner to face the new system. When he arrived in the H Blocks, the smug new Governor and Head Prison Officer were waiting. They told him to strip and put on the prison clothing. Nugent replied with these famous words, which went down in contemporary history, “You'll have to nail prison clothes to my back, I'm a republican political prisoner.” He was then escorted to his cell and given a blanket to wear, thus began the Blanket protest which would last five whole years. Kieran Nugent will always be linked to the prison protest, that he was an ordinary volunteer was even more poignant. He represented the volunteers of the working class 'army', his lonely protest initially represented the republican struggle. He was akin to old Tom Clarke in gaol in England on his own in the 1890s, a struggle of irresistible force against the immovable object, who would blink first? The administration would throw everything at its disposal against the prisoners as the British Government saw it as the 'IRA's last card.' It would take five long years of the blanket protest, dirty protest and hunger strikes before it would be resolved. Kieran Nugent laid the first blow. Sadly in later years, after his release, his life would spiral in a downward twist. He wouldn't be the only person in that community with drink-related problems during the conflict, and sadly one morning he was found dead, poignantly on his own, just as he was all those years on the blanket.

In early August a real tragedy happened in Andersonstown, an IRA unit was moving through the area when they were spotted and chased by an Army armoured patrol. The Army fired over 60 shots and hit the driver of the car. The driver, Danny Lennon, an IRA Vol who was in the Cages with us, died immediately. The car careered off the road on to the footpath, where a mother, Anne Maguire, was walking with her three children: Joanne, John and Andrew. The three children were killed and Anne received serious injuries. It was a horrendous tragedy made worse by the Army claiming that the IRA had killed the children, an obviously false lie taken up by the media and politicians for narrow political gains. It was a disingenuous ploy to damage the republican base, and though it created the phenomenon of the 'Peace People', it would soon disintegrate through personal disagreements and financial issues, not before Corrigan and Williams received the Nobel Peace prize, but they became a footnote in the story of the conflict. Danny Lennon was given an IRA funeral several days later, where it was emphasised that he was already dead when the getaway car hit the children, not that this lessened the suffering of the families involved, either the Maguires or Lennons. Danny had been driving the car which was turned into a deadly human projectile after he was shot, his fellow Vol John 'Green' Chillingworth was arrested, beaten by soldiers and would eventually receive 20 years in the H Blocks. It was one of the saddest incidents of the whole conflict. Anne Maguire, the mother, survived but never got over the deaths and five years later tragically took her own life. Recently there have been suggestions that some of the children were killed by Army bullets, and not the car navigated by an already dead Lennon. Like many events of the conflict we will likely never know the truth. Everyone wanted peace but the cynical misuse of the incident was contemptible.

This was highlighted less than two months later, when the British Army killed young Brian Stewart, his skull fractured by a plastic bullet during a riot in Turf Lodge. He was only 13, like the Maguire children, he was an innocent victim of the conflict. The people of the area around the Stewart home rallied to the family with support and it was made clear to the Army that they weren't welcome in the district. Barricades were erected and the area was tense as the family mourned the young boy. At his funeral, several of us carried the coffin down through the estate; it was our way of saying we were there in support of the family, as indeed the IRA would have been in Andersonstown, but the Maguire family were manipulated by vested interests that saw an opportunity to discredit the republican cause. In the immediate aftermath of the Maguire deaths, a call for peace went out which swept the island. Two women appeared as the voices of this new 'movement'; Betty Williams and Mairead Corrigan, sister of Anne Maguire. They captured the moment and organised marches for peace all over the place: up the Falls, Derry's Walls and the Shankill and Markethill. At first, it was spontaneous and great outpourings of grief mixed with a coming together of people who had been divided by the conflict, seemed to be creating something special that might bring peace. But it wouldn't last, within a few months, the cracks began to appear. A major march was organised for the Falls, the heart of republicanism. It was controversial for many reasons, but went ahead albeit with a smaller crowd than expected. It was followed by a republican march which brought over 10,000 to the streets; it was colourful, vibrant, youthful, and a defiant message that peace wasn't just about defeating the IRA. Ironically, the straw that broke the camel's back was the death of Brian Stewart by the Army. Corrigan and Williams appeared on the news the next day and refused to condemn the Army for the killing, it was a fatal mistake for the 'Peace People'. They were invited to a meeting at the community centre in Turf Lodge by the local Women's Group, where once again they refused to condemn the murder of the young boy by the Army. The women of the estate were appalled by their attitude, and let them know in no uncertain manner as the meeting broke up into chaos. Williams and Corrigan were in danger of physical attack and ironically we came to their aid, sheltering them from abuse, and indeed taking abuse from our own people for protecting them. A shot had to be fired in the air to settle the seething crowd, as we pushed the two 'Peace Women' through the back of the parochial house into a waiting van to take them to safety, yes safety, their lives were in danger after their reckless remarks.

In regards to the Army murder, the community were incensed at a lack of sensitivity; it appeared for the first time that the 'Peace People' only saw peace as the defeat of the IRA. The next night on the news Corrigan apologised to the people of Turf Lodge; she was from a nationalist area and understood, on the other hand Williams still refused to blame the Army. The first seeds of division were being sown. Ironically the two women said they owed their lives to the actions of 'paramilitaries' the previous night, men they didn't understand.

For the next few months, Turf Lodge was in a state of turmoil. The Army were kept out of the area as the barricades were strengthened, any sign of foot patrols on the edge of the area brought an instant reaction from youths firing stones and bottles, and IRA Vols launching waves of attacks at any available target. The women of the area organised street protests and vigils for all killed in the conflict, not just selective condemnation, it was a month of complete unity between the people and the IRA, the fish in the sea. While most people abhorred violence, there was an understanding that the IRA was only one part of the conflict. There was also the reality that in these areas the IRA weren't 'terrorists', but the sons and daughters of neighbours and friends; the postman or the bus conductor, the butcher or the barman. The IRA was part of a community who sheltered them, the 'Peace People' fell into the trap of not understanding that simple fact. I wrote a long article for Republican News at the time which I dropped into Editor Danny Morrison. It just highlighted the connection between the women of the area and the republican cadre which was prosecuting a 'war' against the British Army, and how the IRA couldn't survive without that support. Funnily enough, I finished it with a quote from Fidel Castro, it was deleted, just a little too Marxist for some at the time. I was interested in getting involved in the political side at the time, indeed very interested in the publicity and journalistic side of things, but as it was, my full attention was on the military side,and that would continue for a while yet.

A fortnight later, we headed down to Dublin for the Sinn Fein Ardfheis at the Mansion House, the iconic venue where the 1st Dail met in 1919. As we settled into our seats with other delegates from our local Cumann, word started circulating that three volunteers were killed in a bomb at the gas works in Belfast. The next morning it was confirmed that two of the Vols were Joey Surgenor and Frankie Fitzsimmons, who were released just six months earlier, and had shared the Cages with us for the previous five years. It was devastating news, and we waited with trepidation for word of the third member of the group, all thinking it was another comrade from the Cages who was inseparable from the boys. As it turned out it wasn't him, but another Vol, Paul Marlowe, it made for a sad weekend.

After the final session of the Ard Fheis, I headed out to Sandyford to meet up with a little old lady who had also been writing to me in the Kesh. Of all the women who had written to me over the years she was the most fascinating, then in her 80's, she personified the republican struggle. She had lived an amazing life; was a runner at the GPO in 1916; an observer at the 1st Dail in the Mansion House in 1919; a member Cumann na mBan during the War of Independence; a volunteer during the Civil War; and was in the Four Courts just before it was bombed by the Free State Army with British guns in 1922! She also held Cathal Brugha's hand as his life ebbed away at the back of the Gresham Hotel. She was imprisoned and went on hunger strike. She then worked for De Valera as a journalist in the Irish Press in the 30's, even though she detested him. She canvassed for Republican candidates in elections in the six counties during the '50s and remained a staunch republican all her life, even holding a black flag on O'Connell bridge the day Bobby Sands died, just a few years before her own death, a great woman. I sat fascinated as I listened to her talking; she was like the old woman in the Titanic film as her mind goes back to that night in 1912, when the big ship hit an even bigger iceberg. Maire Comerford was no doubt living history; she talked about Pearse and Connolly, Mellowes and Collins as just ordinary guys she knew. She also spoke to me about her sadness during the civil war, and how their dream of a Republic was fading away. It was wonderful spending a few hours in her company, I left feeling convinced that our republicanism was no different from 1920, that those in power criticising us were afraid that the people would also come to that conclusion, especially in the Republic, thus Section 31, 'Heavy Gang', Special Branch, lip service to the national question, and the reality that 'armed struggle' in 1970 was the same as in 1920 and opened up too many questions and few answers. I left Sandyford that evening with renewed conviction having spent an evening in the company of a wee old woman who had done exactly the same as us in 1920. Maire presented me with a copy of her book, '1st Dail' and also signed it for me; I cherish it to the present day.

The following week, another incarcerated writer was released from Armagh gaol and a party was held in her parent's house, where I had first seen her back in August '69. It was the beginning of a relationship, which had first begun in the gaols, writing to each other. At the party that night was her brother Kevi, and several other members of the Auxiliary IRA. They were a sort of reserve Vols who looked after 'policing' matters, usually investigating anti-social behaviour and dishing out punishment beatings which included kneecapping. It wasn't the most appropriate justice, but in the prevailing situation it was the only solution, and supported by the community. During the night half a dozen of them asked to talk to me in the kitchen, all saying they wanted to join the IRA full time as active volunteers. I warned them of the dangers involved: the threat of imprisonment and death, and set in motion their acceptance into the 'army'. For most of them in due course it would mean years in the H Blocks, and for Kevi, her brother, it would also mean death.

A week later loyalists delivered a blow to the leadership of Sinn Fein when they killed Maire Drumn in the Mater hospital, where she was in for an eye operation. A former soldier and UVF member who worked at security in the hospital set in motion the murder, and was later jailed. Maire Drumn was originally from South Armagh and married to Jimmy who was the most interned republican in the north over the years. She was a fiery character, exhorting young people 'not to throw stones but to join the IRA'. On the other hand, Merlyn Rees the Sec.of State declared, "she was like the woman at the guillotine during the French revolution, knitting and enjoying it."

In the middle of November, Patrick Smyth was shot dead in Short Strand. He had been in the Cages with us and wasn't long released when he was killed. Former comrades had taken the drastic action, because when arrested years before, he had given information during interrogation which led to a 'doomsday' dump of weapons being discovered. He had never been forgiven, initially, he was ordered out of the district but when he continued to return the decision was made to execute him. Such were the horrible decisions made during conflicts. I had known, and was friendly with Patrick during our time in the Cages. Considering the role of major figures within the IRA as informers in later years for financial gain, Scap, wee Denis, Sandy Lynch and Sean O'Callaghan, it makes one wonder if those who break during interrogation are of the same breed. Conflict is cruel, it starts off with the highest of convictions but can descend into unscrupulous actions; participants all end up in the gutter, in the trenches, behind the barricades, on the ditches, even in the corridors of power, it also corrupts.

At the end of November, another soldier was killed in Turf Lodge. Andrew Cocker a member of the Welsh Fusiliers was was shot by a sniper from the INLA. There was serious rioting taking place in the area when he was killed and an Army helicopter overhead followed the INLA guys to a house where they dumped the weapon. The Army sent in ground troops to raid the house, the weapon was thrown out the window and 'spirited away', as were the volunteers to safe houses nearby. My old mate, 'Hack' Smith, was later charged with manslaughter, even though he was at work at the time and had a stone-cold alibi. However the Special Branch threatened to gaol his wife, and put his kids in care, so he signed a statement against his better judgement and was back in the H Blocks for 12 years. Such were the dirty tricks at work during the conflict: informers, blackmail, betrayal, framings and murder, life destroyed on all sides.

1977 began with a string of explosions and sectarian murders. It was the time of the Shankill Butchers, a UVF gang based in the Shankill who went on a horrific killing spree against ordinary Catholics. They would pick up at random, and drive them to their death, but it was the modus operandi of the gang which shocked a hardened society into disbelief, the UVF gang used butchers knives to inflict a horrific death on their victims. It's beyond comprehension that any human being could inflict such death on another human being because of their religion, all because of a confused religious intolerance which was part of their community. The UVF picked up innocent victims as they walked home after a night out across the darkened streets of Belfast, mostly across Millfield between the Falls and Shankill, or at interface areas in north Belfast. Three or four would prowl the area in a black taxi, and attack any individual they thought was Catholic, usually decided by the direction they were walking. They would attack the victim with an iron bar and drag them into the back of the car. Sadistically they would tell the victim that they were going to kill them as they drove to Glencairn or another loyalist area. They would then engage in a murderous hysteria as they stabbed their victim, cut their throat, threw them out of the car and shot them. It was absolutely horrific and sent fear through the streets of Belfast. To be honest, these were not the actions of political activists fighting a 'war' against republicans. They were psychopathic animals with a vile hatred for Catholics that is hard to fathom. They were based on the Shankill road and the leader was Lenny Murphy. This guy was evil personified; he poisoned a fellow prisoner in case he gave evidence against him in '72; murdered another loyalist on stage in front of 200 people in a club on the Shankill; and in the most horrific killing, he tried to decapitate an old guy they picked up with a spade. Even reading the book 'Shankill Butchers' would make your stomach turn, and the worst thing about it was the support they were given from their community. These men weren't fighting for Queen and country, they were sectarian bigots with an unimaginable hatred for Catholics. How a community could accept them is definitely beyond the comprehension of even the most hardened individual. It took many years of police work, and the survival of a victim to bring their reign of terror to an end, and the IRA would, eventually, catch up with Lenny Murphy.

Recently a former UVF vol and now a city Cllr, Billy Hutchinson, brought out a book essentially quite similar to this about life at the time. He had served

15 years in the Cages for killing two innocent catholics on the Falls, he had no regrets and claimed his actions prevented a United Ireland, tbh it's pretty warped thinking? But he represents a socialist working class loyalist segment in society which we need to reach out to in a new Ireland if we are to embrace a new society together.

Whatever about the moons aligning and another phase in life looming, it was with certain trepidation that I welcomed my future wife home from Armagh gaol. The relationship that had begun as a sort of 'pen-pal' friendship between the gaols was blossoming on the streets. She was four years younger, petite, blonde, and I wasn't the only admirer, the Army were also interested. Between her release and Christmas we were 'lifted' three times in just six weeks. Ironically each time we were on our way to get a Chinese takeaway, and it became a standing joke in our closely-knit group, "going for a curry tonight". The first time we were stopped in a 'borrowed' car near Milltown cemetery, and she was held for 24 hours while I was held for three days in Castlereagh holding centre. Among a myriad of accusations they were throwing at me was that we were a sort of 'Bonnie and Clyde' and were going to plant a bomb. There were a couple of inaccuracies in their line of interrogation; there was no bomb and we were on a mission no more menacing than to pick up chicken fried rice and chips. Two weeks later the Kings Own Scottish Borderers were at it again. Driving down through Gransha we turned on to the Glen road near the Glenowen bar, and lo and behold there were the heroes of Bannockburn in situ. Once again it wasn't any tax, insurance or even speeding they were interested in, and two big burly 'Jocks' who looked like they would spend an odd Saturday at Ibrox, jumped in the back seat and told me to drive to Fort Monagh as two jeeps accompanied us. As we drove up the hill for whatever reason, I just stuck the boot down and sped by the entrance to the Fort, with Turf Lodge and safety in my sights. What we would have done with 'Robert the Bruce' in the back seat is another thing, but it didn't matter as one hit me with the rifle butt while the other half strangled me and forced me to stop. It didn't really matter, just a little act of defiance, although maybe the two Ronald MacDonalds in the back seat might have had a different opinion, especially if they had ended up ensconced with the 'natives' in the Marty Forsythe club!

Inside Fort Monagh the IO put a brown bag over my handcuffed hands, but I managed to slip it off to his annoyance later, he was hoping to find traces of fertiliser which wasn't for growing Daddy's roses. So once again it was 24 hours for her, and three days for me, this time in Crumlin Road gaol, in the basement of 'D' Wing' converted into an interrogation centre. They tried to get the owner of the car we had 'borrowed' to say it was taken at gunpoint, but he informed them that he had loaned it to us, the civilian population would never let us down. Over the three days an interesting little incident happened, when I met Roy McShane going between interrogations. We spoke for a few minutes; he was Head of the Auxiliaries, the sort of military police of the IRA. He told me he refused to speak for the whole three days as if to impress me, trying to give me an impression of Tom Clarke in Dartmoor. Years later, he was part of Gerry Adams security, until it was finally revealed that he had been working as an informer for years and sent into limbo, so much for not talking it looked like he never shut up.

The third and final time she and I were lifted together was close to Christmas. We travelled over near Casement Park, to the Red Barn takeaway, but as we arrived two or three army jeeps pulled in and arrested us. A crowd gathered and a bit of a commotion took place, but they hauled us off once again. She spent the first 24 hours being informed that they would revoke her licence, and return her to Armagh to finish her sentence without remission for "consorting with terrorists", which she took as a compliment. I was once again taken in for nearly four days, this time to Springfield road RUC station, where they thought they had enough evidence to stitch me up. For the first day they questioned me about an incident in the estate recently, and focused on certain dates. I told them I was in Donegal and never saw the Special Branch men again. It turned out they spent the three days contacting the Special Branch in Letterkenny to check my alibi. After the three days or so I was released to my surprise, as I thought they really had something on me. It transpired years later that they had made contact with Gardai in Letterkenny, and the local Gardai went out to the Uncle's pub to check if I really had been there on the dates in question. The two Gardai questioned John and Mick who were probably slightly inebriated; they informed them that they couldn't be 100% sure but that I was up and down all the time. The Gardai were happy enough with that and left saying, "the nephew is innocent as far as we're concerned". In later years I got to know both Gardai, I appreciated that little helping hand back in the day. One has passed on now and the other, a staunch Mayo man who has suffered over the years like all Mayo people, for him (and Mary) I'd love to see them embrace 'Sam' and as the Saw Doctors would croon, 'to win just once'! After three arrests in six weeks, and ten days spent in interrogation cells, I felt things were closing in, so never stayed in our house from then on. This brush with destiny was the last time I would ever be in the inside of a British prison, if the RUC Special Branch had got their way I would have been returned to the H Blocks and languished in a cell covered with excreta, wearing a blanket, regular beatings and anal searches by sadistic screws, the late 70's and early 80's a horrific time in the goals as the prison conflict reached a crescendo with the hunger strikes, I was within my fingertips of that scenario!

Another phase that the conflict went through later in the 1980's was the introduction of Supergrass trials. The RUC, Army and Government thought they had broken the back of the struggle when they managed to turn members of different organisations into major informers. The RUC dubbed them 'converted terrorists', and great numbers from both republican and loyalist organisations ended up in gaol on remand for a myriad of charges. They would spend many months and years in gaol before the collapse of the whole charade. Obviously the main target was the IRA, but every group was affected: INLA, UVF and UDA. The numbers arrested reached hundreds, 600 to be exact. The first affected was the IRA when Chris Black turned informer and implicated nearly 40 IRA volunteers. UVF informant Joe Bennett implicated dozens of fellow volunteers and Harry Kirkpatrick implicated 25 INLA volunteers. In all, over two dozen informants brought the hundreds of fellow comrades to gaol in the period. It was a difficult period for everyone concerned, families were abused in their communities, some were kidnapped and held as ransom, and many were ostracised. The word informer in Irish society is a dirty word, it has a historical significance, to be classed as a 'tout' is the most degrading epithet to have made against anyone. The shame, especially within republican communities was soul-destroying and degrading. The informer had sold his soul to the devil, like Dr Faustus, his family were devastated and had to be moved out of their communities. The informer would be resettled in England or wherever it was felt safe and many never saw their wives or children again. It was a heavy price to pay for selling out your former comrades and schoolboy friends, informers in Irish society were regarded as the lowest of the low.

While Scap was the most infamous informer of them all, Raymond Gilmour would run him close. During his trial a slogan painted on a wall in Derry read, “I knew Raymond Gilmour, thank fcuk he didn't know me.” Of course informers were not exclusive to the recent conflict, they have been part of Irish history down the centuries, and the bane of would-be revolutionaries, who were sold out and suffered long years of imprisonment as a result of the action of touts. One of the most famous cases was of those who turned informer after the killings of Lord Cavendish and Thomas Burke in Dublin in 1882. Cavendish was Chief Sec, and Burke Permanent Undersecretary, they were killed by the ‘Invincibles’ a republican splinter group. Five were hanged after several others turned Queen's evidence. In later years, some of the informers were tracked down and killed in revenge; I think one spotted on a boat to South Africa! During the end game in the recent conflict it was revealed that two senior IRA members had been informers all along: Fredrico Scapittici and Denis Donaldson. Fredrico 'Freddie' Scapittici who was head of the 'nutting squad' the IRA security unit, had done severe damage to the movement before he was outed, and amazingly escaped the ultimate punishment. Denis Donaldson wasn't so lucky; after he was outed he was shot dead at an isolated cottage in Donegal. Whatever makes informers tick is hard to fathom, the money might be good, but there has to be a death wish in their complex mind-set.

Informers are a rare breed, remember nobody sets out to be an informer, they might be caught in compromising situations with a married woman or maybe child abuse, maybe facing 30 years in gaol and see a way out, all are working class youths and possibly never had a job, the financial motivations cannot be overlooked, for some Walter Mitty types it is a chance to get out of a humdrum life in a rundown estate, for all these reasons whatever these people say it has to be taken with a pinch of salt, they would sell their granny. Much has been made of the fact that their actions could have directed the IRA in a certain direction, personally I think that's a Fleet St journalist's fertile imagination; these people while definitely harmful were never in a position to dictate the overall political direction of the Movement.

A strange anecdote about the killing of Denis Donaldson, the old secluded cottage he was shot outside had been owned back in the 20's by a Free State soldier who was on duty at Drumboe the day four IRA vols were executed during the civil war, apparently the actions disgusted the soldier and in later years the cottage became a 'safe' house for republicans on 'the run', it's a strange conundrum which adds to the mystique of the 'execution' of Donaldson?

The early part of '77 was seriously violent. The Turf Lodge area had been in virtual turmoil for months and the place became a sort of no-go area for the British Army. We had a kind of freedom to operate that was denied in many other areas in Belfast. Whereas we had Kings Own Scottish Borderers or Green Jackets, Ballymurphy had the Paras, and it was always difficult to operate when they were in situ. One day, one of our volunteers fired and hit a Para on the Whiterock, and the next thing he knew his mates were charging across the fields separating it from our estate. There was something abnormal with the Paras, and I suppose that's what led to them slaughtering people in Ballymurphy and Derry in previous years. Other republican areas of Belfast were struggling at that time; the ceasefire of '75 had damaged the movement, and it came the closest to defeat in the 30 years. Turf Lodge and Andersonstown became areas where we could make living uneasy for British Army units, with constant harassing of their patrols and many casualties. The only way they could operate in the area was by sending in massive foot patrols of 150 men, walking parallel throughout the estate trying to block our escape routes after an attack. But whereas we had local knowledge, they were ham-fisted, smashing up houses in the pursuit of volunteers or looking for weapons.

The Marine commandos landed for a four month tour of duty. They were considerably dysfunctional as well, if not as psychopathic as the Paras. Once, after one had been wounded, they spotted from a helicopter, the house where the Armalite was dumped, and raced to raid it. The volunteers jumped over the railings to the next house, and walked calmly up the path as the Marines came charging down, kicking the door in. They found the rifle, but the volunteers had escaped. Regular bombing teams would leave the estate for various targets around the city. Once a six county co-ordinated attack took place, and many bombs and hoax car bombs left the estate, causing disruption which tied up the Army and RUC for several days. It was a hectic time: full-time volunteers, part-time, auxiliaries and Cumann na mBan, Fianna, were all involved in taking the 'war' to the British Army and the RUC, who had been pushed to the front line in accordance with the policy of Ulsterisation. Many RUC men would pay for it with their lives.

The role of women in the struggle changed as the years moved on, many of the more militant women pushed to be able to join the IRA and leave Cumann na mBan, it was a situation replicated during the War of Independence and indeed during Easter Week, many of the women then resented being treated as nurses, cooks, messengers etc and wanted to take up arms like their fellow male volunteers. Similar happened during the 80's and is personified by the actions of Mairead Farrell who was killed in Gibraltar. Ironically Farrell's niece, also Mairead, who I've met here in Galway and is a rising star in constitutional republicanism, was elected as a TD at the last Dail election in the Sinn Fein tsunami, the ballot box and maybe not the armalite bearing fruition!

One RUC man had a very lucky escape in Turf Lodge. One day his car was hijacked on the Monagh Road and he was held and taken to a block of flats by a single armed volunteer, as his car was to be used in another action. The quick-thinking RUC man knew his identity would be discovered when his gun and documents were found in the car, so he punched the young volunteer, jumped down from the flats and ran like hell down the new road to Fort Monagh and safety, a lucky man. A would-be prison officer had a lucky escape when his letter of application was intercepted at the post office. He was brought to the same flats, where he too jumped out the window but nearly killed himself in the fall, it was considered enough punishment. Prison officers became major targets as the Blanket protest set in, and a greater number of prisoners joined the protest. The warders were the weak link in the system, they lived in the six counties and although mostly in loyalist areas, they had to drive to work or socialise in pubs and hotels. The IRA began targeting them on a much bigger scale, and there were plans to really target them on a massive scale, which if successful might have broken the Government's resolve to defeat the prisoners as it was a relatively small number of warders killed allowed the system to continue with the aggressive decision to destroy the prisoners' morale and defeat them, no more than the small number of British soldiers killed wasn't enough to change British public opinion's view that their sons shouldn't be sent to Ireland. The conflict was in its 8th year now, it was taking on the form of permanency and there didn't seem any way out. The British Government had settled for Ulsterisation and Normalisation whilst the IRA had settled into the 'Long War'. Ordinary people on the streets had also settled into a sense of acceptance, this was the way it was going to be for the foreseeable future. Already the conflict had lasted longer than WWI, WW2, War of Independence, Civil War, 1690, 1798, 1916, and it was to last a whole lot longer.

For a period in 1977 the struggle took on a more left-wing revolutionary philosophy, and a more socialist approach took place, akin to our erstwhile 'enemies' in the Officials/Workers Party. But housing conditions, grants for farmers or rates in the local Council weren't on the agenda, it was more akin to the Italian Red Brigades or the Bader Meinhoff approach to capitalism. Over the span of a few months, the IRA executed several Business magnates; Jeffrey Agate, Director of Du Pont in Derry, and English businessmen, Donald Robinson and James Nicholson. Whether the targeting of businessmen proved a bone of contention with the well-heeled supporters of the IRA in America, or just a logistical disengagement, the targeting of businessmen was removed from the ever-increasing list of 'legitimate targets'. The Provisional movement was a broad church of individuals from all quarters in Irish society: working-class city kids, conservative farmers from the Mournes, country people, city slickers, left-wingers, right-wingers, apolitical, those in favour of abortion, same-sex marriage, divorce, and those against. In England it had the support of working-class Irish and trendy leftie Socialist Worker types who formed the Troops Out movement, in Scotland the Irish Diaspora, victims themselves of vicious anti-Catholic bigotry. In America, again a broad cross-section of supporters, but a significant section of pretty wealthy individuals who would be as likely to be Republicans as Democrats. It took delicate handling by the leadership to keep all groups onside.

Essentially, the Movement was a working-class organisation, those with PhD's were few and far between. In fact, most would never have seen the inside of a University in the early years, except maybe checking out Queen's as a possible target. I had thought about going back to college after release, but to be honest, it was long before the epithet 'Mature Student' was in vogue, and the reality was I didn't know one person who was at University, or indeed even one person who was ever at Third Level education. Previously Queen's had been a bastion of Unionism and middle-class unionism at that. I wouldn't think many kids from the Shankill ever went to Queen's either. I never entered the hallowed halls of Queen's until about 2010, when I visited with a Galway academic who was giving a talk on the peace process. Some of the academics I met were shocked to hear that I grew up a few miles away as the crow flies, but had never been inside the centre of learning. Of course, by that stage it was a changed place, the majority of students were nationalists, and God Save the Queen was no longer played at Graduations.

Easter 1977 witnessed another feud between the IRA and our revolutionary 'friends' in the Official IRA. On Easter Sunday, as their Parade formed up at Beechmount, the UVF had planted a bomb which killed a young 10-year-old boy called, coincidentally, Kevin McMenamin (same name as my future son.) The Officials strangely concluded that the Provos had planted the bomb, and a full-scale feud erupted throughout Belfast. An Official was shot dead in Turf Lodge, and gun attacks continued over the weekend. We had headed to Donegal for a few days, and returned to find out that our volunteers had come under severe pressure from the Stickies (Official IRA) over the weekend, as the 'Stickies' sought revenge. These internecine feuds brought nothing but devastation to the republican communities, and after negotiations ended the bloodletting, it was met by a sense of relief from the whole community. Feuding with other groups was a distraction for the IRA, besides casualties, it was also time-consuming and also allowed the real enemies: the Army and RUC, to sit back and allow republicans to wipe each other out. The Officials were able to sit back and stay armed to the teeth, and while they had withdrawn from the armed struggle, they had no qualms about turning their guns on fellow republicans.

The 'Officials,' if they were serious about non-violent ways and working-class unity, should have dumped their weapons. But they held on to them, and had a burgeoning armed wing who sought regular ‘donations’ from banks the length and breadth of Ireland. These ‘donations’ also funded their political wing, who morphed from the Republican Clubs to the Workers Party, to Democratic Left with a posse of TD's in the Dail. In their previous guise their illicit activities went as far as counterfeit fake dollars made in North Korea, flooding the USA. Maybe in their own minds they were undermining the capitalist system, but in reality, it was gangsterism at the highest level and there was no political thinking behind it. Fittingly the group would disintegrate into oblivion in future years with little electorate support and no political validity.

I knew many Officials and it was hard to comprehend how people, who were fervent republicans at one stage in their lives, had dissolved into this group, so at variance with the communities they lived in. In the six counties, they had become almost unionist in their thinking, and the most severe critics of the IRA, the world works in strange ways. Some of the members of the Officials were neighbours and friends; big Adam Bell was the elder brother of my friend Jimmy, we would have played football together in our youth, sadly he died in recent years. Martin Lynch was a leading light in the Officials local fiefdom, but in later years he would become a great playwright bringing some brilliant theatre to the city, writing for radio, film, T.V and stage. He wrote many plays about the working-class roots of the place, the shipyards, dockers and Mill duffers. Ironically he also wrote a play about life in the Cages, 'The Chronicles of Long Kesh.' It was brilliantly written, based on interviews with some ex-prisoners, maybe it could have been better written by people who spent many years in the Cages and the H Blocks, before and after the Hunger strikes. It was just ironic that it was written mostly about the Provos but penned by an arch-enemy.

At the beginning of May, Paisley and his cohorts tried to bring the place to a standstill once again with another 'workers strike.' But lightning wasn't about to strike twice; the Army and RUC were better prepared and moved against the strike, the public response wasn't anywhere near the levels of '74, and possibly the lack of enthusiasm from the loyalist paramilitaries was a vital component why the strike failed. Many working-class loyalists, they saw through Paisley's manoeuvring and weren't prepared to follow him, which in the past had led to their imprisonment in Long Kesh. It was a blow to Paisley, but he was a survivor and would live to fight many another day. After dealing with the loyalists the new Secretary of State Roy Mason turned his undivided attention to the IRA; bringing in extra troops, increasing the numbers of RUC and UDR men and sending in the SAS. He described it as "squeezing the IRA like toothpaste", to which the phantom wall painter on the Whiterock road replied, "Stone Mason will never break us." There was a sort of mutual respect, he was a tough miner facing down working-class republicans, and in the next few years both would go down into the trenches.

The summer continued with attacks on British Army foot patrols, it was a crazy time. Our unit was involved in a lot of activity against Crown forces, some of the unit had been arrested after Easter. Unfortunately, under interrogation at Castlereagh Holding Centre, they all signed incriminating statements which sealed their fate in the non-jury Diplock courts. It was disturbing for us, as we had drilled into them that preparing for the interrogation was all part of a volunteer's life, but it's difficult to get the message through, until you actually experience being in an interrogation centre with violent Special Branch interrogators. It's a frightening, lonely, nervous three or seven days, on your own, pressurised by skilled manipulators. Their ability to extract statements from broken volunteers was crucial to Mason's plan to destroy the IRA, it was a war on many fronts. On the streets, the place was a virtual wild west at times, army foot patrols and ASU's confronting each other at the end of the barrel of a gun. Many close encounters took place, once we almost came face to face with a soldier running towards us, we dove over a fence and lay on the ground looking up at him, with a weapon lying just feet away in the dark. Another time, upon meeting a foot patrol at the flats, time appeared to stand still, before we bolted through the warren of flats, soldiers in pursuit. Luckily a door opened and we calmly sat down to have tea with a little old lady, as she made use of the brush cupboard for a good hiding place as the soldiers ran aimlessly by.

Luck ran out for two volunteers after an ambush at the bottom of the estate. A soldier was shot, but on the run back, another foot patrol cornered Matt Lundy and Billy Green who was also shot. Earlier that day Billy had bought Mars bars, and was owed 50p by everyone, 20 years was a long time to wait for his change. Brendan O'Callaghan from Andytown was an officer in the 1st Batt, he called up to the estate the next day to get a report on the incident, "this fcuking place is like Vietnam", he commented. A week later he was shot dead himself at the Whitefort bar near Casement Park, by British soldiers as he went to 'arrest' anti-social elements. This was the beginning of the 'Hoods', thieves, druggies and parasites on the community, Brendan lost his life protecting the community from these gangsters. We went to his funeral a few days later, it was so sad to see his young, attractive wife and kids crying, as they were handed his black beret, gloves and the tricolour which had draped his coffin. That evening there were gun battles in Andytown and Turf Lodge, there was revenge in the air.

Around the same time, I foolishly decided to stay the night at my parents' house, and just as luck would have it the Army raided the house at 4am. My parents were again distressed, I took as long as I could getting ready and whispered to my Dad to check the back if there were soldiers there. Looking through the back window he nodded in the negative, opened the back door and I bolted out. I jumped over Gallagher's wall, about three garden fences and crawled up to the back door of another house, where the occupants let me in. Soldiers were running about everywhere and an armoured car was actually sitting outside this house. I stayed there for hours drinking tea, and talking to the couple, coincidentally the man of the house had worked driving trolley buses with my dad in the 1950's. It turned out they had raided loads of houses that night and lifted several volunteers. I never stayed at home again. My dad, like everyone's dad was my hero; a quiet gentleman, a driver all his life and an avid gardener. He never drank, but smoked like a trooper until a heart attack at 59 put an end to the Players plain. He possibly saved my life that night. As I bolted out the back door a soldier followed me and raised his rifle to fire, but my dad, who had never hit anyone in his life, punched the soldier, knocking his aim askew, and I got away. My Dad never mentioned it until years later, he's passed now over a decade, I think of him a lot.

Around the end of July, internecine feuding between the Officials and the IRA was back on the agenda. It was vicious; four men were shot dead and 18 injured as the two groups flexed their considerable muscles. One of those killed was Tommy 'Toddler' Tolan who was one of the seven who escaped off the Maidstone back in '72, he was married just three weeks when shot by the Officials. Toddler was a local legend in Ballymurphy, who along with Jim Bryson, brought the 'war' to the British Army. It was soul-destroying that both had been murdered by so-called fellow republicans, and even worse, by a group who had downed arms and were taking no part in the armed struggle, but were still able to use weapons against fellow Irishmen. The killings disgusted the nationalist community, and a mechanism was set up where further feuding would be avoided. Sensible heads would get together with intermediaries and thrash problems out, rather than resorting to killing and dying. Hopefully, this would be the last feud between the groups. I knew Toddler on the Maidstone and actually met him at Kelly's bar at the top of the Whiterock, just a week before he was killed. A likeable guy, a character, volunteer soldier, that he was murdered by these charlatans posing as revolutionary socialists was disgusting, they did more harm to the republican struggle than the Army and loyalists combined with their virulent vitriolic condemnation, and it was hypocrisy of the highest order.

That summer of '77 was hot, both literally and metaphorically. While the sun made the river Lagan like a Belfast Riviera, on the streets blood flowed like 'a bright red rose.' These were the same streets where Connolly tried to unite Protestant and Catholic workers in 1907 against the unionist business class who exploited them. Ultimately he failed, as did socialists before and after him. While the national question dominated events, it would prove impossible to unite the working class in the six counties. Connolly would understand that and faced the wrath of Labour for joining the physical force movement in Easter Week, whereas they would have had no problem if he had returned to his British Army unit at the Somme.

On the Falls road today, there is a new Connolly centre where he once lived. It's quite appropriate, as a tribute to a thinker, but also an activist with a gun. Connolly was not just a placard holder, he understood the divisions in northern society were not so much sectarian but a division on nationality, and as long as one sector remained loyal to the Crown there would always be division. While so-called revolutionary socialists adhered to the philosophies of Marx, Lenin and Trotsky, we recognised the words and writings of James Connolly to be more consistent with the Irish situation, "if we remove the English army tomorrow it will be futile if we don't remove the business class."

We had read loads of left-wing tomes in the Cages, the bookshelves would be teeming with Karl Marx, Engels, Trotsky, Lenin, Chairman Mao, Castro, Che Guevara, Liam Mellowes, Connolly of course, Peadar O'Donnell and Frank Ryan. It made sense to us that society should be fair and equitable, with every person treated equally, that was what a Republic was all about. Unfortunately, after Independence, it didn't work out like that. While the leaders in 1916 were far-sighted in their ideals to protect "all the children of the nation equally", many of the progressive thinkers like Connolly and Mellowes were dead. After the civil war, an elite cohort took power; they were mostly of a business class and protected their own. The new state became a capitalist system not unlike what it was previously, under the British. The ideals of those who formed the 'Limerick Soviet,' or were on the side of small farmers or the landless and working class, were lost in the mayhem of the civil war. The two sides of that conflict formed the two biggest political parties, FF and FG, and they have dominated the state ever since, mostly made up of a business class, and the once hard- fought ideals of genuine republicanism and socialism were lost.

In August, for the first time since the conflict started in 1969, Elizabeth Battenberg/Windsor visited the six counties. This was all part of the 'normalisation' process, which the British Government were making huge plans to implement. The visit of the Queen presented great logistical problems for the Army and RUC, as the IRA said they would make her visit one to remember. The week before the visit saw riots, bombings, burnings, shootings, and one day of a complete shut down as the IRA, anticipating a massive clampdown from the Army, sent volunteers on bombing missions all over the place, before republican areas everywhere were sealed off and military roadblocks blocked exit and entry to anywhere a potential threat existed to 'Her Majesty'. On the first day of her visit 20,000 marched down the Falls carrying a large banner bearing the slogan, "Not Our Queen", before being denied entry to the city centre. It ended up with massive rioting, the petrol bombs, water cannon and plastic bullets used providing stark contrast to the almost English like village welcome on the other side of the city near Stormont. The TV cameras had a field day with footage of a divided community, Elizabeth II, great, great granddaughter of Victoria the 'Famine Queen', for the first time since the conflict started she was setting foot in a part of the UK where half the inhabitants weren't her subjects, there was no chance she would be driven along the Falls Road in a British version of a Pope mobile!

As part of our unique republican welcome, posters were put up all around West Belfast in shops, factories and pubs with the legend, "Queen Elizabeth doesn't work but receives 2 million per annum; the fictitious 'Elizabeth Queen' is a cleaner and earns 20 pounds a week! On a more serious note, the Marine Commandos were patrolling Turf Lodge when 19-year-old Neil Bewley was shot dead and three other soldiers injured in a gun battle. The Marines went berserk afterwards, attacking anyone on the streets, smashing up houses, arresting anyone they thought might be a suspect. The IRA unit was able to escape from the immediate area with the help of local people. Queen Elizabeth might not have accepted it, but her presence caused the death of the Marine, as much as the IRA. In reality these working-class soldiers were cannon fodder for a Government, who much like the US Government has been at war around the world for much of their existence. Young Neil Bewley was just the latest fatality from a foreign army to fall in someone else's country. We would wonder at times, do they not understand that if we reversed their thinking, there is nothing that would make me want to join the Irish Army and patrol streets in Derby or Nottingham, shoot innocent English civilians or claim a piece of their country. Do the Israeli soldiers ever think about that in Gaza, or the US soldiers in Iraq or Afghanistan? It has to be in your psyche, and it's not in ours although at one stage between Waterloo and WW1 over half the British Army were Irish, but that's another story. Most came from families steeped in military history and loyal to the Crown, that sore in Irish society festered until 1918 when anti conscription would put an end to it although 200,000 went to the Somme and Ypres with 49,000 losing their lives 'for King and Country'. Unfortunately for Neil Bewley, that day in August '77 would be his last day in the service of 'Queen and Country'.

Immediately afterwards, the Marine Commandos made massive swoops on safe houses all over the area. Many Vols and ordinary civilians were arrested and held for seven days; degraded and beaten as the Special Branch tried to force confessions to the death of the soldier. At one stage, twelve houses were raided in one night, and only timing and luck prevented us, the intended targets, from falling into the net. It was difficult to move around the estate, the Army presence became suffocating as they tried to locate various people on their wanted list. Their presence became so intrusive that the only hope was to move out of the area for the immediate future, till things settled. I didn't know it then but my days in Belfast were coming to an end. To make matters worse, in a sense, although back in the Kesh for 20 years was the ultimate, but she was pregnant and we were due to get married the next month and as my Mum observed, “the honeymoon was over” in many ways. A few days later, while walking through the town we met up with another Vol who informed us that Bobby Sands and Joe McDonnell had been arrested with others after a bombing and gun battle with the RUC on the Lisburn Road.Seanna Walsh wouldn't last any longer, and would spend the best part of the next 20 years in Long Kesh. An avid Irish language enthusiast, he is now a

Sinn Fein Cllr within a nationalist majority. Once upon a time Paisley's daughter used to spray air freshener when Alex Maskey, the first Republican since partition, took his seat at Belfast City Hall after the Hunger strikes. We are now in changed times indeed.

The end of the summer '77 was a hectic time for all of us, we were coming under severe pressure from the Marine Commandos. They would enter the estate from three different approach routes, maybe 100 soldiers at a time, patrolling the streets parallel as armoured vehicles sped through the estate. It was getting difficult to operate; the Army was closing down the escape routes through the back gardens, helicopters were in the air constantly and undercover soldiers and police were operating covertly. There was always a small group of £10 touts who handed over small bits of information, putting their lives at risk for the price of a few pints. Other more dedicated informers were working for the Army and it was a constant battle to flush them out before they did any real damage.

One such 'player' was Alexander 'Sandy' Lynch. He was only a kid at the time, but must have been compromised. One night he dropped us off and a few minutes later was shot in the leg after going through a checkpoint further up the estate. He had been driving a car used by us during the day, and the Special Branch must have let him go free if he would co-operate with them, like Scappaticci and Denis Donaldson. It's hard to fathom how he went about it, but over the next decade he was a rising star in the Movement, all while working for the RUC as an informer with an ear to the leadership. It took a long time to suss him out and God knows what damage he did to the IRA in the meantime. Eventually, they would catch up with him and during interrogation, he was submerged in a bath with electric prods attached to his body. His future wasn't looking bright, when the Army burst in the door of the house in Andersonstown rescued him, and arrested several IRA Vols along with Danny Morrison. He was the Sinn Fein Press Officer during the Hunger strikes and the guy who coined the phrase, "who will object if we take power with an Armalite in one hand and a ballot box in the other" Lynch survived while the men lifted were jailed and at the trials it was said that Lynch apparently was one of the most important informers the British ever had within the IRA.

Informers are the lifeblood of counter insurgency, used in colonial situations the world over. The British have always been adept in their use in Ireland, many, many times throughout history informers have sold out for the 30 pieces of silver. It's difficult to understand the mentality of these people, on the surface they are part of the community. They live among the people they grew up with, went to school with, played football with, went to their first disco with and met girls. They probably married locally, and their children born in the community and their parents and extended family would be living close by. Yet they give it all up for dubious financial reward and a constantly threatened existence. Trying to get into the mindset is fascinating, first of all the disloyalty to their community, friends, comrades if they were involved in the IRA. How they continue to live this double life is strange, passing information, meeting with their handlers in some dingy hotel in the other side of town, their lives compromised by the Army or RUC. They live in a dirty seedy world; compromised at some stage, maybe broken during interrogation, some maybe caught in dubious situations which allowed a form of blackmail. Some just enjoyed the lure of the filthy lucre, but for the rest of their lives, they live in fear of the day when a young guy with a gun appears at their door, in their relocation in England or wherever. Justice comes in many forms. Whatever makes these people tick, could it ever be worthwhile to sacrifice your whole life? Your family disgraced, never able to set foot in your home place ever again, always remembered as a low life who sold out his friends and community. The legacy of the informer is one of deceit, deception, disgrace and dishonour.

The end of August 1977 was a sort of poignant time in my life, we were under severe pressure on the streets from the Army, Gerry and I, and indeed several others were staying in different 'billets' each night trying to keep one step ahead of the prying eyes of the Crown forces. At this stage also I was starting to have doubts about the career path I was pursuing. I was also in a relationship and concerned for both of us, if we continued the way things were it was only a matter of time before I was arrested again, and this time it would be for a hell of a long time. I was also concerned for her safety, she was on the fringes of activity since her release and to be honest I was trying to keep her away from getting more actively involved. I suppose I had a vested interest in both of us staying free, liberty is a many-faceted thing. At a local level, things weren't going our way at the time, the unit had been broken up a bit, damaging our strength. Many volunteers had been arrested, we had more close escapes in recent months but our luck was sure to run out. I couldn't confide in my closest friends, but I was determined that I wasn't going back to the H Blocks. Then one morning, after a night when many houses were raided, I took a black taxi down to Castle Street, the train to Derry and a Lough Swilly bus across the border. I had decided it was time to go.

It was one hell of a decision. I was firmly committed to the armed struggle, if anything my time in Long Kesh had created the republican within me, and it would stay with me for the rest of my life. I wasn't turning my back on the armed struggle by any means, but I needed a break away from it all, and it was also about self-preservation. I had sworn to myself that I would never go back to gaol, and although my continued activities in the past two years should have laid lie to that theory; luck, instinct, experience and knowledge had all helped me and others to stay ahead of the posse. I began to ponder the future and what was going to happen. I thought of my parents, they had suffered enough, and I couldn't bring more torment for them. They knew I was back on active service, and they understood but my mum said one evening, "you know if you get put away again we'll be dead when you get out." It was a spine chilling moment, I could see the tears well up in her eyes and I had to turn away. Her love was unconditional and unadulterated, she would always have my back, but there is only so much she could take and I couldn't inflict any more heartache on her.

At the time I began to seriously think about my role within the Movement. I was a volunteer, we all were, but the percentage that were actually involved in the military side appeared to be getting smaller, while there were countless numbers who suddenly had positions with the movement that didn't involve taking up weapons or driving bombs into the city centre. There suddenly seemed to be loads of guys who were 'Intelligence Officers'; some were needed of course, but they would never be at risk being caught with anything, so the chances of going back to Long Kesh were slim. Others would be 'local policemen', again never under any real threat of being lifted. Many would become career republicans, but like de Valera never fired a shot in earnest, and of course, there were the 'thinkers' who would all become community workers and politicians in later years. The 'struggle' became a way of life for many of them, maybe for some it gave them a life, but it wasn't for me.

Now saying that, I'm not including the many thousands of dedicated volunteers who sacrificed everything, spent long years in gaol, were marginalised and demonised, but at the same time, to use a term coined by hunger striker Lawrence McKeown, were, "unrepentant Fenian bastards." They embraced an ideal that while still aspirational, rather than de facto reality, and brought suffering and death to many. They spent long years in the H Blocks, naked wrapped in a blanket in a cell covered in shit, with regular beatings by warders and endured four years of unending depravity from 'Screws' who were in the main, loyalist bigots. That many didn't break and lose their senses, like Tom Clarke's fellow inmates in the 1890s in England is amazing. The 'Blanket Men' were the strongest of republicans, who put fear into the loyalists and the 'Screws'. They survived with their dignity intact, while many of the warders and loyalists descended into a world of alcohol, drugs, depression and depravity. In later life, republican prisoners became leaders in their communities; strong-minded individuals who followed through on the original 'community ethos' created in the Cages back in the mid-'70s. The 'Long War' created a new society, but it was a long struggle to get to that stage.

One final observation on the 'long war' was the contribution made by so many ordinary people, the little old woman who had 'war' thrust on them and they responded with vigour and courage. As well as the strategic support many gave, there were so many incidents which while having a serious side to them also lent to a facetious side like a time when a woman walked into a room and reached for a weapon under a pillow and fired it by mistake as a volunteer turned pale as the bullet whizzed past his ear and left a hole in the wall and a Celtic tea cloth as it would ricochet around the room! Another time when a unit were preparing a bomb and suddenly British troops landed in the front garden as they left by the back door, the old dear was calmness personified as she carried the bomb down the stairs and planted it in her bin in the back garden for the boys to retrieve it later! One incident which was quite hilarious was when the Brits raided a house in the middle of the night, there was a new baby in the house and a weapon was hid under the baby in the cot, as the Army searched the house one went towards the cot but the Mum shouted at him not to waken the baby and fortunately the soldier complied, a close encounter! Other incidents brought a bit of hilarity to the situation, once a unit were robbing a Bank on the Falls, as they entered the building and held staff up, one of the boys jumped on top of the counter but it was an old bank and he fell through the woodworm ridden counter, needless to say robbers, bank officials and customers had trouble keeping a straight face! In another incident an IRA unit were robbing a bank, the getaway driver was sitting in a car when another IRA unit hijacked his car before he had a chance to say anything, and needless to say he had some explaining to do as his unit walked back to base! In another incident an IRA vol was driving a bomb into Belfast city centre when the 200lb bomb detonated prematurely, the driver walked away from the scene holding just the steering wheel without a mark on him, miraculous for him and I suppose the city centre! While not wanting to trivialise the impact of violence, these things happened and no doubt there is a million other stories from the 30 years of conflict, and I'm sure guys who were in the trenches in WW1 or Vietnam could tell similar stories, at the end of the day it's the human experience which survives to tell the tale.

DONEGAL - A WHOLE NEW WORLD

Donegal was idyllic in comparison to Belfast. We eventually settled in Termon, a small rural area just 10 miles from Letterkenny and only a mile from my Mum's home place at Doon where the blacksmiths cottage still stood, and a short distance from Doon Well, a Holy spot where pilgrims would go to pray and search for a cure for ailments. It was also a sacred rock, where the Chieftains of Ulster were crowned from 1200, the first one Eignechan and the last one, Red Rory O'Donnell in 1603. After independence republicans would hold Easter commemorations there, and in the modern era the local PP Fr Pat would hold ceremonies on New Year's Eve, leading groups walking barefoot around the Holy Well.

I arrived in Donegal on one of those 'soft' days as they say in that part of the world, it wasn't a strange place to me by any means, and I had been visiting the 'Hills' since I was a kid. I knew the place well, it was my maternal home where my grandfather was the local blacksmith, the uncles had a wee pub and a few acres of land, the old cottage where my mum was born was still there as well and an aunt had arrived back from England to live in it. It wouldn't take me long to settle into the place. We got married at the end of October, many made the journey down from Belfast to join up with a lot of Donegal friends. A lot of guys who were on the run in different parts of the Republic ended up at the wedding reception, as indeed did my sister's pipe band. We had invited six of the Joe McKelvey but the whole bloody band landed down for the craic. During a break in the evening, the band started up and brought the house down, with stirring renditions of several rebel tunes, it led to a perplexed proprietor, Englishman John Lilley, phoning athlete Hugo Duggan his head 'bouncer' to come down quickly, "the place is full off fcuking Provos." Lilley made his fortune buying up hotels which were bombed in the 6 counties and after renovation reselling at a massive profit, in later years he went to live amongst the Mafioso in Marbella; sadly Hugo, a great sportsman passed away recently.

We settled into life in a small flat, over the next few years our children were born; Padraic (Paddy), Ciara and Caoimhin (Kevin) and life moved on. I would eventually live in Donegal for almost 30 years, but the one major regret I had was that we hadn't moved further west to Gaoth Dobhair and immersed ourselves in the Gaelic language. It had been part of my life when I was in the Cages, and I'm sure I would have embellished my grasp of the language and the children would have been native speakers, but it wasn't to be. To be honest I hardly spoke a word as gaeilge since, even though Termon was a lar

Gaeltacht, and a lot of subjects were through gaeilge in the National school. Ironically my friends Gerry and Angela sent their kids to gaeilscoileanna in Belfast and they became fluent, whereas my kids living in the Republic have hardly a word. It was a form of cultural revival in the 6 counties which took place throughout the conflict; it definitely helped the language revival in Belfast, whereas in the Republic it was felt to be a chore just needed for valuable Leaving Cert points, and to get a good job in the Gardai, Civil Service or Brussels. The rise in gaeilscoileanna throughout the country is an interesting phenomenon, while it hopefully shows a greater interest in the language there is a perception that it's greater in middle class areas and certain suggestions that a form of racism and pragmatism might be at play as in there is less chance of foreign migrants attending gaeilscoil and a 10% bonus in LC points? I would seriously like to think that this is untrue and the love of our native tongue is the defining reason?

The first few weeks after we both started living in Kilmac, we had a few interesting visitors. One night the new Garda Sgt Eamonn Doherty arrived down for a social call, he introduced himself as the new Sgt to the area. It turned out he was a full cousin of Martin McGuinness, although he told us that he didn't have any sympathy, just understood things in the six counties better than your average Garda from Mayo or Clare. He told us that he had been reading through a file on us, up in the wee barracks near the football pitch, and he informed us that as long as we kept our noses clean we would have no trouble from him. Then we had the tea and a sociable chat. We both kept our end of the bargain and never had any problems over the years. Sadly Eamonn passed away in recent years, we were always good friends, both involved in underage football training the kids, and we played a bit of O-40's together in later years. He was a good guy who would never do you a bad turn; local gardai in rural Ireland were a different breed than armed Special Branch, political police and 'Heavy Gang' members who went out of their way to harass republicans in the 80's.

The following week we had another visitor, two, in fact. One was an IRA volunteer who was the first to escape in Belfast back in '71. Gerry Fitz was shot by the Paras but was spirited out of the hospital by white-coated 'doctors' and took up residence in a hospital south of the border, in later years he would be shot again by Gardai during an attempt to kidnap Prince Charles billionaire friend, Gaylon Weston, and survived. The other guy was a member of the Army Council; it was also a social call but needless to say the agenda was slightly different. They offered me a 'job' that I felt, with great difficulty, I could, and would, refuse, I needed space to clear my head. So our first few visitors within weeks of arriving in Donegal couldn't have been more different, that I could stay friends with all of them for the next 30 years says a lot for us all.

The conflict would never be far away from us, just a few months later in February '78 a bomb attack at La Mon hotel near Stormont went disastrously wrong. An inadequate nine minute warning from the IRA left no time to clear the place, and 12 innocent civilians were murdered in horrific circumstances, burned to death in a fireball, with another 30 badly injured. It was indefensible and sickening just like Birmingham and Omagh later, 'war' is so cruel. The British Government has committed many such horrific killings over the centuries, and it was wrong, just as it was wrong for the IRA, although that's scant consolation for the families of the bereaved. After La Mon, the Army arrested over 20 republicans, including a good friend Eddie Brophy from Turf Lodge, while most were released Eddie was charged, possibly to satisfy public opinion. He was eventually acquitted with his barrister successfully arguing that while he was in the IRA, he had nothing to do with the bombing. Years later he was seriously wounded when loyalists shot him in his city-centre shop, which heralded a premature death soon after. Eddie no more or less than those killed in the bombing, was a victim of the conflict.

In May another young teenage joyrider, 17-year-old John Collins, also from Turf Lodge was shot dead by the Paras when he careered through the checkpoint at Andersonstown Barracks. There wasn't any sympathy in the community for the joyriders, but being summarily murdered for stealing a car is a fairly severe penalty, the Paras didn't take prisoners. Sad news reached us in June '78, Jim Mulvenna who had been in the Cages with me, was on an IRA operation with two other volunteers when they walked into a trap set by the SAS, after an informer had sold his soul to the devil and betrayed his friends. The three Vols were shot dead, riddled with hundreds of bullets in a premeditated ambush, the target was a Post Office Depot in a loyalist area and an innocent Protestant was also killed in the shooting spree by the Army. We were moving into an era of 'shoot to kill' by the Army and RUC, Jim had been shot previously and had a colostomy bag during his years in the Cages. Like me, he was an avid reader and loved history; he was a good guy and the fourth to be killed since we were released, after the deaths of Frankie Fitzsimons, Joey Surgenor and Danny Lennon, all within two years. Jim's cousin, Paddy Mulvenna, had also been shot dead by the Army in '73, along with Jim Bryson in Ballymurphy; the conflict was taking its toll on everyone.

Around Easter '78 we got word from Belfast that her brother Kevi had been sentenced to 13 years, he would spend the next 9 years in the H Blocks, naked in a cell with only a blanket as he took part in the protest, he never took a visit for 4 years as he refused to put on the prison uniform, he was a determined young man, I wouldn't see him again until the mid '80's after release from prison.

By the end of the decade another Turf Lodge man would be killed. Ronnie Bunting was an interesting character; a former member of the Official IRA he was the son of Major Bunting, a close friend of Ian Paisley and involved in many of Paisley's activities at the start of the conflict. Ronnie was the first non-Catholic/republican to be interned, and later joined the INLA, so he wasn't short of enemies: the Officials, Provos, Loyalists and the British Army. The identity of who killed him is still controversial, but it was most likely the UVF/UDA in collusion with the SAS. The killings (another republican was killed with him) took place close to Turf Lodge, an area where it was unlikely that loyalists would enter unless under protection from the Army. After his death, his Dad, while totally against his son's political beliefs said "he had a sense of social justice and fighting oppression and injustice." He was an intelligent guy, studied at Queen's and was a teacher. His killers battered his door down with a sledgehammer at 3am in a strong Republican area, it all pointed to British Army involvement in the murders.

The first few years weren't easy; small kids, little money, working nights and trying to get a lift home, city kids in a country environment, but there was peace! My involvement with the newly formed football team was a godsend in those early years. Once we went to Arranmore Island and the whole team got pissed, Dicey our tee total Manager wasn't impressed. Another time we went to Dundalk to see Celtic, we took a long way round by Sligo 'just in case' and it took about two days to get back, wee Harry said he got back from a Republic game in Prague quicker! Many times we would end up in the Talk of the Town after games the south side of Donegal, it would take two hours to get there, the pints would be flowing and it would be the wee hours before we got home. The guys I played with remain friends to the present day, Paul, Fred & Harry, Pat, Tommy, wee James, Neil, Raymond, Frank, John, Jimmy, Josie, all alive and kicking, the latter metaphorically. But sadly, we lost big Andy Quigley from Ballybofey recently, the first to go.

At the end of 1980, events in the H Blocks were coming to a head and seven men went on the first Hunger Strike. H Block Committees were formed all over the country, and I became Chairman of the local committee. We organised protests, put up posters, went to marches and even painted an H-Block sign on the old viaduct down Barnes Gap. The strike came to a head near Christmas with Sean McKenna on death's door. OC Brendan Hughes called the strike off to save McKenna's life after documents from the British appeared to accept a form of political status. There was relief all around that no one had died, but in the light of day, it was soon realised that British duplicity had once again reared its ugly head, they had deceived the prisoners. Once again, it was back to the protest and the new OC Bobby Sands laid out plans for a second Hunger strike, this time to the death.

On the 1st March 1981, Bobby Sands started fasting, thus the greatest battle between the British and the IRA took place through the proxy role of the prisoners. It was a battle of wits, Thatcher refused to back down and the prisoners were determined. Ironically the IRA Army Council was against the strike, but the prisoners contrary to popular belief within British circles were in control and the strike would be to the finish. It's well documented that ten prisoners would lose their lives during the protest: Bobby Sands, Francis Hughes, Ray McCreesh, Patsy O'Hara, Martin Hurson, Joe McDonnell, Kevin Lynch, Kieran Doherty, Tom McElwee and Micky Devine. It was a horrendous year and 60 would lose their lives on the outside: civilians, soldiers, police, loyalists, republicans. It was the darkest of times, immoveable object against irresistible force, and despite Bobby Sands being elected as an MP and Kieran Doherty a TD it didn't make any difference. Thatcher believed that the IRA were 'playing their last card' and refused to budge, it was the saddest of times for the parents of the Hunger strikers, they suffered to the end.

The strike was called off in October '81, much to the relief of everyone: relatives, republicans, the general public, governments both in London and Dublin, and of course the prisoners in Long Kesh. It had been an unbearable time for everyone, but mostly the prisoners; they had endured four years on the blanket protest, excrement smeared on their cell walls, no visits, beatings from the 'screws', unbelievable boredom stuck in a small cell 24 hours a day with nothing to read, and then a summer of death as their ten comrades, one by one died on the protest. The Hunger Strike period was one of great difficulty for everyone, it disrupted life on a massive scale. Protests on the streets brought conflict between the Gardai and republicans, culminating in a massive riot at the British Embassy in Dublin. This brought consternation to those living in the Republic who felt the conflict might envelop them.

What the Hunger Strikes brought, which wasn't expected, was the imminent arrival of Sinn Fein and republicans on the political stage. Bobby Sands' election showed the world that indeed the IRA had massive support and they weren't this tiny 'terrorist' organisation, but a movement with great support from ordinary people throughout the length and breadth of the country. If people really thought about it, how could a guerrilla group prosecute a 'war' for 30 years without the support of the people, all over Ireland, ordinary people supported the 'armed struggle' by building 'dumps' underneath their houses or in hay sheds, kept men on the run, providing logistical support which was vital, that was how the 'war' continued for so long.

I faced a terrible dilemma during the period of the Hunger Strikes. I had extricated both of us from the heat of the conflict in Belfast, we were married and had two kids with another due just as the strikes ended. I was Chairman of the local H Block Committee, involved in all the protests the length of Donegal, and had spent a few weeks canvassing for Joe McDonnell in Sligo; once having a verbal altercation with Government Minister Ray McSharry in his home base of Strandhill. He was obnoxious, saying we were all "supporters of violence". The little old ladies at the polling booth were shocked, Strandhill was a beautiful, rather well off area and it would normally be tea and scones during elections, not aggressive opponents metaphorically sparring. Little did I know then that many years later I would be back in Strandhill, playing the beautiful links.

My dilemma, of course, was of a much higher level of intensity. While I was now domiciled in the Republic, it was a few short years since I had been involved heavily in the 'armed struggle' and it was difficult to let go. Just because I had taken a step back didn't mean that I was any less convinced that the 'armed struggle' was the only way forward to bring about the end of British rule in the six counties. Certainly, I didn't want to go back to gaol, and the longer I spent in Donegal the decision made even more sense, but personal safety wasn't exactly the number one response to our activities since 1969. As the long hot summer of 1981 slowly progressed, with death after death in the H Blocks, my mind was swimming against the tide. I, along with many other volunteers realised that the only way to hit the British Government hard, were attacks in London. Bringing the conflict to their door appeared to be the only way to stop the procession of deaths from Long Kesh. It was heart-breaking to watch families suffer as their sons were carried out of the gaol in a coffin. I thought it over and over in my mind and the only conclusion I could see that made any sense was to volunteer to go to London as part of a bombing team. It wasn't an easy decision; I was nervous, frightened, as I understood all the implications, but I just couldn't sit back and watch this procession of death continue.

At this stage six strikers had died. I knew Bobby Sands, and had met Joe Mc Donnell on the Maidstone and big Doc would die soon, so I knew three of the strikers personally, it was soul-destroying. I made the decision after discussing it with an escapee, and then the process began. I met another escapee from an English gaol, the pitfalls were spelt out, this was no vanity trip, death or gaol again were the likely options. Finally, I met up with the member of the Army Council that I knew, he again drew a literal diagram of how things worked in England; it was dangerous but they could get you out of the country if things went wrong, but there was also the likelihood if caught of facing up to 30 years in an English prison. This was serious stuff, just as the old IRA guy who recruited us in the early days had spelt out in clear fashion, we faced death, gaol, isolation, demonization and torture. They always spelt it out critically so that you understood, if you weren't up to it, it was better to drop out now than later, or maybe even compromise an operation with lack of conviction. I had a few weeks to think about it, and it was probably the longest time of my life. I weighed everything up, we had a new life in Donegal and what I was contemplating could totally destroy our lives. There was a chance I could kill or be killed, there was always that chance. There was also the reality that if you were caught, it was going to be at least 20 years in gaol. If I was jailed, by the time I was released our marriage would be over, children grown up and my parents would have passed on. Crucially my wife had said that if I went, she would take the kids back to Belfast. Despite everything, I was still convinced that this was the only way to help the Hunger Strikers, but when I put everything in perspective I just couldn't do it, I couldn't throw my whole life away. I didn't need to make excuses, these were life-changing decisions. I informed my contact within the Army Council that I had decided not to go, he understood and wished me luck, my days of 'armed struggle' were over.

To be honest the decade between leaving Belfast in '77 until '87 was a time of soul searching for me, in those years while I settled into life in Donegal were challenging to say the least. While life went on relatively normal, my kids were born, I was working, playing football at weekends, even working at the turf in the summer, but I felt pangs of guilt that I had left the 'struggle', I didn't need to, there was no disgrace in walking away from things, but regularly I would contemplate getting involved again, the Hunger Strike period was the most intense but for many years I fought against my best intentions to lead a normal life, it wasn't easy, I was mixing with and meeting fellow republicans on a regular basis, the difficult times were of course as each hunger strike died, but also when volunteers were killed by the Army in Derry and Tyrone, especially some of the guys who were on the run and based in Letterkenny. What was the hardest for me was that life on the surface just went on as normal while the 'war' continued in the 6 counties, of course in the background Donegal contributed greatly to the 'struggle', my conscious was in turmoil as to whether I should contribute once again, the major problem was that I wouldn't be prepared to just play a bit part but would embrace the armed struggle in its entirety, that bedevilled me for a decade before I could accept my future would take a different path.

Another four Hunger strikers would die before it was over. 1981 always appears to me to be a long dark depressing year, when, to paraphrase the Wolfe Tones in their tribute to Joe McDonnell, "everything is lost and nothing won." Its 40 years from those painful days for everyone. For one person in particular, it was a life-changing experience and not for the better. My sister Bernadette was 25 at the time and engaged to Paul, an Irish dancer of some repute. She had a nice job down the city centre in Belfast, and was a member of the Joe McKelvey pipe band. She was very musical and played the pipes, fiddle and tin whistle. She took up the fiddle after my grandfather in Donegal who was an exponent of the art, she loved the music and regularly headed off to Clare and the Willie Clancy festival to mix with other traditional musicians. Lots of times she would arrive in Donegal with the pipes in tow, some of the lads would ask her to play, and she would rattle out some rebel stuff and then in the middle of it the 'Sash my Father Wore', which definitely confused the locals. Bernadette was a republican in the purest sense, dedicated to preserving the language, music and culture. She wasn't involved in the IRA or anything, but played at various H Block marches during the Hunger Strikes, that was as close to political activism as she got.

When Bobby Sands died, she was asked, along with a male piper, to play at the funeral. She had no hesitation in offering her services with pride for a young man who had sacrificed everything, in a dignified and principled manner to his death. On the day of the funeral, Bernadette was brought to a house where she met up with the armed Colour Party, all masked, and they drove to Twinbrook where the massive crowd of 100,000 were waiting. It was possibly the largest funeral Ireland has ever seen, similar to Daniel O'Connell's 'Monster' rallies in the 1840s to repeal the union. The colour party in military fatigues, black berets, masks and gloves, escorted the cortege to Milltown cemetery; Bernadette and the other male piper walked just in front, the iconic picture of them leaving Twinbrook emphasised the vastness of the crowd. At Andersonstown the cortege stopped, and an armed guard stepped forward and fired a volley of shots over the coffin in time-honoured tradition, then the procession continued on to Milltown for the final ceremonies. It was a highly tense day for all concerned; the TV pictures flashed around the world, the colour Party, the armed salute, the political leadership, Adams and McGuinness, the military leadership in the background, and the pipers. It didn't seem significant at the time but these film clips would come back with a vengeance for Bernadette.

Thatcher had no sympathy, "Bobby Sands was a convicted criminal and took his own life," she told the House of Commons, a mixture of the xenophobic misunderstanding of the Irish psyche, and a personal vendetta against those who had killed her friend Airey Neave at Westminster. There was no way out, the Hunger Strikes would continue. A week later Francis Hughes, a legendary guerrilla fighter who lived on and off in Letterkenny in the preceding years died, he was 25. Once again Bernadette received the call, and led the cortege around the hilly townlands near Bellaghy as he was laid to rest, it was going to be a long hot summer. Just nine days later, the news came that both Ray McCreesh, 24, and Patsy O'Hara, 23, had died, and Bernadette was off to South Armagh and Derry city respectively. The crowds might have been smaller but the pain was the same, for everyone it was an exhausting, it was the darkest of times.

The following month or so was a period of negotiations between all parties in the equation. If goodwill had existed on the part of the British Government events might have panned out differently, but Thatcher believed that the "IRA had played its' last card" and she was going for the jugular, how wrong she was. In early June the prevailing mood of sadness and despair was lifted temporarily as eight volunteers escaped from Crumlin road gaol. In a carefully planned operation they shot their way out the front gates. I knew four of the lads: Tony Sloan, Dingus Magee, 'Fat' Campbell; and Joe Doc who had been in Cage 18 with us. They had been part of the 'M60' unit who were arrested after a siege, after killing an SAS soldier the previous year, weeks later they were all sentenced to 'life' in their absence. By that stage, they were all safely in the Republic where they would have varied 'careers' thereafter, Joe Doc made it to New York where he became a cause celebre in the Irish community. Like all escapes, it gave a great boost to the republican struggle, especially as it came during the Hunger Strikes.

On the 8th July Joe McDonnell, 30, died after 61 days on strike. Two days later Bernadette made the short journey over to Andersonstown for the funeral. As she played the pipes near St Agnes chapel, British soldiers moved in to try and arrest the colour party. There was pandemonium as the baton-wielding soldiers fired plastic and lead bullets in a desecration of the funeral cortege. It was a despicable action which would be repeated over the next decade, yet no Army or RUC funeral was ever attacked; a principle of any war allows for the burial of combatants on all sides, obviously that wasn't the British approach. The morning of McDonnell's death a young Fianna boy from Turf Lodge was shot dead by the Army. John Dempsey was only 16, and his Dad, Jimmy, was in the Cages with us. His young son was shot by the Army as they tried to burn down the Bus depot near Andersonstown Barracks. He was killed just three hours after McDonnell died. His Dad Jimmy, not long released from Long Kesh, took his son's death really badly, he had missed him growing up during his years in the Cages, and then just as he was building a relationship with him, the son was gone. Every death is the same, every parent grieves the same, it's the horror of conflict.

Just three days later, Martin Hurson was the latest hunger striker to pass away; he was a year younger than McDonnell and lived at Cappagh, Tyrone, a strong Republican area. He died after only 46 days on strike from dehydration, the shortest time of any of the strikers. Bernadette again made the journey to the Tyrone hills, and while this time the Army stayed away, it was still the same sorry, sad journey to his final resting place, where a volley of shots was fired over the grave. Six men had now died, and still there was no sign of any ending of the strike or movement by the British Government. The first chink of light came when the family of Paddy Quinn took him off the strike after medical consultations; a way out of the impasse at hand, and encouraged by Fr Faul it was the beginning of the end for the strike, although unfortunately, another four strikers would die before it was over. This has caused a debate in later years within republicanism and caused heartache for the families as to whether the strike could have ended earlier. This theory has been put forward by certain individuals within the republican 'family', it's a total falsehood and has no credible sources, it's also been driven within the dissident element of republicanism and various individuals who resent the path that the Movement took in the 90's.

The following day, former Derry GAA star Kevin Lynch died, aged just 25, after enduring 71 days on strike, the longest of any of the men at that stage. Bernadette once again was on the road to Dungiven, as the INLA man was given a sad send-off with local GAA clubs to the fore. Once again masked men led the salute, marching defiantly with a volley of shots breaking the Derry air, as the pipers delivered sad laments in the summer sunshine. The following day the macabre litany of death continued as Kieran Doherty, aged 25, died. He was the longest on strike at 73 days, and had been elected TD for Cavan/Monaghan which brought the Government of Charlie Haughey down. I knew 'big Doc' from the streets in the '70s, his death appeared sadder as a letter agreeing to a deal with the British Government was allegedly in transit, but this transpired to be 'fake news.' Bernadette once again played the pipes with her male compatriot, as the coffin made it's the way through Andersonstown, followed by thousands of friends and comrades on the long slow march to Milltown. Whatever the political intrigue going on, the nationalist community stuck with the strikers to the end.

Less than a week later, the 9th death took place; big Tom McElwee, only 23, died after 62 days, another Bellaghy man like his cousin Francis Hughes. Once again, Bernadette and her fellow piper led the cortege through the Co. Derry village, accompanied by the colour party and masked armed guard. Shots were fired, the 'Last Post' played and there was a silent dignity as footsteps trod the country lanes, the process had become a regular spiral of death. Within 12 days, the final act of a horrendous year of tragedy took place, as Derryman Michael Devine became the last Hunger striker to die. Aged 27 and a member of the INLA, he was the 10th to die in Long Kesh, it was probably the saddest and most futile of the deaths, as it was felt that the strike was on its last legs at that stage. Bernadette made her way to Derry via Donegal, spending the day before in Termon where we lived. She was exhausted by the whole series of events, but had a certain pride in her little part in events. I drove her up to Buncrana the night before the funeral, and Cllr Eddie Fullerton brought her into Derry on the morning of the funeral. Eddie himself would die at the hands of the UDA with British collusion a decade later; we spent a few hours in a wee pub at the end of the main street the night before, as Bernadette played a few tunes there was a little light relief, in the midst of the horror all around us. The funeral in the morning was the final episode of a summer of death. Micky Devine received full military honours from his comrades in the INLA, the ordinary people of the Bogside, the Creggan and Donegal came out in their tens of thousands, and his wife and children looked on forlornly as Bernadette played the lament of the dead.

1981 was the saddest of years, as well as the 10 deaths on Hunger strike, 61 died on the streets in the same period: innocent civilians, soldiers, RUC, UDR. It was a year of fear and tension, but out of it came the politicisation of the republican struggle and eventually the ceasefire, peace process and Good Friday Agreement, thus it mightn't have all been in vain. Unfortunately for my sister, events afterwards took a course for the worse. In her workplace, which was mixed but predominantly loyalist, she was recognised from those TV clips as the piper at the funerals and started receiving death threats. She was told she would be picked up in a black taxi, taken up the Shankill and her throat cut. It was the time of the Shankill Butchers and she had to cross the bottom of the Shankill to get home in the evening after work. It was a frightening period for her, she received little or no support from the managers who were mostly loyalist, and eventually she had to leave the job she loved. Over the next few years her relationship to Paul, whom she was engaged, petered out, and the music that she loved and which brought her so much enjoyment also went by the wayside, as she recoiled into a world of her own. She was protected by my parents, but they were unable to help her. Finally, a bomb meant for the Army went off nearby the house and blew in the front window, just seconds after she left the room. Her nerves were shattered, the sister and Auntie who took my kids on shopping sprees in Belfast when they were young, was never the same again. Conflict always has victims, it's the nature of 'war', but not all victims of conflict are physical.

To be honest, I personally welcomed the end of the Hunger Strikes with great relief. It had been one awful year, for a generation it was life-defining. For the strikers themselves their young lives ended, for the families, it was heartbreaking and for society in general, it was in turmoil, the Hunger strike was the story of 1981, just like the Miners' strike and the Malvinas/Falklands, there was one common denominator: Margaret Thatcher. The Tory PM, the 'shopkeepers' daughter', the lady 'not for turning'. She apparently refused to negotiate with the prisoners and let them die, just as she let 300 Argentine sailors die at the bottom of the South Atlantic sea, and just as she destroyed Mining villages the length and breadth of Britain; Scottish, Welsh and English, mining towns with their own unique history. Thatcher destroyed their communities and turned vibrant societies into industrial wastelands, ghost-like mines reduced to underground dungeons holding the tales of history. The Mining communities, the Hunger strikers and the Argentine cadets faced the wrath of the 'Iron Maiden', her hatred of socialism, Irish republicanism and Latin America was palpable, yet paradoxically she had allowed negotiations with her supposed enemy, in our case the back channel which was at play right through the hunger strikes, indeed the whole way throughout the conflict.

It's a historical distortion of fact that the British are regarded as the home of democracy, parliament and liberalism. The reality is that they invaded more countries than anyone else, and raped, robbed and plundered property and human lives to build up their Empire. Those who resisted, like the Indians, Cypriots, Arabs, Turks, Scots and Irish were regarded as barbarians, unfit to rule themselves, their language and culture destroyed, their lands stolen by military force. Thatcher fed into all that, but in Ireland, as in the other countries she would fail. The prisoners defied the prison regime, and eventually achieved all of their demands, Republicans controlled the wings in the H Blocks as in the Cages, they were recognised as political prisoners all around the world, and the British failed in their effort to defeat the prisoners and by default the IRA.

Within a few years they would take revenge on Thatcher and the Government. Mortars were fired at 10 Downing St, in the centre of London, and only luck prevented the entire British Cabinet from being wiped out. The IRA then bombed Thatcher in Brighton at the Tory Party Conference, just the width of a wall between the toilet and bedroom saved Thatcher from death. Finally, the largest escape in penal history in Ireland, UK and Europe, saw 38 prisoners take over a H Block and escape from the gaol. ' The Great Escape' was the IRA answer to Thatcher, that she would never defeat them and all three events were revenge for the deaths of the Hunger strikers. My brother in law Kevi had survived the years of the Blanket protest and Hunger strikes, and he was one of the guys who held the warders while the 38 escaped the gaol in the food van. The escape would never have worked without their actions, which in turn led to them receiving heavy beatings from revengeful warders who had lost a friend during the escape.

We were well domiciled in Donegal when Kevi was released in '85; he had served nine years of a 13-year sentence. Four years on the blanket, in a cell covered in excrement, regular beatings, he never took a visit in the four years, refusing to put on the prison uniform even to see his Mum. After release, like all fellow prisoners, it took a while to settle back into normal life. He came down to visit us several times those two summers, it was the space and freedom he needed from the Belfast goldfish bowl, we toured around the beautiful scenic county: Gaoth Dobhair in the Gaeltacht, Downings and Atlantic Drive, Inishowen, Errigal, Killybegs, Glencolumcille. He brought a cousin one time, a Marist Brother domiciled in New Zealand, they loved it especially one day I brought them to help me turn the turf at Glenveagh! Between midges and back-breaking work, there was a slight disagreement in the camp, the Marist cousin thought it was wonderful back to nature, and Kevi reckoned it was worse than the H Blocks! I had long talks with Kevi about what the future held for him, I encouraged him to stay with us for six months and clear his head, and then make the decision as to what he wanted to do, but like the decision I made a decade earlier he insisted he was returning to the 'armed struggle', fate would not be kind to him, he had less than a year to live.

The '80s were difficult times in Donegal economically, many of the young lads emigrated to London and the US. Work was scarce but I managed to find a job in a German light engineering company in Letterkenny who made car parts for Opel mostly. It was a small company with around 120 employees. I had tried for years to get into Unifi the giant American company. but each time I was knocked back, eventually I found out why? I knew the Personnel Manager, met him at his house, and he told me that a retired Garda Special Branch officer was head of security, and he had blocked my application because of being in Long Kesh in the '70s. A bitter vindictive Garda, he couldn't see the person, just the political connections and considering what the Gardai got up to in later times in Donegal with the whole McBrearty fiasco, it was a bit rich from a 'guardian of the peace'!

Nevertheless, I started in Sigro which later morphed into Kirchhoff, and for my sins spent almost 20 years there, to say it was mind-numbing would be a mild interpretation. The work was monotonous, repetitive, soul-destroying and damaging to your brain cells to say the least, but on the other hand, it paid the mortgage, helped bring the kids up, kept a car on the road and allowed a certain lifestyle. All things being equal, let's say it was a necessary evil which was required at the time. But I hated it right from day one, conveyor belt stuff, thousands of pieces of a motor vehicle going through our hands, spot welding, big second World War presses shaping bumpers and what not, and then 'targets', fcuking targets, 5000 a day, 600 an hour, Jesus when I think about it, I have nightmares. Many years later I met a republican friend and he suggested I would have been better staying in Long Kesh. Saying that he was on the Dole at least I had regular employment, I valued that lifestyle. But to be fair to Kirchhoff, they gave me a job when others ignored me, and it wasn't all doom and gloom. There is a camaraderie within a factory situation, our Union rep used to say that's what kept the places going; the bit of craic, slagging, jokes played on each other, football team formed, golf societies, they all helped to get us through the week. Not everyone can be a consultant, but then that is the crux of the matter, and a lesson for all young people; education is the only way to get on in life and not end up in a dead-end job. I had other ideas about what I wanted to do in life, but leaving school at 15 wasn't the brightest thing to do. I always had the dream of going to University, I loved reading and writing and that's what made it so difficult in the factory environment. Some people spend their whole lives in such an environment, thank God after 20 years a chance came when I could work my 'escape' from the factory, but that was many years ahead.

The '80s were passing, the kids were getting big, we were both working and life was good. I had decided to stop drinking when the kids were small, and didn't drink right through the '80s. It was a personal choice, and didn't bother me in the slightest to the extent that I would hardly go near a pub, even during Italia '90! I was working full time in the factory, then worked weekends in the Milford Inn, one of the busiest nightclubs in the county, and would also spend a lot of time in the Bog; cutting, turning, fitting, bagging turf for the winter fuel. I actually got to love the time spent in the Bog, it was really back to nature, as the New Zealand monk described it. This fuel dug out of the ground had lain there for millions of years, originally covered in forest and then gradually turned into bogland. We would go out, maybe six of us, and spend a day or two cutting the turf by spade; one man cutting, one-man 'in the hole' throwing it out, and one-man 'spreading' it. Two teams of men working together cutting down three levels, it wasn't for the faint-hearted, it was back-breaking stuff. But we would cut enough to provide fuel for the whole winter, maybe 1000 bags, Arthur Scargill would be dismayed, we never bought coal during the '80s. During the day we would have a few tea breaks, boiled the tea on a wee turf fire and the eggs, sometimes in the same water, much to the dislike of John Ban, who one day exclaimed that 'the water was poisoned'.

Over the years I met many characters in the Bog, working with myself or the Uncle: the aforementioned John Ban, his brother wee Tony the accordion man; Moriarity from Kerry; Paddy 'Dominic', Charlie Bob, Barney Charlie and young Charlie; Hudie Kit and Eddie Paddy John, sadly all deceased. They were 'real bog men' and regular visitors to the Uncles 'Mountain Bar,' after a hard day working at the turf. As for us 'blow-in's': Dan and wee Pat, both from Glasgow, big Neil an ex-soldier from Athlone, and myself, we were considered city slickers domiciled in wildest Donegal. We were new to the Bog and the 'local yokels' wouldn't think we were great 'bog' material, but we could mix it with the best of them, although right enough Moriarity wasn't too impressed one day, when he saw wee Pat with gloves on. On another day we were having the tea and the discussion got up about the turf; good turf or poor turf, white turf or dark black, turf off the rock which was like coal and threw out better heat on a cold winter evening. As we supped the tea and scone bread, big Neil declared, “aye that's a good turf,” holding a perfect specimen in front of us. Dan responded, “Would you know a good turf then,” it brought hilarity to the situation.

In September '85, a married couple were 'executed' in Turf Lodge as informers. Gerard and Catherine Mahon were shot dead in a little entry just beside my mothers’ house. They were low level 'touts' recruited by Special Branch, then compromised and paid with their lives. Many informers were just that, £10 touts, but these two had been recruited by estate agent Joe Fenton who was running a spying system for the RUC Special Branch. He was shot dead 4 years later, but many IRA operations were compromised by the actions of these people. Ironically as it turned out they were all under the direction of Scappaticci who was involved in the IRA Army Council. These street touts were all small fry compared to 'Scap', yet he was allowed to fester within the Movement for many years and even lived to tell the tale, possibly his personal contacts helped to save his life because a TV reporter was able to catch up with him in broad daylight in Andersonstown after he was outed, how the IRA 'nutting squad' which 'Scap' presided over for years weren't able to locate him is an interesting footnote to the dirty side of the conflict.

I had the experience of 'informers' or alleged 'informers' during my time in Belfast: CharlieMcIlmurray, Sandy Lynch, Anthony McKiernan and Denis Donaldson. I knew them all, ordinary guys, but caught up in a web of deceit, or were they? Denis seemed straightforward, he publicly admitted they had been working for the British for years, and as Gerry Adams observed, ‘he knew the penalty’. But for Charlie and Anthony, it's not so clear cut who made the judgement, who provided the information to seal their fate, all suffered the ultimate decision. When it transpired that the British covered up leading informers like Scappaticci and ‘Sandy’ Lynch by sacrificing lesser lights, it muddies the water, what would an ordinary volunteer know in comparison to someone who had the ear of the Army Council? Those who gave information which delivered the Loughhall ASU or Gibraltar into the hands of the SAS, were operating at a high level within the IRA, they possibly fingered lesser volunteers for death and survived the conflict. Many are still walking about living the good life while ordinary Vols lie in a cold grave.

In Belfast, a feud had developed between several factions within the INLA. Following their internecine feud with the Official IRA, this was the last thing they needed, but in an organisation which wasn't exactly structured properly, egotistical individuals with a powerful urge to dominate others led to another internecine feud, which brought more horror to the streets of West Belfast. From 1914, when the Irish Volunteers split, we had the split that brought the Civil War, the split in Sinn Fein which saw the birth of Fianna Fail, and in 1970 the split in the IRA which saw the birth of the Provisionals. In 1974 the Official rump, which had been left after the split with the Provos split once again, and the INLA was formed. Now a decade or so later, the INLA split once again and the IPLO was formed, each fragmentation led to further feuding, shooting and death. In February '87 a childhood friend of mine, Micky Kearney, was shot dead during the feud between the two factions within the INLA. He was 33 and married, with five kids and another child on the way who would never see his Dad. Micky and I had grown up together, we went to football games at the Oval in the mid-'60s, he was one of the guys I sat on a wall near the flats in Turf Lodge in 1969 and thought about the future, Micky was the second to die. He received a 12-year sentence courtesy of the evidence from Harry Kilpatrick, who was one of the first 'Supergrasses' in the '80s but it was overturned on appeal. The feuding between the two groups was hard to fathom, they were small groups with grandiose titles, and it wasn't difficult to be a 'General' in a tiny grouping. That was probably the downfall of the group, there were too many budding 'Generals', all wanting power, and it didn't make for a cohesive unit. Certainly, there were many brave and dedicated republicans within the ranks, but there was also an element who were loose cannons and defied discipline. The INLA certainly laid claim to many powerful incidents during the conflict, three of their men died on Hunger Strike, a much bigger percentage than the Provos. They claimed spectacular hits like Airey Neave at Westminster, and planned to attack Charles and Diana's wedding parade at Buckingham Palace, but their downfall was the power lust of several leading members. They also spawned such mavericks as 'the border Fox' Dessie O'Hare and ‘Mad Dog’ Dominic McGlinchey, who had found the discipline within the IRA difficult.

During the latest feud in February '87, Micky disregarded his own safety to go and visit his wife and kids late at night. The IPLO faction was waiting for him, and shot him dead in New Barnsley, another death, but he was just the first of another needless feud. As well as his role in the INLA, his day job as a spokesman for the IRSP also sealed his fate. I've thought long and hard about all these young guys I grew up with, how their lives were cut short in their prime, but what did any of us know about political conflict or armed struggle? When things kicked off in 1969, we were ordinary kids like in any other city, as far as I remember nobody came from a republican family. In effect the republican Movement would be defined as a close group of families in Belfast, volunteers' fathers and grandfathers would have been involved and in gaol as well in the '20s, 30's, 40's and 50's. There was a tight-knit bond which made for a cohesive unit, as befits a secretive organisation, the closeness of the family connections made for tight security within a small minority in the nationalist community. This, of course, would change during the '70s as it became a massive guerrilla army, involved in civil resistance and street protests leading to the eventual 'armed struggle.' As was the nature of this communal resistance, the IRA became a more open 'Army'; volunteers would be on the streets carrying weapons without masks, and while it was great to be able to operate like that, the downside would be that the dogs in the streets knew who was involved, giving the £10 touts a field day.

As 15 year olds, I suppose we were prone to getting involved in the conflict, and indeed many of my childhood friends did get involved, spent many years in gaol and were killed and I may as well say, they also killed others. But likewise many others did not get involved, and made their way through the mayhem unscathed. Whether those who became involved in 'armed struggle', eventually led a better or worse lifestyle in future years is hard to know Those who got involved were more likely to become politically active, working in community activities and maybe had a greater interest in international events, history and the Arts, more than the average guy in the street. But in saying that, there are some who became alcoholics, unemployed and lived a life in Social clubs drinking their way to oblivion. Some found their way into gangsterism, their children anti-social thugs and joyriders. It was like every urban society, and people live different lives, the conflict in the six counties threw an extra mix into things which we could never have foreseen. As I get older I think a lot about the guys; Norman, Kevi, Micky et al, they never really lived. I wonder how their lives would have panned out, what would they be doing now; the pension years beckoning, playing golf maybe, enjoying life, the grandchildren all around them. Sadly only Micky had kids but they have all grown up never knowing their Dad. The conflict has many unwritten stories, part of my journey in writing this is to relate the stories of young people I knew, and never made it this far in life.

April '87 brought the killing of Larry Marley, shot by loyalists at his house in Ardoyne, he was only released the previous year after spending 14 years in Long Kesh. His funeral became a major confrontation between the RUC and the nationalist community in Belfast. Three nights of rioting after his death left the Ardoyne in a tense place, then the RUC blocked the funeral if there were any signs of Republican symbols, tricolour, beret and gloves, so the family brought the coffin back into the house. There was a standoff for three days amid outrageous thuggery from the RUC, the family were dignified and young Lawrence, now a History Lecturer, stated there would be no funeral until the RUC pulled back. On the third day, the RUC pulled back enough to allow the funeral to go ahead, and when the cortege entered West Belfast the crowds were estimated 10,000 strong. The tricolour, beret and gloves were put on the coffin and the RUC stayed well away, as the slow procession headed to Milltown and eventually, after three days, Larry was buried, it had been devastating for the family. Larry spent all of his time in Long Kesh trying to figure out how to get out of the place. In 1975, he was one of twelve who escaped from Newry Courthouse after charges for previous escape attempts were brought, and was on the run for a few years before being caught travelling the motorway between Newry and Belfast. Back in the H Blocks he was in charge of the escape committee, and was the central figure in the massive escape in ’83, a slap in the face for Thatcher, the largest escape in prison history on these islands.

April also witnessed the deaths of two other IRA Vols, but in vastly different circumstances. Finnbar McKenna wasn't long out of the H Blocks, when he was killed throwing a bomb at Springfield road RUC station. A well-liked Republican, who along with his Dad, who had been interned on the prison ship Al Rawdah in the 1940s, they had helped defend the Lower Falls in August '69. The other death was Charlie McIlmurray who was shot as an informer. He had been involved and was charged with the murder of a soldier, but the charges were dropped and apparently he was compromised by Army intelligence. I had known Charlie, and it's just hard to get your head around that anyone would turn informer. By the turn of the year another friend would meet the same fate; Anthony McKiernan, who had been in our Cage in the Kesh, was also shot dead as an informer. He was a likeable wee guy and we spent the entire time of imprisonment in the same Cages. Apparently the IRA said he had compromised 'operations' and the Army admitted he was an important informant, but can we be sure if either is telling the truth? If Scappaticci is head of internal security and he's a top informant how can you believe anything that came from a source like him. Also, the Army could have ulterior motives suggesting an IRA volunteer is an informant in a bid to sow dissent within the Movement, the subtract to the conflict brought out the worst in human behaviour on all sides.

THE DONEGAL DREAM TAKES ON A WHOLE NEW SHAPE

Christmas 1987 was a milestone for us as we were domiciled in Donegal for a decade. Kevi came down for a few days, at this stage he was back fully in IRA activities. I tried again to get him to stay for a time, but he couldn't wait to get back. He would never see Donegal again, he had three months to live. 'Beware the Ides of March' the famous cliché allegedly uttered by Spurinna the soothsayer before the slaying of Caesar has connotations for March 1988. In the first few days of March an IRA active service unit left Belfast bound for the little British controlled part of Spain in the Mediterranean, Gibraltar. Mairead Farrell, Dan McCann, Sean Savage and another female volunteer weren't going on a sun holiday, but to target a British Army marching band which had ceremonial duties on the 'Rock'. Unfortunately for the volunteers, and fortuitously for the Army Bandsmen, the operation had been compromised by an informer working at the highest level within the IRA, a high level 'tout' who had the ear of the Army Council and was reporting back to the British Government. There has been speculation ever since, as to who delivered the volunteers to the SAS death trap: someone further up the gravy train, take your pick. They've never been publicly identified, but their actions set in motion a string of events which will never be forgotten.

The volunteers had planned to leave a bomb close to the parade ground in Gibraltar. On the selected day they crossed the border between the 'Rock' and Spain, and reconnoitred the area. Unbeknownst to them, they had been under surveillance the whole time and as they prepared to walk back across the border, they were ambushed by a dozen SAS men who shot them dead in broad daylight. The volunteers were unarmed and could have been arrested, but the British Government intended on sending a message to the IRA that they weren't for taking prisoners. It was a clinical shoot to kill policy which was in full force back in Ireland at the time. A 4th volunteer, Siobhan O'Hanlon escaped the SAS murder gang and in later years became a political activist, though sadly she died prematurely. Mairead Farrell had been OC of the female republican prisoners in Armagh when my ex-wife was there in the mid '70s, and was later caught again in an operation with Kieran Doherty who died on Hunger strike, and Sean McDermott who was shot dead. She was a political activist, who no doubt, had she lived would have been a future TD, MLA or Cllr. Ironically her niece, also Mairead, was elected a TD in Galway this year; Dan McCann was an experienced Vol who had been in Long Kesh and was the eldest of the unit. Sean Savage, the youngest, was a nephew of Billy McKee the first OC of the Provisionals in Belfast in 1970. A dedicated group of republicans wiped out in one fell swoop; the actions of the SAS would have major implications in the weeks ahead.

After a difficult week of negotiations, republicans hired an aircraft to take the bodies home, with Sinn Fein's Joe Austin accompanying them on the long, lonely journey back to Ireland. From the airport, the IRA took over arrangements for the journey back to Belfast. As the cortege passed through Balbriggan, Drogheda and Dundalk, thousands of ordinary people lined the streets to pay their respects. They may have been 'terrorists' in the eyes of the British, but not to ordinary people in Ireland.

Back in Donegal, I was preparing to go to our football club monthly meeting, I watched a bit of the RTE News at 9 before I left, as they showed coverage of the slow journey home. During the meeting an uncle arrived telling me to ring a Belfast number, that someone had rang and said it was urgent. I tried several times but no answer, and I went back to the meeting, not thinking anything untoward. Arriving home after ten, she cried out, 'someone had been shot dead in Turf Lodge', quoting the Army, 'a known gunman'. Suddenly the penny dropped, she also had a premonition, "I think its Kevi." I could see it on her face, she knew it was Kevi. There were no iPhones in those far off days, and we had no landline, so I raced over to the local pub, 'the Lagoon' to ring my friend Gerry, and Sheila let me use their house phone. Gerry confirmed that Kevi had been shot dead by the Army during an attack on soldiers who were surrounding Sean Savage's house, which was just across the road from my parent's house. Apparently Kevi and two other volunteers were preparing to attack the Army, when a soldier spotted them and shot Kevi 5 times in the back and he fell dying. Local women took his rifle away before the soldiers reached the scene, but they preceded to abuse the body and 15 mins later, just before the ambulance arrived, Kevi died.

I returned to the house, she was in deep shock, it was a traumatic experience which would come back to haunt us in a few years' time. We immediately started to pack up clothes for the journey to Belfast and then awakened the children. They were only ten, nine and six, we let them stay in their pyjamas and brought a quilt for the back seat. We informed a few of the neighbours, they had already heard it on the news but didn't think it would be so close to home. After midnight we headed off on the sad journey to Belfast, at the Cosquin checkpoint where six soldiers were killed a few years later, the Brits posed the usual perfunctorily questions and we headed on towards the Glenshane. It was a foggy night as we passed the Ponderosa, we had to take it slowly, every half hour the news came on the radio, "A suspected gunman was shot dead by the Army in Belfast tonight." The moment was surreal, we listened in silence. Arriving in Belfast around 3 am there was a relative calm;

neighbours rallying around, people stood quietly chatting on the streets, feral youths strolling about awaiting British troops. IRA Vols mingled with family, it was going to be a testing few days, little did we know what lay ahead.

Earlier in the night, the RUC had broken the code of respect at funerals by hijacking the hearses once they crossed the border and blocking off the mourners. They then raced to Belfast with each hearse accompanied by ten RUC jeeps; they didn't want a massive outpouring of support throughout the six counties. In Belfast at least 10,000 were waiting on the cortege at Kennedy Way, the RUC had different ideas. With the bodies of the Gibraltar three back at home, Gerry Adams and other members of the Republican leadership arrived at the house in Turf Lodge around 4am to sympathise with Steven and Rita. It had been a long day for everyone, while the dead volunteers 'rested', so did everyone else, it would be the calm before the storm.

On the Tuesday Kevi's body returned home. The previous day he had been renovating the house with a few friends, they had tumbled the living room wall into the hall to make a larger room and had intended finishing it the next day, as they were ready for a pint in the club; alas the next day would never come for him. Tuesday morning would see comrades and friends help tidy up the house for the wake, they did sterling work and had the little house ready for the evening as people started gathering to sympathise with the family. As he was an IRA Vol there would be massive numbers visiting the house over the next few days, it's always a difficult and stressful time for the family, but also they gain strength from the support of the community. There was an IRA Guard of Honour beside the coffin at all times: black berets, masks, black gloves, white shirts, black trousers, the six men guarding their fallen comrade, taking turns with other volunteers who rested upstairs. I met some of them on their rest period, just young guys, the same as we were 20 years earlier: idealistic, dedicated and committed. Every day they ran the same risks as Kevi did, and now with the whole community, they mourned him.

On Wednesday morning we headed over to Andersonstown for the funerals of those killed in Gibraltar. I met two friends, Gerry and his brother Jim, and my sister Bernadette who had played the pipes at the Hunger strike funerals. We stood outside St Agnes chapel where the cortege of Sean Savage and Dan McCann had joined Mairead Farrells' for the funeral liturgy. Unbeknownst to everyone, apparently one guy sat in the pews that wasn't there to mourn; several rows in front of him sat his targets that day, Gerry Adams and Martin McGuinness. The lone loyalist gunman Michael Stone had set out to target them, but didn't get a chance, so he bided his time. The funeral procession then made its way down past Casement Park on the road to Milltown cemetery. Republican Ireland came to pay their respects to those murdered in Gibraltar; thousands upon thousands, the largest funerals since the Hunger strikes almost a decade earlier. As the piper who played with Bernadette at Bobby Sands funeral led the way, it was conspicuous that the usual Guard of Honour and Colour Party were missing. The coffins were draped with the flag of the Irish Republic and gloves and beret atop the coffin but high-level negotiations between the British Government the RUC and Army, the Church and through contacts, the IRA, a deal was struck that there would be no colour party and shots fired over the coffins, in return, the Army and RUC would stay well away from the funeral route, it was a decision which would have major implications.

The massive funeral procession finally arrived at Milltown and the ceremonies were taking place when suddenly, as the first coffin was being lowered, dull thuds sounded, followed by explosions all around us. Gerry, Bernadette and I were about 20 yards from the graves and as the thuds and explosions continued we thought mortars were being fired from the 'Village', a loyalist area just across the motorway. There was utter pandemonium as the bereaved families fell among the headstones and mourners took cover. Republican leaders called for people 'to stay down', then about 50 yards away a long haired guy with a cap was spotted with a gun. Young people surged forward towards him, he fired off shots and the first guy fell. He proceeded back down a path towards the motorway with a large number of young people following him, my mate Gerry was one of them, as was Seanna Walsh who had been in the Cages with us. I lost my sister in the chaos and didn't see her again until later that night. I stood there watching all this madness unveil in front of me, it was crazy stuff. Much later when I thought back on it, I presume being domiciled in the Republic for a decade had detached me from all of this, or else I might have been with the crowd chasing the gunman. Being part of a society in conflict makes you oblivious to danger, the young people who chased the gunman did so without fear for their own lives, in a normal society, and you would take a rain check!

Michael Stone became a walking hero within loyalist circles that day for his kamikaze attack on the funerals. Whether he had a death wish, was suicidal, astonishingly brave or just nuts, it's hard to know, but to launch a one-man attack on a 20,000 strong crowd at an IRA funeral was beyond comprehension. Stone continued down towards the motorway, firing at the young people and throwing the odd grenade. The youths were catching up on him but three would die at his hands from gunshot wounds. His stated intention to target McGuinness and Adams was hyperbole, like all loyalist assassinations, any Catholic would do. As Stone reached the motorway a white transit van which had been sitting there the whole time suddenly pulled away, it was later discovered that it belonged to the RUC. Suggestions that it was an escape van for Stone were never substantiated, whether he acting on his own, or had help within the security forces will never be known. Stone eventually ran out of bullets for the handgun, threw his last grenade, which failed to explode, and the chasing group finally caught up with him. He was beaten, a car was hijacked and Stone was being bundled in to face community justice when suddenly the RUC arrived and saved his life. It was the most amazing day in the whole conflict; world news headlines showed this happening in broad daylight in a Belfast cemetery. The world was in awe, the six counties were spiralling into a crescendo of violence, with no end in sight, not this week anyway. Stone was taken away and eventually would receive 30 years in the H Blocks for his attack on the funerals, which saw two civilians and an IRA Vol killed. This would lead to another day of madness which brought Belfast to the verge of insanity.

Eventually, I made my way from the cemetery back up to Turf Lodge and the wake house. The news, of course, was on everyone's lips and every news programme. There was a sadness about the wake house but also pride, with hindsight it's hard to fathom what happened. Kevi was 31, he had a lot of living to do, all IRA Vols understood that they could lose their lives at any time, most that were killed didn't make 30, and similarly British soldiers faced a shortened life. Looking back on it now 30 years later it's hard to know was it worth it, life is so short that we want to live as long as possible and enjoy life. Would we make the same decisions now? I'm not sure. Of course, over 3,500 people were killed during the conflict, the same goes for all of them. They all wanted to live, they were cut down in their prime and they never lived to see a new society with peace of sorts. We can't change the past, it is what it is.

Was it worth it? Is any conflict worth it? I just don't know, time will tell. I've thought long and hard about this over the years, we didn't live in a normal society, I've discussed it with various friends: football teammates, work friends, neighbours, politicians, Garda friends, golf buddies, my partner and children, why did we make the decisions we did and they didn't. The conclusion we always arrived at was that ‘environment was everything’. If I had been born in Termon in north Donegal, I would have joined the local GAA team and maybe been a County Minor in ‘69, if any of them had been born in Belfast and lived in Turf Lodge they would have joined the Fianna in ‘69, eventually been involved in 'armed struggle' in the IRA. It was as simple as that, a ‘quirk of fate or an accident of birth’, as my partner Mary would say. There is no way we can change our past, everyone is on a voyage through life. Do I have regrets? No. Would I do it all again? I don't know. Let's leave it with the overused idiom, c'est la vie.

It was a long night, thousands of people must have passed through the house over the few days. I met many old friends and ex comrades, most I hadn't seen since the Cages, but the bond we had created was preserved.

Some had been back in the H Blocks again with Kevi, some still involved and committed as ever while others had hung up their 'armalites' and were living a relatively quiet life. We chatted long into the night, as the Guard of Honour stood to attention around the coffin. Outside the Brits stayed away, and the streets were quiet, the crowds had drifted away, but many stayed and sat up during the night. I never slept the three nights and on the last night I sat with Rita, Kevi's mother. She didn't say much, she was in a sort of a trance. At about 6am she walked over to the coffin and suddenly let out a high pitched wail like an old banshee. She screamed her son's name and cried, then sat down again beside the coffin. It was a really surreal moment, the 'Irish Mammy' and her lost son, a bond broken. I took a walk outside, it was a bright Spring morning and overhead a British Army helicopter hovered. We wondered after what happened at Milltown if the Army would move in for Kevi's funeral. We would have to wait and see.

Finally, the time came to carry the coffin out of the house one last time. The streets where Kevi grew up, played football, went to school, started work, went to his first disco, met girls, had his first drink. The streets he knew so well, knew all the neighbours, this was his home, yet a foreign soldier riddled him with bullets just like a scene from Gaza, the British Army no different from the Israeli's. One questions who had the most right to be on the streets of Turf Lodge that night armed with a rifle; a young guy who grew up there or a foreign soldier, a paid killer. As we emerged, carrying the coffin into the Spring sunlight, there were thousands gathered on the street; neighbours and friends, republicans from all over Ireland, camera crews and news reporters from around the world. They sent reports around Europe, the US and Middle East, it was a week of all weeks.

Gathered behind the hearse, the coffin was placed on a ‘catafalque’ of sorts, family and close friends surrounded it. The Sinn Fein leadership were there, Gerry Adams and Martin McGuinness et al, also present were the IRA leadership; a Vol. stood forward and placed the beret and gloves on the flag of the Republic which covered the coffin. Hundreds of IRA volunteers took their place amongst the thousands in the procession to the local chapel, there was no colour party but a volley of shots had been fired earlier to pay the IRA's final salute. The deal for the Army/RUC to stay away pro quid with no colour party held firm, it had arrived after a decade of shameful scenes when the RUC/Army attacked Republican funerals, there would have been sanctimonious outrage if it had been the other way around. We walked from the house, down the streets where Kevi grew up, turned down the Gardens, where I used to live and passed my parents’ house, just across from Sean Savage's house, then the entry where Kevi was shot down. The cortege slowed for a moment then we carried the coffin into the chapel as Fr Denny gave a homily which sent shivers down the spine. It was no misplaced condemnation, as he said it as it was for the people of the parish, "is it any wonder the youth of the area vent their anger, frustration and desperation, by throwing stones, petrol bombs, hijacking, burning vehicles or even joining the IRA."

Not sure if his sentiments went down well with Cardinal Daly in his 'palace' in Armagh, but they certainly resonated with the people of the area. Kevi was no terrorist, he was a member of their community and the British Government couldn't comprehend that. After mass we took the body on its last journey through the estate, down by Norfolk and past Andersonstown RUC barracks. As intelligence officers filmed everyone at the funeral, the cortege entered Milltown, and amid massive security by the IRA after the previous day's events, Kevi was laid to rest in the Republican memorial plot. An IRA officer gave the beret, gloves and tricolour to his mother Rita. It was almost the final act of a harrowing week so far, unfortunately there was still worse to come. Almost unbeknownst to us, as we retired to the Felons Club across the road from Milltown for some 'refreshments', we heard and then saw marching bands, banners, swirling pipes and drums; the parade went marching by, Kevi was buried on St Patrick's Day.

In the prologue to the book, I have written about events on Saturday at the funeral of IRA volunteer, Caoimhin MacBradaigh, and the deaths of the two soldiers who drove into the cortege. I don't need to repeat it here, but it was one of the most spine chilling days of our lives. There were no winners that day, but maybe it was the beginning of the end. The day after the chaos of the funeral we drove home, over the border and back to Termon; to peace and tranquillity, really a different world, how could anyone in that small rural hamlet understand what we had just experienced? We were part of that idyllic community now, we enjoyed life 'in the Hills.' Our children were growing up there, it was just so different from the urban jungle we had just spent a week in. Our kids didn't quite comprehend what they had just been part of; their Uncle shot dead by the British Army, the funerals of three Irish people butchered in Gibraltar, attacked by a crazed gunman, and another three people killed. Their Uncle's funeral with flags, berets and gloves on the coffin, shots fired in a nearby street in salute and then another funeral and two soldiers killed, absolute mayhem. In their young minds, ten, nine and six, it must have appeared like something from a horror movie. It certainly wasn't something that children should be exposed to, the worst they would be exposed to in Termon was their school GAA team losing a match, or maybe a bad summer making it hard for dad to save the turf.

What do we say to our neighbours? They had seen it all on TV, many had Republican sympathies and understood, but there was a cohort who were virulently anti-republican and didn't want northern politics impinging on their

'Republic', a 26 county one at that. They were happy enough to ignore what was happening 20 miles up the road. Saying that, we never ever had any problems with anyone regarding the 'north', but there was a serious detachment from it during the conflict. People just didn't want anything to do with it, probably understandable as no-one wants conflict, but it is still part of our country annexed by Britain. As time went by and the peace process kicked in, there was a definite softening of opinions, and people talked more about events in the six counties. The absence of killings brought a new awareness of what actually happened during the 30-year conflict, so much so that by the time of the 1916 commemorations in 2016 the Republic was able to celebrate the sacrifice of Easter Week in full grandeur without any fear of being accused of commemorating violence, how the War of Independence and Civil War are to be commemorated is a different story. It was difficult for a Fine Gael Govt. But they eventually sensed the mood among the people and upped the commemoration process, how they commemorate the Civil War is going to be interesting, they have already got off to a bad start by trying to commemorate the RIC which proved to be a disaster, how they explain their role in the death of 77 republican prisoners during the civil war will be problematic for them? Even recently the presence of a Govt Minister at a ceremony to commemorate the founding of the Northern statelet has caused major controversy after President Higgins refused to attend?

After Gibraltar, Kevi and the soldiers' deaths the killings didn't end there, less than two months later we got word that Hugh Hehir was shot dead by the Gardai after a post office raid in Feakle, Co Clare. Hugh had been in the Cages with us in the '70s, he had been sent to the six counties, and was operating in Belfast when he was arrested with Joe Doc in the New Lodge, and both ended up in our Cage. A big guy, he used to walk around the Cage in the summer in his bare feet and apparently did the same in the Burren at home. A likeable big man, he was always referred to as 'Hughie Hehir, the man from Clare', he was the first IRA Vol killed in the Republic since Tom Smith during an escape in Portlaoise in 1975. Ironically, I now play golf with an ex Garda who, at the time, was working in the area where Hugh was shot, the contradictions in life.

A few months later Brendan Davidson 'Big Ruby' was shot dead at home in the Markets area. UVF men dressed as RUC arrived at his door, pretending to serve a summons and he was killed as he opened the door. Brendan was a brilliant big guy, who was also in our Cage in the '70s. The British dirty tricks department tried to sully his name. Ironically his good friend Anthony McKiernan, who was also in our Cage, was shot dead as an informer. It once again poses the questions; where was this information coming from, who was disseminating it, what people were in charge in Intelligence sections in the IRA and the British side, and who was benefitting casting aspersions on certain individuals? Two more guys who were in Cage 18 with us dead, the list was getting longer.

It wasn't just Republicans who were being killed. Several months later UDA leader Jimmy Craig was killed by fellow loyalists. He was a controversial character, who had also been in the Cages, in Cage 19 beside ours, he was in charge of the UDA Cages and Gusty Spence the UVF Cages. Craig had built up quite a reputation within loyalism; he had been charged with the murder of Maire Drumn in '76 and allegedly ordered the murder of Jack Kielty, the comedian Paddys' Dad, after he named him in a television programme on extortion. Craig built an empire of mafia-style gangsterism; living the high life while extorting protection money from up to 100 building companies, they either paid up or couldn't operate. Ironically what brought Craig's demise was his relationship with the IRA, within the Cages he was always on friendly terms with leading republicans, and the theory is that he passed information to the IRA on leading loyalists who were later killed: John McMichael, Lenny Murphy et al, who were involved in the sectarian murder campaign. It was a strange relationship but sometimes in conflict, strange things happen.

Two years after Kevi was killed, our marriage collapsed. Something inside her head clicked after Kevi was killed, she was never the same again, and she was prepared to destroy the lives of our children and myself, all for what? The kids are the most important people in your life, and they were happy; Padraic and Ciara were preparing for Secondary and Kevin at National school. The boys were part of the local GAA team, they had loads of friends, it was idyllic living in rural Donegal: Marble Hill and Downings beaches close by, Lough Salt just up the hill, Letterkenny 15 mins away and Derry 40 mins. What was there not to like about it? Only she can answer that.

At the start of October, I went up for the weekend. By this stage she was back in Belfast and had the kids with her. I picked Kevin up at school and something happened which would change our lives forever. I was sitting in the car waiting, when in the rear view mirror I saw him walking down with two little Belfast friends. He was laughing and happy as all kids are on a Friday, but I saw something else. I realised that in six months he would just be another wee Belfast boy, Padraic and Ciara would be at secondary school creating their own future, and I would be in Donegal on my own. Just then I had what I can only describe as an 'explosion' in my brain, a light bulb moment as they say, I realised that this was a life-changing experience, and at that precise moment I decided to bring the kids back to Donegal, whatever the consequences.

She was in Dublin for the weekend, ironically at the Sinn Fein Ard fheis, her thoughts were far away from her children! I never regretted anything I have done and feel proud that I put our children first. How she has lived her life since without them is hard to comprehend, but on the surface after 30 years, it looks like she didn't care. That Friday night the kids came around to my mum's, we sat up and I told them I wanted to take them back. Kevin said right away he was going back, Ciara said she would follow us soon. Padraic took a bit longer to convince, he told me years later it wasn't that he didn't want to go, but he had just started secondary in Belfast, had already made a lot of friends who he played football with after school, and the thought of starting it all over again was the problem. We sat talking till midnight, there were tears again and Padraic had a massive headache, eventually he said he would go back. He was the eldest and probably most affected emotionally. He was also the clincher to the deal, if he had said he wasn't going then I don't think it would have worked, so when he said 'I'm going' I was overjoyed. The boys stayed with me in my Mum's that night, while Ciara went around to the other Granny's and said she would pack all the bags and have everything ready when we arrived the next day. It was like a military plan organised to perfection. Despite a short confrontation with Rita and some of her family we headed off the next day, it was a nervous two-hour journey to the border at Killea, but finally as we crossed over to Donegal there was relief, we arrived at Termon exhausted, it's been 30 years since but I've never regretted one moment.

I spent the next week getting the boys back into school, Kevin was fine and slotted straight back into Scoil Naisunta an Tearmann, but Padraic had to start all over again at St Eunan's, It was difficult for him and the first few months he struggled, ironically he was bullied and got shingles, many an evening I would find him tapping on the window in his bedroom. I felt for him, he was deep and kept everything in. He cried the most, but he stuck it out even when I offered to bring him back. Kevin was younger and it was easier in national school. Saying that, I had informed Eamonn, the Sgt, that there was a chance that she would get people to lift the kids at school, she had threatened to do so. The Gardaí kept an eye on the schools and the teachers were informed so between us, we were alert to anything she would do. At the same time a solicitor informed me that no court in Donegal would send my kids from rural Donegal back to West Belfast in the middle of a conflict. In life, I have always gone with my gut feelings and for the past 30 years I've always felt I did the right thing, as the old saying goes, "you can't kid the kids." Her disgraceful behaviour abandoning her children proved me right and how any mother could do it is beyond comprehension. My oldest boy Padraic was 11 at the time, he's 43 now, his so called 'Mother' hasn't seen him since, there's not much more to say! A few months later Ciara arrived down on the Derry train, as we crossed the border into Donegal at Killea she said she wasn't going back. I shed a few tears, the kids and I were reunited, and always would be, life was good.

THE 90'S, THE CHILDREN AND I

I was always a 'socc-ar' man as Eamonn Dunphy was wont to say. I played the 'beautiful game' from when I was 8 years old, my friends all played soccer and I just loved the game. Unfortunately, there was no GAA club where we lived, so I never played gaelic football even though when I went to St Mary's soccer was banned, I just didn't get into the GAA. At the same time, my kids were growing up and the boys, like everyone in Termon, joined the local GAA club and started to blossom in the new underage set up. I had no interest in the GAA previously, but once the boys started playing, I started going to their matches and the interest grew. They were great years, Termon reached their first underage county final and Padraic was top scorer. He was a very good footballer and should have achieved more, but sometimes life takes over. Kevin then came along and the talent was obvious from a young age.

For the next decade, I was heavily involved in underage football: both soccer and gaelic, moreso soccer of course but I never missed the boys play at either game. To get involved in any sport is imperative for children, unfortunately, the modern era has produced a generation which is stuck in a bedroom with a laptop, iPad, iPhone, 500 so-called friends on FB, Playstation or Xbox, sitting up half the night playing Grand Theft Auto, just harmful to their intelligence. Physical fitness and exercise has taken a back seat to these video games, a dangerous situation. Children who get involved in physical contact sports benefit from a certain fitness level, a camaraderie within a team structure and become a part of something bigger than the individual. It's essential we encourage our children to embrace field sports, rather than become brain dead computer nerds.

So the '90s were all about the children as they grew up, went to secondary and played football. I eventually went back to work at Kirchhoff, they had been good to me, understood the circumstances and kept the job open. I might have hated the place but it paid the mortgage, helped bring the kids up and gave us a certain standard of living, all in all, it was okay. I got on well with Sean who had taken over as General Manager, he was just out of his time as a tool maker when I first started but he rose through the ranks rather quickly. We always got on well, both 'nordies', his father's pub was burnt by loyalists in Limavady in 1969, and they moved to Greencastle, near Moville, a place I used to look across to from the roof of Huts at Magilligan when I was interned in the early '70's.

At the start of the 90's Giggs and I started taking an interest in the small white ball game. He was one of the first guys I met when I finally moved down from Belfast in the late 70's, we played together for Lurgy for a few years before he headed off to London and Canada for a decade to make his fortune, which he did along with Noreen in Harley St, and now they were running the Village Tavern and had one hell of a year during Italia '90. And then came the golf. There was no golf course near us, and we knew nobody who played, but as the football careers wound down, golf would take its place. We had a 'swing' probably more like Maria Bailey than Rory McIlroy, but we could manage and soon were 16 handicappers. Our drives mightn't have been a thing of beauty but we could scramble with the best of them and our putting would yield as many pars as bogeys; 40 pts on the Links wouldn't be every day, but we had our days in the sun, and the rain, wind, hailstones, and thunderstorms. There was always the 19th hole awaiting, and pints of the black stuff or red wine. They were great years, learning the game of golf where Paul McGinley learned his stuff, and wee James Brogan was the maestro. You can't turn the clock back, but we had some wonderful times at Dunfanaghy. At the end of December '94, just before New Year's Eve, my first grandchild was born, Oisin Lee, making me a Grandad at 41, and my parent's Great Grandparents. Wee Ciara was just turning 16, so was quite young, but these things happen. Ciara obviously had to leave school to look after the baby, the boys were still at St Eunans, while I was back at work. It was a bit hectic but we just mucked in and helped each other, you know in that Irish way Oisin just became one of the family.

My Mum was a great support to us during those years, she would arrive down from Belfast with a big black bag full of food. She helped support the children who had no mother, we were indebted to her on many occasions and it was so sad to see her fall into Alzheimer's within the decade, it was just so unfair. She was the quintessential 'Irish Mammy', she had a heart of gold and was generous to a fault. She lived in Belfast for 60 years, but that old cottage in Doon was her home, she loved Donegal and her heart never left the old blacksmiths cottage near Doon Well.

In 1991 Sinn Fein Cllr Eddie Fullerton was shot dead by loyalists in Buncrana. It came during a period when loyalists were targeting Republican political targets. Eddie was a popular guy who I had canvassed for during a European election campaign in the '80s, he was also the guy who brought my sister into Derry to play the pipes at hunger striker Patsy O'Hara's funeral. He was larger than life, had a big mad beard and a voice like Paisley, and had spent half his life working in Scotland. His loss was felt within republicanism in Donegal, but he had created a base which Pearse Doherty and Padraig MacLochlainn would build on in later years. A week later another Cages man, Lawrence McNally, along with two other Vols, were killed by the SAS in the village of Coagh, Co Tyrone. Over 200 bullets were fired into their car which went up in flames, and the bodies were virtually incinerated. Lawrence had been in Cage 18 as well, a jovial character and part of the country/city divide, we got on well and the news from Tyrone was devastating. Incidents like this only highlighted what we had left behind, I still felt the same as I had 20 years previously, but I wasn't prepared to die for it, life had moved on. Tyrone was hit particularly hard during those times, a theory that it was to divide the IRA is untrue, it's just the way it was, Derry and Belfast were subdued by this stage, Tyrone was very active and South Armagh as always was in complete control of affairs, an attractive plan to create a buffer zone along the border might have been wishful thinking but certainly if Tyrone and South Armagh had their way there would never have been a ceasefire!

In early '93, a good friend from the Cages was shot dead by loyalists, presumably acting with information passed on by rogue RUC men and Army Intelligence. Alan Lundy was from the Ardoyne and spent the 70's in the Cages, a genuinely likeable guy, we spent many an evening shooting the breeze in Cage 18. He was articulate, and a dedicated republican. In May that year he was building a security porch for Alex Maskey, another Cages guy, who became the first Sinn Fein Cllr in Belfast since 1920, when loyalist gunmen driving by fired at him and chased him into the house, before shooting him and searching the house for Maskey, who they failed to find. Alan Lundy died on the spot and the killers escaped. Maskey had several murder attempts made on his life, and was seriously injured once. In the City Hall he was the victim of abuse from Unionist Cllrs, he strode a lonely path in the City Hall before being joined by other Sinn Fein Cllrs in later years. Eventually he would have the honour of being Lord Mayor, and seeing Sinn Fein become the largest Party in the modern era.

In October of the same year, an IRA unit targeted a shop on the Shankill, where intelligence suggested that the UDA, namely Johnny Adair was holding meetings above it. The intelligence was correct, but the meeting had ended early and most were gone by the time two IRA Vols entered the shop. The bomb exploded prematurely and one of the IRA Vols was killed along with eight civilians and a UDA member, it was a disaster for everyone. 14 Catholics were killed in revenge by the UVF/UDA over the next few weeks. One of those killed in the Shankill bomb was Sharon McBride, many years later I met her husband at a 'Victims Conference' in Hammersmith, London, chaired by Mary McAleese. He wasn't a bitter guy, but wanted to find out what really happened in the dirty war. His life was shattered by her death, as were so many others, like all victims, he deserves to know the truth. The people on the Shankill deserve it, just as much as those in Ballymurphy or the Bogside.

Sport was always a big thing in our lives. In the early '90s, my two boys were getting seriously involved in football, both soccer and Gaelic. They loved the game and embraced it fully, both were talented and would make shapes in both sports. In '96 Padraic (Paddy), as well as sitting and achieving good grades in his Leaving Cert, was also playing well for Termon GAA club and selected for the Donegal Minor team. He was on the panel which won the Ulster Championship and League, and lost by a point to Laois in the All Ireland semi-final at Croke Park. Kevin was also making shapes in football, he won an All-Ireland U-14 medal with St Eunan's in Gaelic, was attracting attention with Kilmac in underage soccer, and was also playing for a team in Derry. Within a six month period in '94 he was called up, along with Declan Alcorn, for a trial with Celtic and then went over for a week on trial with Aston Villa, Gary Shaw was scouting for Aston Villa, who he won the European Cup with in 1982, and wanted to bring Kevin over to Birmingham. It gave me an insight on how professional clubs in England operate, within a week they had organised for Kevin to travel over for the trial. He played three games, including one against Rangers which he enjoyed, and performed well, but Peter Withe, former England International and Head of Youth Development at Villa, thought his height (5'6') would go against him, which would be a problem over the years.

English football is all about 6'4' athletes who can run all day, and it passes down to League of Ireland, and indeed the Republic international team, the skill factor is missing as these robots play football the English way. Leaving school early, Kevin went on an FAI course in Dublin for a year, Letterkenny's Anthony Gorman had been on the first one with none other than Roy Keane a decade earlier. He then joined Finn Harps and was part of the Youth team which went two years unbeaten, winning the Ulster Cup and League. He then played a part in the only Finn Harps team to win the Ulster Senior League, and finally a senior medal with Harps as they defeated Ballymena in the North West Cup. But as much as he loved the soccer, his heart was in the GAA and his first love, Termon CLG. Over the next decade, he would develop into a brilliant corner forward, totally left-footed, he would score for fun, becoming the leading scorer in the county for several years. At 17 he inspired Termon to Intermediate victory, and then in the 2000's he played a major part in bringing the team to two County finals. Unfortunately they lost, but for a small club like Termon to even get to a County final was magnificent. The new millennium would be a very successful time for Kevin, or 'Wappa' as everyone knew him, a nickname given to Padraic at St Eunan's and passed on through the ranks. Kevin would play ball at the highest level and defy those who said his height would hinder him. I've always believed that height or the physique doesn't matter, it's what you can do with the ball if you have a football brain, you can more than make up for anything else.

Golf had become a big part of my life during the 90's. We were playing in Dunfanaghy and all over the place, with the Muckish Ramblers. We were also playing with our golf society in Kirchhoff; we played every Course in Donegal,

Tyrone, Derry, Sligo and a few in Scotland, Germany and Gran Canaria, it was a brilliant time. I have great memories of golf Courses that were absolute gems: Slieve Russell, Galway Bay, Ballyliffen, Rosapenna, Murvagh, City of Derry, Rosses Point, Balmoral, Maspalomas and Salobre in Gran Canaria. It wasn't just the courses, but the people I played with; absolute gents, the best of friends to this day; Giggs, Basher, John Mac, the Deer Hunter, Boyd, Dermot, wee James, Lua, Roger, Nigel and the Derry wans in Dunfanaghy; then big Mick, Denis, Eugene, Trampas, Putchy, Terry, Pat, Gerry and more Derry and Strabane 'wans' at Kirchhoff. These guys, and others too numerous to mention, were part of a great time in my life. We travelled the country, golfed, partied, drank and had birdies and pars galore.

The old Clubhouse in Dunfanaghy saw some great nights; the Catscan Classic and a marquee so beautiful Captain Lua described it as a 'Bordello', the Ramblers dinner dance in the Lagoon, Enda (RIP) bringing the house down with rock and roll, wee John Orr striking his drive through a flower pot in Cavan and presented with it at the dinner, the flower pot that is not the ball! An unnamed Rambler battering a fellow golfer's Garda car after he closed down his disco and the boys suggesting, "you should have used a 9 iron" when he arrived in the clubhouse the next week;Giggs throwing the ball over whin bushes at Portpatrick in Scotland and sinking the putt, wee James was oblivious to his extracurricular skills. We gate-crashed a wedding in Enniscrone and mixed with H&W employees in Belfast, went to nightclubs in Westport, Stranraer, Portmarnock, Sligo, Clydebank, Playa del Ingles and the Lagoon, once leaving hard-line Prods at Lisburn and meeting up with hard-line Provos in the Felons Club. Another night, landing in the middle of New Buildings in Derry at 3am surrounded by Union Jacks after leaving wee John Orr home. In Portnoo, with Declan Bonner, Packie Bonner and Daniel O'Donnell; with Paul McGinley and the Garda Commissioner at the Catscan Classic; or with Sean O'Rourke, Iggy O'Muircheartaigh and the NUI Galway Alumni society at Salthill. Golf brings you to the most amazing places and meeting the most amazing people, it's been a wonderful 30 years playing the little white ball game.

The early 90's would see many feuds between the various smaller republican and loyalist groups. In the early days Dominic McGlinchey, Francis Hughes et al were based in Letterkenny. Hughes, of course, died on Hunger strike whilst McGlinchey, Dessie O'Hare, 'the Border Fox' and others, faded into the obscurity of dissident republican politics. As the years went on the groups imploded amid feuds of a horrific nature, both McGlinchey and his wife were shot dead, and Hughie Torney, a guy I was in Crunlin Road with in '71, was among many killed in INLA divisions. The late '90s would see the end of the IRA campaign to force the British to withdraw from the six counties, it was a difficult few years as the politicos tried to negotiate the barriers to a peace process, while within republicanism were many who weren't happy with the direction that Adams and McGuinness were leading the republican movement, it was a delicate operation, just as difficult as it was to prosecute a war for the previous 30 years.

The IRA held a convention in Donegal, just as Sinn Fein held a conference in the Clanree in Letterkenny, to decide to end the war. There were problems bringing everyone along with the new initiative and many prominent republicans were side-lined if they disagreed with the new road to 'freedom'. It was imperative that the Movement did not split, and that guns didn't come into the equation. Gerry Adams has come under criticism over the years for his part in the conflict; whether he was in the IRA or not, his economic nous or lack of it, but the reality of it all was that there would never have been peace without his efforts. The Good Friday Agreement brought new arrangements for the whole island. The new millennium would be a different age, the Republic would become an economic powerhouse with the Celtic Tiger and in the six counties, the guns were taken out of the equation. After a century of division, it was a whole new world.

The new millennium came and went with a bang, or even without a bang, as the forecasts of planes falling out of the sky as computer systems collapsed, proved to be hyperbole from people who should have known better. In the summer of 2001 I had another grandchild, Tiarnach, a wee sister for Oisin. She would grow up into a wonderful young lady, and just this summer finished 2nd year at College in Sligo, it's hard to believe she will celebrate her 21st next summer. The children were now young adults with girlfriends and boyfriends, I was still in Kirchhoff making car parts for Opel, playing golf at weekends, and enjoying life. My parents were ageing and so was I, the conveyer belt of life. The Kirchhoff Golf society headed to Gran Canaria for a week of drinking and a little golf, it was a fun week. More grandchildren came along in the noughties, Rionach, Alanna, Oran, Cian, Rian; I came from such a small family, two sisters who never married and no brothers, so it was nice to see the family growing all around me. The summer of 2002 saw the latest edition of the beautiful game's showpiece, the World Cup was being held in Japan/Korea. Three of us, John Mac, my son Kevin and I headed to Gran Canarias, we knew the craic would be mighty and we brought the golf clubs as well. We stayed in Maspalomas, in the Dunaflor near the golf club. By a quirk of fate two women from Galway were also staying in the Dunaflor, Mary and niece Ciara, who had just graduated as a teacher; they hadn't intended meeting up with three Donegal lads on tour. I was reading 'The Ragged Trousered Philanthropist' and Mary was impressed, first impressions can be lasting.

One night we went to a pub and met the girls, it was a long night but the start of something special. I was still working away in Kirchhoff, a lot of us were heading for the 20-year mark. One day Sean, my boss, came out to my machine and said, "You didn't tell me you were a Grammar schoolboy", I replied, "didn't think it was relevant." He replied, "well it is, you're the only person in here who did." Apparently, on a slow day in the office, he was flipping through files on employees, pulled mine out and noticed that I had gone to St Mary's in Belfast. He then said to me, "get yourself out of here and go back to college." Now maybe it was a gentle way of getting rid of me as I wasn't exactly employee of the year busting a gut to make targets in the repetitive crap of factory life but I prefer to think it was a genuine offer from a good friend. So for the next year, he paid for me to attend computer applications courses to get up to speed in modern technology, and also to get the feel of being back in a classroom after 35 years. Sean lit a spark which Mary massively encouraged, she suggested that I go back to University as well but at that stage, I was just happy enough being able to turn the PC on. Little did I know then that within 18 months I would be heading to NUI Galway full time. Life was going to turn full circle, I would soon embark on an amazing journey which would be the best years of my life.

2003 would prove to be a momentous year in my lifetime. I cleared my mortgage on the wee terraced house in Termon. Kevin was the last of the kids to leave home for London and Boston, Mary and I were at the beginning of something special and Celtic made it to the UEFA final in Seville against Porto managed by Jose Mourhino. Earlier in the year I thought that Celtic might make it to the final so booked flights to Faro for Mary and I, and wee Oisin. We stayed in a small village near the Spanish border, Manta Rota, and drove up to Seville on the day of the final. 80,000 Celtic supporters were in town and we actually met up with some Belfast guys, including John Bradley from Turf Lodge, brother of Angela, old friends, old republicans! As it approached kick-off time we headed to a wee pub mixed with Celtic and Porto fans and watched the game there, it was a disappointing end but that's football, big bad Bobo was sent off and Porto won in extra time, with the financial doping in modern football will we ever see Celtic in a European final again?

We walked back to the stadium to get the car and head back to the Algarve, but decided to just sleep in the car till morning. I walked over to the stadium, kept on walking, entered the stadium and just kept walking through the place. I ended up in an executive suite where people were still having drinks, I had shorts on and polo top, the Spanish barman queried; "quieres un trago" and handed me a glass of Prosecco, it was very welcome on a hot night. I recognised two guys standing beside me: Jack McGinn former Celtic Chairman and Brian Wilson, a Labour Government Minister under Tony Blair and a former Celtic Director. I got chatting to them and we had a few more drinks as we lamented the loss earlier. Before we left Brian and I were given two large posters commemorating the final by the Maitre D. Considering future events, I'm so glad that we got to spend the week with wee Oisin, we could never have imagined what lay ahead, how life would pan out for him, those were precious days in Seville and the Algarve.

During the week in the Algarve I got a phone call from big John (Trampas) to say that the Germans had finally decided to give us redundancy. For those who took it a whole new world opened up. I had spent almost 20 years in Kirchhoff, that's a big chunk of anyone's life, I hated it but to be honest the craic with the boys could be mighty at times. We had a football team and a golf society, an annual dinner dance and we also got a chance to visit Germany every so often. They were based in Olpe, near Cologne, the home of 'Krombacher', and at Christmas every year we could have half a lorry filled with Krombacher arrive in Letterkenny. In return we would send them smoked salmon, which was a delicacy there and quite expensive. Of course, the Customs and Excise were oblivious of all this going on; it's hard to beat the Irish way of doing things. Funny I met a former commander of the IRA in Donegal years later, we were chatting about life and I told him I had taken redundancy after 20 years in Kirchhoff, he replied, 'You would have been better going back to the H Blocks'! Black northern humour at its best.

In the last six years of my time there, we built up a relationship with the Kirchhoff family and our work's golf society. One day Joachim the 'main man' was looking at our golf notice board, he then asked Sean about us. He was probably slightly surprised that we played golf as it was still elitist in Germany and only for the wealthy. Sean told him about our Society, and the next thing we got an invitation to organise a weekend's golf that June when they were over for their AGM. So that's how a great friendship began on the golfing links around Donegal and further afield. The first time we brought them to Portsalon, Ballyliffen and Dunfanaghy, they loved it, and for the next six years it was repeated in various golf courses like Rosapenna; City of Derry; Rosses Point and Strandhill. Joachim, Laura and the four sons were golf aficionados and just loved that week playing some of the best Links courses in the world. Sadly both Joachim and Laura have passed in recent years, they were lovely people, once when they opened a new extension to the factory they spent an hour chatting to a few of us in our overalls about the golf and ignored the 'suits', great times which made the weekly slog on the machines bearable.

So that was it, after almost two decades, I took my leave off Kirchhoff. I can't say it was with a heavy heart, I would miss the craic with the boys but as for the daily routine, oh God. I must say this mightn't be everyone's feelings on their time on the factory floor, one thing I must say I appreciated having the job in the first place. Donegal was no heaven in the '80s industrially and economically, it created stability in our life path and provided a regular pay packet. Donegal for all its beauty can be a difficult place to live, unless you're a wealthy farmer's or business man's son or acquire a job in the Civil Service, Gardai, HSE, Eircom or ESB. These jobs were like gold dust then, and you wouldn't get in unless you had family connections to FF or FG. The jobs were given out as part of patronage, even jobs on the road in the County Council, clientelism existed in a big way, jobs translated into votes and the political parties looked after their own.

Kirchhoff as well as giving me full time employment also gave me one of the funniest moments in life. Terry Dunlop and I headed up to Lisburn for a golf day; it was invitational from the oil company who supplied Kirchhoff. We had a wonderful time, beautiful course, lovely evening meal, drinks etc. The funny thing was that everyone else was from engineering companies in the north; Sirocco, H&W, Mackie's, all good Ulster Prods and in their midst were Terry and I, the two token Fenians. Afterwards Terry headed back to Derry, whilst I headed over to West Belfast to the Felon's club with a friend, talk about out of the frying pan into the fire. But there was a sequel to the story. Later in the year, we were playing Dunfanaghy during Open Week, and Giggs and I were playing with this old guy, Payne, Wayne or something, he was a retired British Army Major, the sort you might find strolling around Dunfanaghy on a pleasant summer's evening. Walking along the 1st fairway Payne told me he was from Hillsborough. I said I knew it and that I was up golfing in Lisburn recently, "the Oil Company who deal with us invited a few of us up to play." and what does the old man reply, "oh so you're in oil Paddy". Well Raymond had palpitations and whispered to me, you should have told him you were in the Kesh', just down the road from Hillsborough but not known for its golf links! It was a funny moment which actually came back years later when I was at a wedding in south Galway, hurling territory. A nephew of Mary's was getting married and on both sides of the family there were Doctors, Consultants etc, so a lot of medical people at the wedding. About three in the morning I was in the loo, when an uncle of the bride came in. We got chatting as you do and he said to me, "I suppose you're a medical man as well Paddy", and old Payne's words came back to me, I replied, "...no actually I'm in oil'!

We went to Thailand for my 50th, and word came through that Termon had made it to their first Senior County final after 40 years in existence. Apparently the semi-final was a wonderful night in Donegal town, there was a big Termon crowd at the game and in the first half they could hardly believe what they were seeing, within a 20 minute period Termon were three goals up all scored by 'Wappa', my son Kevin. In an exquisite display of football he blew MacCumhails away, with goals of quality scoring 3-4 in the process and a Darren Gibson thunderbolt put the Termon boys en route to the final. Termon held on in the second half for a one-point victory and at the final whistle the crowd surged on to the pitch, nearly incredulous by what they had seen. The older guys like Johnny, Benny and big Helferty told me they never imagined they would ever see the club in a County final. We got a phone call at the hotel and over the next few hours were on the phone and listening to Highland radio après match. I had mixed feelings, I was so proud that Kevin had played a key role in delivering the club to the final but disappointed we weren't there, but we would be back for the final, which unfortunately they narrowly lost to Four Masters, but that night in the semi could never be replicated. It was a magical moment and put him on the radar for the County team, but still Brian McEniff had reservations because of his height. It would take a change in management before he pulled in the Donegal jersey.

Unfortunately, the County final proved to be a damp squib for Termon. They were playing an excellent team in Four Masters, with a splattering of County players like Karl Lacey and Patrick Dunnion. They really dominated the match, although there wasn't much in the score at the end, it was a massive experience for the whole community in Termon. The place was covered in flags and bunting, the build-up was great with lots of media coverage, and on the day it was the largest crowd at a County final ever with probably everyone in Termon in attendance, we had a large banner, 'Wappa the baby faced assassin will terminate the Masters', a reference to the Irish News report after the semi-final. Kevin was disappointed after the final, the reality was we probably didn't have enough quality players, it's not easy in a small rural area, but the team did the community proud. As well as being disappointed for the team, I was disappointed for Padraic, he should have been on the team. He had played in the winning Intermediate team a few years earlier with most of the same team that would play in two County finals in the first decade of the new Millennium. It was the golden era for the club, but his forte would come in later years, when he became involved in coaching the young players of the future, a dedicated club man in the local GAA community.

During 2003 my Mum and Dad moved back to Donegal, to the old cottage where she left 60 years earlier. Unfortunately, she had developed early Alzheimer's, so after all those years in Belfast they made a final journey over Glenshane Pass and down to Termon and the old blacksmith's cottage. Over the next few years, my Dad was a star as he looked after Mum. It's the worst thing that can happen to anyone, it's not living. Up until she was 75 she could travel up and down to Belfast, and now she was sitting there utterly helpless. It was heart-breaking to watch, I felt for my Dad, as he had to watch his true love and lifetime partner disintegrating before his eyes, it's a horrible disease, worse than anything.

NEW MILLENNIUM, NEW LIFE.

In January 2004 I started a two year course at the LYIT as a computer technician. After attending the night classes in computers, I was interested, but this was a different ball game. There's one hell of a difference between becoming au fait with Word, Excel, Spreadsheets in comparison to Programming, as one Lecturer said to me "it's like being dropped from a helicopter into the sea and you can't swim."I spent the first six months Programming, I was getting to understand binary computer language, but it was difficult, saying that I always think that anything you learn is never wasted. In September, I transferred to a Computer Applications course. This was much more like it; in fact, I should have done this first before the programming, the classic cart before the horse!

2005 would be a momentous year for me in many facets of life. My relationship with Mary was blossoming and my visits to Oranmore increasing. I had applied to NUI Galway as a mature student, to take a BA in History and English. On a sadder note my good friend and neighbour wee Pat McGrattan got whacked by cancer and was dead within five weeks. He was only 49, it was a devastating blow. He had met wee Teresa, a Donegal woman, and moved over from his hometown Glasgow a little while after we had arrived in Termon. The first night I met him was during the World Cup '82 as Scotland played Brazil, "are ye watching the game?" he said in an accent which almost impossible to decipher, but we became friends for the next quarter century. He was a great Celtic man; we would spend many a weekend in Glasgow during the '80s and '90s, and nights down in the Inishowen outpost of Glengad watching games on STV, just 12 nautical miles across to Scotland!

Pat was a gentle sort, a red leader in John Brown's shipyard in Partick, he would morph into the local painter in Termon/Kilmac. There wasn't a kitchen or bedroom he hadn't painted before his sad demise, just give him a wall to paint, a jar of coffee and radio and he would paint to his heart's content. Pat's sudden illness and death came as a shock to everyone; neighbours Frank, Peggy, wife Teresa and I comforted him as he died in his little sitting-room. He lies just a few yards away from my parents in the little Termon graveyard and as I pass between their resting place and wee Oisin, I always share a moment with Pat and tell him the Celts are doing well, he would like that, RIP.

As we neared the end of the 1st year on computers, big John and I visited an education forum in Letterkenny, strolling around the various stands advertising their colleges. A lady asked were we interested in history, and brought us over to their stand where the imposing poster advocated the Great

War of 1914-18, the War Graves, Somme and Ypres. To be honest up to that stage, while having an avid interest in history the escapades of imperialist armies slaughtering each other in the mud of the Verdun or the heat of Gallipoli didn't do a lot for me. They were running a course, one day a week in Derry about WW1, and the clincher was the offer of a week fully paid to visit the war graves at the Somme and Ypres at the end of it. Now John and I hadn't a lot of sympathy for those who took John Redmond's advice and fought with the British Army, against fellow working-class Germans at the western front, but it was off to Ypres we were destined, with another 30 students. It was an eclectic group: former UDA, UVF, British Army, UDR, IRA, Musicians, Poets, Writers, Shinners, Teachers and a CEO in the HSE, we were a real mix, and to be honest it was one of the best weeks of my life.

The first week was a bit of a surprise as the 'International school' was in the loyalist Waterside, based in the old Ebrington barracks. It was the brainchild of Glenn Barr who previously had been a leading UDA 'general' and a leader of the UWC strike in 1974 which brought down the power-sharing Executive. He had teamed up with Paddy Harte, the Fine Gael TD, in building the Peace Tower at Ypres and the Peace school, and organised trips from schools from all over Ireland. His son Craig and a traditional musician from Inishowen, Tracey, were running the Peace school, and welcomed us the first day, then ran informal introductions for the whole group, it was fascinating. There was Seamus who resembled a Bogside republican but was a career soldier in the British Army for 30 years oddly enough from 'Londonderry'; Nigel a part time UDR man; Raymond a UVF Vol who spent 13 years in Long Kesh; Jim a school Principal who had been in the UVF youth; myself an IRA Vol who spent 6 years in the Kesh; big John whose grandfather and granduncle both served in WW1 and he had the medals at home; a Sinn Fein organiser from Buncrana who looked like Johnny Adair; and Joe, HSE CEO, and Kathleen who were heading to Rome for the Pope's funeral a day or two later. It truly was an eclectic mix, cross-community, cross border, and we all blended well together. It was 2005, the 'war' was over and for the first time in 35 years we could sit around a table and talk without the usual tensions. For eight weeks we did just that, and then the week at Ypres, it was an experience to be savoured.

The first day in Derry was as interesting as it gets. At lunchtime I joined Seamus, Nigel, Jim and Raymond; two Long Kesh 'graduates' in this exalted group of former combatants in the recent conflict. We all shook hands and ordered the chowder and ribs, it was a good start to the day. At the end of the eight weeks, we made the journey to Ypres for a week in Belgium sunshine. It was a great time, each day we would travel to various war grave sites, then in the afternoon back to the peace school in the round tower, where we would discuss various aspects of war and conflict. We would then head off for dinner and a few glasses of the best French wine, and as everyone headed off to bed the 'conflict quintet' and big John would continue the discussion into the wee hours, with loads of red wine flowing. The debates were interesting, informative and challenging but never once did we ever fall out. The fact we had matured enough to talk and engage with people we might have tried to kill in a previous time, says a lot about how far we have come.

We visited Thiepval, Poelkapelle, Guillemont, Passchendale and Messines ridge where the Allies exploded 20 ton of explosives under German lines, the slaughter unimaginable. We saw Tynecot cemetery, the largest allied war graves site, 12,000 little white headstones and 60,000 names on a curved wall, men who were never recovered from the muck, squashed by tanks or blown to bits. It was a moving experience, we visited a German war cemetery, Spanbrokmolden, hidden away behind trees, dull, dark, the French didn't even want them buried on their soil. It was a sad site, we also came across the little hillside cemetery where Eric Bogle sat beside Willie McBride's grave and penned the famous anti-war song, and big John and Sam sang it, a very poignant moment. We visited Poelcapelle, where John Condon was buried, allegedly the youngest soldier killed in WW1. He was a young farmer's son from Waterford, only 15 when he was gassed at Mousetrap farm nearby. The whole group sang the song, 'John Condon', "wee lad who'll not grow old, heroes that don't come home, here they lie in Belgian fields, and Picardy." Also during the week, we had to move hotel. Loyalists had arrived to negotiate a truce during a UDA/UVF feud in Belfast and David Irvine was there, as well as some top UDA men. It was felt best to move us in case any incidents took place; with a few Johnny Adair lookalikes about it was a wise decision, these sectarian psychopaths would think nothing of going for the jugular of any Fenian they found.

On the final night, we had a lovely evening. Glenn Barr was there and the head of the IDA, we went to a lovely restaurant for the meal. The IDA guy sang Boolavogue whilst Glenn Barr sang Danny Boy, it was that sort of night. We left Belgium/France with a greater understanding of WW1, but still divided on opinion why 250,000 Irishmen fought in the war for Britain and 49,000 lost their lives. Mary McAleese has tried to cloud the waters by suggesting that they were Irish soldiers but the reality is that they weren't, when they put on the uniform of the British Army they were British soldiers. The only Irish soldiers to fight in the period 1914-18 were the volunteers who took over the GPO; it's unfair to history to be revisionist with the truth, let's say it as it is and work it out in a truthful manner. Of course many joined for a myriad of reasons, adventure, travel, excitement, peer pressure, famously for 'a pair of boots' and purely economic reasons, the country was coming down with 'fish wives' who were getting the 'separation money', and maybe a minority who believed in the fight to free small nations? Part of the problem in Ireland has been families who had connections to the British Army for generations, they had conflicting interests when it came to the independence struggle, many of these families, not all, were pro British, there might have been a tradition within the family of serving the crown, i.e. when the British were marching republican prisoners through Eyre Sq in Galway after Easter 1916 this pro British element were out on the streets attacking the prisoners, many would have been the wives receiving the 'separation payment' and their husband's away in Flanders, like the soldiers who came back from the war they were on the wrong side of history after 1921!

Returning from the Somme and Ypres, I faced up to a busy time. Within a month I had to head up and down to Galway several times. First I had to take an aptitude test at NUI Galway, in the Aula Maxima, the old part of the University built and dedicated to Queen Victoria, 'the Famine Queen' in 1849. Next was an interview with a panel of academics, then I had to deliver a 2000 word statement outlining why I wanted to return to University at 50. They don't want any time wasters, or people who will drop out after the 1st Semester, as indeed the actor Martin Sheen did that Christmas. When a letter arrived from the University, I opened it with bated breath, it read, "You have been accepted as an undergraduate at NUI Galway on a BA for the Academic year 2005-06." It was incredible news, 36 years after I had left school in June 1969, I was returning to full-time education, as an undergrad at a prestigious university at 52, Ciara was also starting her Nursing Degree programme and wee Tiarnach was starting National school. Three generations going 'back to school' at the same time, it was a very proud time for all of us.

Entering the hallowed corridors of the University was an emotional experience. I had never been anywhere near a university in my whole life, for me it was an incredible experience, everything was new. I laugh about it now as I talk the university language, but when I started I didn't even know the difference between an Undergrad and a Postgrad. The first days in University were a settling in process, the place was massive, 17,000 students and 5000 staff, it was like a small town. The campus on the edge of Galway city centre is a beautiful site, Arts concourse, Aras na Gaeilge, Hardiman library, Moore Institute, the Kingfisher Leisure centre and of course the Aula Maxima, a wonderful old building full of history, dating from the Famine era.

In 1916 the college had academics and students fighting on both sides during Easter Week, also in 1920 Michael Moran, IRA Commander in Tuam, was executed by Auxiliaries on the college grounds, it's history wasn't all academia. The university was vast; it took a month just to find where we were. Eventually, I picked my subjects; English and History which were close to my heart, and spot on if I wanted to pursue a teaching career, Celtic Civilisation which I found interesting, and Social and Political Science to satisfy my interest in politics. It was a good mixture and each one contributed to my overall experience in college.

Before we kicked off on the lectures, we had a sort of induction day where some senior lecturers gave us talks about college life. Mary Liddy, the mature student officer gave us our first essential tip, "If you're parked illegally get out and move it, you'll be clamped." Hubert McDermott, Head of English Department and the eldest lecturer at the University gave a wonderful talk about college life. He said "there's a mystery about college outside the walls, but you'll come in and experience it and realise there's no mystique at all, but you won't tell anyone, and so the mystique continues." He was a wonderful guy who I got to know very well, a master of the language, a witty guy, you could listen to him all day.

Then Rita O'Donoghue gave a talk on the practicalities of college life, the do's and don'ts, she brought the house down with her advice to, let's say the more mature guys, "When it comes to Easter and exam time if a pretty young thing in a denim mini skirt and heels snuggles up to you in the college bar, it's not your body she's after, it's your notes'.

The first few months were a whole new learning process, Lectures, in large auditoriums holding several hundred, smaller tutorials with a dozen or so, taking notes, writing assignments, spending hours in the library. It was a whirlwind start, and of course, meeting up with new friends. Over the years there would be loads, at first, there was 'the Last of the Summer Wine' an epithet handed to a group of female mature students I hung out with by musician Damien Quinn: Kath, Moya, Colette, Ruth, et al. We all came together at a later stage in life and everyone made it through the BA and further, sadly Moya has passed in recent times, a lovely wee woman from Spiddal, in earlier life she worked as secretary to former Provisional IRA leader Sean MacStiofain whilst working in Conrad na Gaeilge in Dublin.

One mature student we didn't expect to meet in college was the actor, Martin Sheen. Despite having made over 200 films and being a very wealthy individual, he had left school at 15 without any qualifications and decided like ourselves that he would go back to college and attain a degree. Coming from an Irish background, and a regular visitor to Ireland he decided on an Irish university and NUI Galway became his college of choice. He made it clear from day one that he was serious about this, didn't want to be treated any differently from other students, and wouldn't be giving any interviews during his time as an undergrad. So the guy who was 'President' in the 'West Wing and slaughtering innocent Vietnamese in 'Apocalypse Now', was now an undergrad with us for a few months in the Fall of '05. Ramon Gerardo Antonio

Estevez was the son of an Irish mother from Tipp and a Spanish dad from Galicia, both migrants to the US. Sheen made a good career move by changing his name and became one of the most successful actors of the modern era. Interestingly for such a man, his computer skills were lacking, one day he asked a friend of mine, Marie Lavin, could she "switch the damned PC on." Marie helped him, and as she was on the editorial committee on the College paper, Sin, she took the chance to ask him for an interview to which he agreed. Marie got one of the only interviews he gave during his time at college, the other with Pat Kenny on the LLS, a great coup for her.

The first few months went by slowly. Celtic Civilisation was interesting; Political Science with Niall O'Dochartaigh; History with John Cunningham and Steve Ellis; and English with Hubert and Daniel Carey. If you think about it, here I was in the halls of academia after almost 40 years of hardship; in the Cages of Long Kesh, and the inside of a bloody factory making car parts, cutting turf in the bog, pulling pints in the Milford Inn, married and separated, children and grandchildren, unrequited love and new love. It was some fcuking journey to get here, but you know through it all I had a dream. I could read Tolstoy and Joyce, knew that I shouldn't have been stuck in that factory for 20 years but c'est la vie, what can you do about it. With no qualifications, a wife, small kids and mortgage, you can't be a dreamer when you need money coming into the kitchen on a Friday. Everyone is on a journey in life, when I reached 50 so many things fell into place that I got the chance to pursue the dream, I never regretted it.

The second Semester brought a shock as Martin Sheen made an exit after Christmas, like his character in the helicopter in 'Apocalypse Now'. I'm not sure exactly what happened, but the next time we saw him was on the set of the 'West Wing', at least Marie got her interview.

Second semester completed, assignments completed, exam preparation completed; we were all ready for the exam season, seven exams in a few weeks, it was tough going but we managed it. The night before my first exam I met Hubert and his wife walking in Oranmore. The next morning before the English exam he strolled around the exam hall as they do and stopped with me, "You know Paddy I told my wife last night that they're even letting people live in Oranmore these days without Letters after their name." I'm preparing for the first exams in 36 years and Hubert comes out with this, but that was his style. He actually might have settled me down, because I found the paper suiting me and at times when I was answering a question about the 'Butcher Boy' I could hear Hubert's voice. He had done that on generations of English students, 40 years he was in NUI Galway, and everyone has a story about him.

As I was preparing for those first exams, we had another few days in Maspalomas playing golf. One day, while having a beer in the clubhouse the news came on, and a picture of Denis Donaldson flashed on screen. He had been shot dead at an isolated cottage near Glenties in Donegal, once again it was a shock although to be honest, not unexpected. I actually felt sympathy for a guy I knew, although more so for his family. They must have had a mixture of sadness and confusion that Denis had brought this shame on them. Within Republicanism there was always a feeling that informers were operating at the top level, many major operations were compromised: Gibraltar, Loughgall. Was Denis the only one who was turned? Sandy Lynch survived as did Scappaticci, in Irish society the word 'informer' is the lowest of the low, it is an image of a scum like character betraying his friends, taking money from the RUC/Army. How anyone as articulate and dedicated as Denis could become an informer is beyond belief, whatever the Brits had on him must have been of massively incriminating proportions for him to betray Bobby Sands, Tomboy Louden and Gerry Rooney, the three guys with him in the iconic photo taken in the Cages before they were released.

Who killed Denis Donaldson? Speculation has been rampant since his death? Was it officially sanctioned by the IRA? Was it dissidents? Will it ever be revealed? There is no doubt that once it was revealed he was a high placed informer his fate was sealed, like all such people who were turned he would have known the consequences but why he moved to Donegal is a mystery? Like Scappaticci was he given a bye?

Denis Donaldson would be the last of those that I knew who were killed during the conflict, almost 40 in total. His demise apart, most were school friends, IRA Vols, ex-prisoners, a brother in law, adult friends and comrades. I have recalled the accounts of their deaths throughout this tome, I think it's important that they are not forgotten. The conflict brought us all to a different place; in 1968 we would have never have known or expected what was ahead of us, as I reflect now it's beyond comprehension. Most died young, most were ambitious and wanted so much to achieve in life, sometimes I think what I achieved in life is for them as much as anyone else.

During the summer of '06, Kevin was back in the US playing for Donegal Boston again. He was a bit frustrated as Brian McEniff hadn't called him into the Donegal squad, despite being the top scorer in Donegal for the past few seasons. Donegal were playing in Division 2, after losing the League 2 final, apparently the new manager Brian McIvor began an extensive search for new players, and sent a message to Kevin in Boston to come back and join up with the panel. Kevin was in two minds, but decided to stay in Boston for the rest of the summer. Kevin came back before Christmas, immediately joined the Donegal panel and started some serious training to prepare for the new season. On the first weekend in January he pulled on the Donegal jersey for the first time in a McKenna cup game against UUJ, and was the top scorer in a horrendous day in Ballyshannon. Coincidentally another young guy made his debut that day coming on as a second-half sub, his name, Michael Murphy. Donegal went on to win the McKenna Cup and Kevin picked up his first medal. He was also named as the Irish News 'Player of the Month', it was a great start to his Inter-County career.

At the start of February we made the long journey to Cork as Kevin and the team flew down by plane, a first for the team. Kevin scored a goal in a first-ever win against Cork in the southern capital. The team was gelling well under McIvor and Kevin was establishing a place as corner forward alongside Brendan Devanney and Colm McFadden. He was scoring freely and the team went on an unbeaten run through the League to the Final, where they played Mayo at Croke Park. In the semi-final versus Kildare, Kevin scored another goal and the RTE commentator proclaimed, “Wappa (the name everyone knew him by, even the RTE guy) scored a brilliant goal, that's why he's making such a name for himself in this season's League.” Kevin landed a monster of a point at a vital stage in the final, in front of 30,000. It was an intriguing game which Donegal won by a few points at the end. There were wild celebrations, it was the first piece of silverware since Anthony Molloy had lifted 'Sam' in 1992, 15 years without an Ulster title as Armagh and Tyrone ruled the roost. The team arrived back to Donegal town to a wonderful reception; despite having some great players over that time, Armagh and Tyrone were just too strong, but it was felt as if this was the start of something special, and people started talking about Donegal as possible contenders for 'Sam' once again.

Unfortunately the luck of the Ulster Championship draw paired Donegal with Armagh in the quarters, with the winners to play Tyrone in the semi-final. It was going to be difficult, but the team were well ready for the challenge. The championship game with Armagh was the biggest match in Ballybofey for years; Donegal hadn't beaten Armagh for almost 20 years. Almost 20,000 packed into MacCumhail Park on a roasting hot day and the match was end to end stuff, with Armagh in control for long periods. Donegal came storming back and in the last minute a move involving Wappa and Devanney led to a high ball dropping in on top of the keeper, and Kevin Cassidy put him and the ball in the back of the net. The goal stood and Donegal had beaten Armagh for the first time in a generation. The semi-final brought Donegal to Clones against Tyrone, the mood among the camp was good, the fans were confident, but Donegal would flatter to deceive. Tyrone were in the middle of three All Ireland's in five years, and were the real deal, they put Donegal to the sword in a deeply disappointing day. Colm Anthony and Kevin were both sent off; Colm for a straight right hook on Brian Dooher, Kevin after smashing the ball into his namesake's Ryan's face on the sideline, after already being booked. It was a dismal finale, followed by defeat to Monaghan in the qualifiers the following week. There was no disgrace in defeat to the Farney men, as they came close to lifting 'Sam' twice in those years, but for Donegal, it was back to the drawing board. Kevin had a great first season in the Donegal colours, he had defied the odds and played county despite his height. In Termon's 50 odd years as a club, they have only had a handful of County players and he's still the only Termon player to play in a final in Croke Park, and the only guy to score a goal there. I was so proud of him, and not ashamed to say that I shed a tear when he busted the net versus Kildare in the league semi at the old Canal end.

In September Dad suddenly took ill and passed and Mum had to go into a nursing home, both left the old cottage at Doon the same day and never returned, you don't want many days like that in life. They were good people who led a valued and principled life, my Mum passed 30 months later, they are buried on the hillside in Termon, and they're always in my mind.

In October I was preparing to head to Malta for a year at the Universita ta Malta. It was another new experience, when I arrived it was sweltering with humidity, thankfully November brought beautiful, cooler weather. I liked the place from day one. I also had an ulterior motive, I was interested to see what it would be like to live in a foreign country with a hot climate and after a year in the southern Mediterranean I knew it was a lifestyle I could adjust to, a seed planted for the future. Sandro, an estate agent got me a nice apartment up in Swieqi near St Julians, and a short bus ride to the University. A neighbour, Simone, had a small bookshop and she would source books for me for college: Joseph Conrad's 'Heart of Darkness and Joyce's 'Ulysses'. I have remained friends with both since, the Maltese are friendly people, not unlike the Irish, they too are an island people with a colonial past. They love football and a few drinks, they either support English or Italian teams. The island, of course, has a strong Italian connection being not far from Sicily, and the British have a big influence having been there from 1800 until the 1960's. The two political parties are also divided like that; the Labour Party has pro-British tendencies whereas the Nationalist Party were founded with links from Mussolini's fascist group, but are very European, the Labour Party not so much.

The first week in Msida, at the University, I met up with Ronan from Limerick who was also out for the year and we became good friends. Soon we would be spending many nights in the Dubliner, the main Irish pub on the island, where we met up with a load of other Irish guys who were out there working: big Tom from Tuam an Engineer, Andy a Dub who worked at the airport fixing big planes, Greg from Waterford teaching in a Language school with a penchant for exotic foreign students! Brian a Tipp man who would land later from India with his hammock and is still there today! A few Belfast guys including Michael from the New Lodge, working in Betfair who were in situ on the island availing of lax tax laws. Interestingly Michael's father in law was an ex RUC man and the Dad a Prison Warder, that was a complicated relationship! Liam Brady's cousin Tom was there as well. Paul, the Manager of the Dubliner was from Tallaght, went out in '89 when the Republic played Malta on the way to Italia '90, and never came back! Along with Carl the Maltese/English owner of the Dubliner, they were Mein Host extraordinaire.

Mary and I made a firm commitment to our relationship by getting engaged on the 29th February, a Leap Year. We had a lovely meal courtesy of Peter and Jackie in Peppino's, then a party in the 'Scotsman' with all the Malta gang: Tom, Andy, Greg, Ylenia, and Ronan et al. The Cava was flowing and Mary sang, 'You needed me', and a wee French rugby player from Cork brought the house down with a great version of 'The Fields of Athenry'. It was a lovely night, the plan was to come back and get married in Malta the following summer, but life got in the way. We're still together though, so it wasn't just a rash decision in the Maltese sun.

I returned to Galway for the final year of the BA, it was tough but flew by. There was also a new cohort of friends, as the original crew had mostly finished up and few if any went on to a postgrad. Ronan came back from Malta and we met up with Michael, Bernie and Joe from Culdaff. We would all graduate the following October; black robes for the men, hats for the women, letters after our names and a 2.1 in the bag, I felt more comfortable in Oranmore now! In May I had organised a mature students trip to Malta, we had a great week; Michael, Ronan, Kevin, Steven 'the Professor' et al, trips to Gozo and the Blue Lagoon, Club 22 and the Dubliner. There was, of course, the cultural side to it: Roman General's holiday homes, Latin Mass in the Pro-Cathedral, Caravaggio paintings and the bombed WW2 open-air theatre. It's amazing what a group of 'Historians' would get up to on tour.

During the year I had applied to do a Postgrad in Teacher Training, PGDE. Places were scarce, but my application must have impressed and I was accepted on the course. We started in September, and it was hectic from day one, you also had to source a school yourself and as I was in Malta working in a language school, I had left it late but found a place in St Joseph's, Garbally, near Ballinasloe, formerly a seminary and an elite centre of learning back in the day, a rugby school which had former Irish Captain Ciaran Fitzgerald in its ranks, and also a boarding school, set in 300 acres halfway between Galway and Dublin. It was imposing and challenging, but I spent the next year there Teaching 1st, 2nd years and Transition Years. I would travel up and down on the new M6 three days a week, and the other two days in NUI Galway, it was a hectic year but I got through it. The intensity of the course was highlighted a few years later when the HEA changed it to a 2 year Masters. An amazing coincidence happened while I was in Garbally, big John Doherty (Trampas) who worked with me in the Ballyraine and Kirchhoff, also on the computer course after redundancy and the week at the Somme, he too went back to College to do a Nursing Degree while I was doing the PGDE, and then by pure chance we both ended up in Ballinasloe out of all towns in the country, an amazing coincidence!

2009 also saw Termon back in a County Senior final for the second time in a decade. It was a golden period for the club, which is unlikely to be repeated for a long time. Unfortunately, the final had the same result as '03 with a powerhouse of Donegal football, St Eunan's, winning out. Kevin was still in the County panel, but as the recession hit he headed over to London to find work and joined up with Tirconaill Gaels, the leading club in London. He would spend four years with them, won two Championships and also played for London in the All Ireland series. The Gaels looked after him well, and he responded by being the leading scorer every year. The downside was that he missed out on the Jim McGuinness era and a Celtic cross.

I went out to Malta to work in AM language school and brought Oisin and Tiarnach out for the summer. At this stage I was living up in San Gwann, Oisin and Tiarnach had a great time in the pool and Tiarnach made lots of wee friends her age that lived there. Oisin was older but he was happy out, he had his Playstation with him which kept him occupied, I'm so glad we had that time together considering what happened a few years later. I would teach in the school in the mornings and then we had the afternoon to stroll into St Julian's. I treasure those memories so much, between Seville and San Gwann they will always be the happy memories I have of Oisin. I can't ever believe that life wasn't good for him; he was a happy go lucky youth, whatever happened it wasn't because of lack of love from family and friends, the mystery will always be there

In October 2010 word came from Belfast that Gerry 'Whitey' Bradley, had taken his life near a Marina at Carrickfergus. 'Whitey' wrote a book about his involvement in the struggle, 'Insider, Life In The IRA.' In the complex world of Republican politics, he had crossed a line by writing about certain IRA operations. For some it wasn't acceptable and he felt he was being ostracised. It's a touchy situation, there has to be a realisation that there are things you can't say, but then many combatants went along with the Boston College initiative to talk about things during the conflict. It appeared foolhardy in the extreme for people who should have known better, as I said there are just some things you can't talk about, especially in republican circles; this was serious stuff, matters of life and death. Whitey might have crossed the line, or might not have, in such a closed tight-knit community it's difficult. Whatever the verdict, it led him to drive to an isolated spot and take his own life, another young guy I knew who sadly suffered and died prematurely because of the conflict. Whether it was coincidental or not, the night Gerry died, the programme about Boston College – 'Voices From The Grave' was aired on television, mainly focused on Brendan Hughes and the UVF's David Irvine. Like the 'Dark', 'Whitey' was a dedicated IRA volunteer, it was a sad ending.

While it was tempting to go straight into teaching, the collapse of the 'Celtic Tiger' meant there was a moratorium on recruiting new staff, so I decided to do a further Postgrad. This time, a Masters (MA) in History. I had originally thought of doing Journalism but stayed with History, so I applied for the MA and was accepted again into NUI Galway, it was to be another long year. I went back to Malta to teach for the summer, and then back to Galway for a final year in academia. Starting in September we were straight at it, Mary Harris was the Course Director, and was a hard taskmaster. We were in a small group which included Bernie, Maire, Vinny et al, it was heavy stuff: Irish, European and World History, studying Documents, researching Primary sources, visiting Kew Gardens the British national archives, and finishing off with a 20,000-word Dissertation, which took all summer and left my time in Malta short that year. In November we had the final graduation, once again with a 2.1, it was a very moving experience and I had achieved way above what I had ever expected, the old Granddad was now a Teacherman.

Ironically my favourite book over the period in college was Frank McCourt's 'Teacherman', it was a wonderful expose of teaching. Long before he became a great writer, McCourt was a teacher in the Bronx, it was tough going but he was up to it. On his first day a student hit him on the head with a ham sandwich and as he bent down to pick it up he thought this was make or break time, so he took a bite out of the sandwich, the kids loved it. Another time he was at a parent-teacher meeting and a big black 'Mama' said to him, "Listen Teacherman, cut out the crap, those old stories about Ireland, my son's going to be a mechanic." McCourt's book was my bible during my teaching years!

BACK ON THE GOLF COURSE AND THE REST OF MY LIFE

During the years at University, one thing had to take a back seat, golf! I had been playing since 1990, mostly in Dunfanaghy and with two societies: the Muckish Ramblers and the Kirchhoff Society. Golf was a big part of my life, but when I returned to college something had to go.

For the next few years I gave talks to new mature students, first years and history classes. I was teaching, mostly subbing, as there was no chance of a full-time job as the Tiger imploded and the recession took a firm grip, also there was an ageist element in vogue? I was happy enough, started working with the State Exam Commission, as Superintendent at the Leaving Cert and then as Examiner for the Junior Cert in English and History. It was quite an interesting period, although little time time for golf! In recent years they have started changing the marking to online following Germany. All exams will eventually be marked like that, it's quick and efficient and all done on a laptop, but like all things with modern technology, there will be fewer jobs for Examiners!

Anecdotally during my first time as Superintendent I was out in Malta working when I received a call from a teacher in a Galway school, “are you here next week?” I replied, “yes, but there's a problem, I'm in Malta,” to which the rather agitated VP on the other end said, “what the f—k are you doing in Malta?” I rearranged a flight back, and was in the school Tuesday, where I met fellow Teacher and sheep farmer John Finn. To this day we play golf together and always have the craic about that day.

On the football field, Donegal won a second Sam Maguire in 2012 beating Mayo; 'Jimmy's winning matches' reverberated around Croke Park, and they should have won another in 2014. Kilmac Celtic were kingpins in the Donegal Premier league, winning two consecutive titles in a row, and just missing out on three-in-a-row on the final day. Kevin contributed to all three whilst commuting over and back to London, the 'wee club' was now a major force in Donegal football and celebrated their 35th anniversary with a dinner dance in the Lagoon. Paddy Crerand was the guest speaker; he was a great choice with his Celtic, ManU and Donegal connections.

We relocated just before Christmas 2014. It's a lovely setting, just beside Galway Bay golf resort, with the Atlantic on one side, forest and park on the other. Both being avid golfers, we had arrived in a wild Atlantic heaven. Unfortunately the best-laid plans and all that, soon Mary was diagnosed with womb cancer. It was a devastating shock but thanks to her Consultant and team she is now cancer free.

In September '15, events 150 miles away were about to unfold that would shake our little family to its foundations. The news that morning was devastating in its finality; my eldest Grandson Oisin had taken his own life. He was preparing for his 21st at New Year, was hoping for a mechanic apprenticeship in the near future. He had bought his Mum's old Honda Civic and was getting it ready for the road, he had good friends, and they all loved cars.

I watched all these young people at the wake with disbelief edged on their faces, their first experience of death, and a harrowing experience which knew no bounds. They will grow up and eventually grow old, but Oisin would always be that 20 year old they knew in their young days, his sister and cousins would in time tell their children about him. He would always be wee Oisin, on the Xbox, playing mad music on the Decks at his 18th, the wee boy at the Celtic final in Seville, the infant I brought to the Naoinra in the old National School in Termon that his great Granny attended in the 1930's, or the 1st Year at St Eunan's and a young black friend he called 'Paddy'. The wee boy I brought to the Scottish Cup final in '99, all these memories.

Three months later we gathered together to remember Oisin on what would have been his 21st birthday. We had a special Mass down at Ards Friary, hundreds of Oisin's friends, neighbours and the local community joined with us in recalling his short life, it was a moving ceremony and Fr Sylvester gave a lovely insightful homily Afterwards, we returned to the little graveyard on the hillside in Termon and his friends released balloons and lanterns into the night air. It was almost New Year's Eve and symbolically it felt like a metaphor for a young life and the old year passing, We were humbled by friends and community being there to remember him.

2016 was all about one thing, the 100th anniversary of the Easter Rising. The State were reluctant at first, but gradually warmed to the idea when they realised that the ordinary people wanted Easter Week to be commemorated in a proper fashion. Almost every parish in the country did their own little thing to remember the men of 1916. In Oranmore the statue and garden in memory of Joe Howley, who was with Liam Mellowes in 1916 and was killed in Dublin during the War of Independence was given a makeover, and in Renville Park a beautiful structure was built with the words, 'Equality, Liberty, Peace.' In Termon the Proclamation plaque was errected on the graveyard wall, and in Kilmacrennan a ceremony was organised by a good friend and fellow golfer, Cllr Michael McBride, with a plaque erected to Pearse, Connolly and all the signatories to the proclamation, their names preserved for future generations.

Just after Easter 2016, I started to have problems with my breathing while out on the golf course. In early August I went in for surgery to replace the

Aortic valve, after nine hours on the operating table and recovery, things didn't go to plan. My heart didn't kick in properly and I was kept going with an external pacemaker for a few days while they decided what to do next. Eventually it was decided that a pacemaker would have to go in permanently. I felt quite nauseous over this period and was in ICU for ten days, but it wasn't all bad, two consultants, Dave Veerasingam and Da Costa, used to come up late at night and chat about golf with me!

2017 was all about recovery, no driving, on the road or golf course, but by the end of summer it became apparent that something was wrong with the aorta valve again; tests showed it would have to be replaced once more, the valve had been infected, a chance in a million? A few weeks later the surgery went ahead, I thought it would be straight forward, but seven hours later I awakened to learn that it was too dangerous to operate and the decision was made to close me up again. This was a severe blow; they told me it was 50/50 to go ahead with surgery which left me perplexed? We got a second opinion and transferred to 'James's' in Dublin. The surgery was a long drawn out affair, I was eleven hours on the table as they replaced the aorta valve and the pacemaker, both had been badly infected. When I came round I felt like I had been hit with a bus, but at least I was still alive. The consultant came in and said, "We did it, it wasn't easy but we managed it". I thanked him profusely, his skilled hands had saved my life, a Mayo man but coincidentally he had trained at the 'Royal' hospital in Belfast, just a few miles from where I grew up!

In total I was in the hospital for ten weeks, it was a long period. I was quite nauseous again for several weeks, but by the end of January I was back home and on the long road to recovery once again. Unfortunately within two months I would be back in hospital, this time it was even more serious, I had a brain haemorrhage! As Mary drove me to hospital I took a massive headache, she contacted the ambulance service and they met us at the Connacht rugby stadium and straight to Beaumont, I remember nothing of the next ten days, Mary was told I mightn't make it. In Beaumont they worked on me through the day and night, the Consultant was Dr Satar, a guy with a big mad beard who had a horrific time himself in recent years. His family in the UK were the victims of a racist attack, and his wife and three children were burned to death, a horrendous act by right-wing racist bigots. Luckily for me, he was able to continue his medical career, but despite his clinical skills said to Mary, "say a prayer" The bleed had stopped but they had to remove a piece of the skull the size of the palm of my hand to allow for the brain swelling, and deposit it in my abdomen for three months, the wonders of modern surgery. Padraic and Ciara were down from Donegal, Mary by my side, and Kevin came over from London; it was a difficult time for them, they didn't know if I was going to make it. After the ten days I came around, I don't know if it was the expertise of the medical team, God's will, the soft music Mary played in my ear every night, or even wee Brian's poetry from our golf trip to Rosses Point;

'......and the love of a baby unafraid,
has existed since time began,
but the greatest love, the love of love,
even better than that of a mother,
is the tender, passionate, infinite love,
of one golf hacker for another.......'

I slowly came around to see Mary and the family around me; it had taken a lot out of me but also them. I found out later there was a major chance that I wouldn't have made it, we take our own mortality for granted but when you're that close you realise that there's really nothing else worth worrying about but your health. What does it matter if you miss a 4' putt or duff a drive, that Celtic didn't make the Champions League or Donegal win 'Sam', that it's raining today or even tomorrow, that Boris and Mi-hal are in power, sure it could be worse it could be Thatcher and Trump. What does it matter if the grandkids don't get 500 points in the Leaving Cert, sure they'll get enough, they're happy and healthy and their whole life is ahead of them, and I'm still alive to see them grow up, that's what is important!

That's the most important factor, that I love them and they me; Padraic, Ciara, Kevin; the grandkids, Mary who has been by my side for almost 20 years now, the most wonderful person I've ever met. She encouraged me to return to University, she encourages me now when my golf is less than perfect. She sat beside me and held my hand as I was at death's door; she encouraged me to get better. A nurse domiciled in Galway, but a true Mayo woman who unfortunately has never met 'Sam Maguire', but she's also the most special lady I've ever known. We're entering the penultimate stages in life, it's for living and we intend to do that. Every day I thank God that I've been given a little longer to share this world with a beautiful person, from the inside out. There might only be one real golfer in the house now but I'll happily be her caddie for life.

I cried a tear, you wiped it dry,
I was confused, you cleared my mind,
I sold my soul, you bought it back for me,
And held me up and gave me dignity,
Somehow you needed me, I needed you.

You held my hand when it was cold,
When I was lost you took me home,
You gave me hope when I was at the end,
And turned my lies back into truth again,
You even called me friend.

You gave me strength to stand alone again,
To face the world out on my own again,
You put me high upon a pedestal,
So high that I could almost see eternity,
You needed me, I needed you...'

EPILOGUE

So, finally, we near the end of 2021, the second year of COVID and the first two decades of the new millennium gone already. Life is short when you think about it, I'll reach the three score years and ten in two year's time, and it's hard to believe. Old Lizzie and I are going to live forever; she had her Coronation the year I was born. In recent times, Martin McGuinness met her and shook hands, and she bowed her head at the Garden of Remembrance, life has moved on. Where have the years gone? 18 in Belfast, 6 in Long Kesh, almost 30 in Donegal and 16 in Galway, to paraphrase James Connolly, "sure it's been a good life Lily', but there's still a bit to go.

Working class heroes, that's a cliché worth examining. They generally don't make the Sunday Times rich list, fly to Morocco with Johnny Rohan, buy a pad in Shrewsbury Road for four million or mix with the posers in Reynard's, but they usually are the salt of the earth: community activists, GAA volunteers, small farmers and working-class kids. Back in 1970 when we took up arms against the British statelet, these were the people who made the difference, many sacrificed everything to change society. They were dedicated, disciplined, honest and principled, they had a dream to create a new society, and in 2021 it is closer than ever, nationalists are in a majority in the 6 counties and the mood for a referendum is growing in the Republic, never again will there be a need for 18-year-olds to take up weapons in armed struggle, 'our revenge will be the laughter of our children'.

Mary convinced me after years of persuading to start this project while recuperating from my surgery. It took a while but eventually I made a stab at it and thus we have the finished product now. I've always loved writing, from secondary school to the Cages in the Kesh, then the years at university when it was a labour of love writing up assignments; writing for the Celtic fanzine, 'More than 90 minutes', and the past four years writing a weekly article for the Tirconail Tribune in Donegal, also uploading articles on my blog and podcast, it's definitely a therapeutic activity; Sunday evening après 18 holes on the golf course and while the Sunday Game is on, rattling the keypad on the laptop, a few glasses of red wine, 2,500 words, finished at midnight and emailed off. It's enjoyable, along with teaching, it's what I should have always been doing, but life just doesn't work out quite like that.

During COVID and Lockdown I published two small books on Amazon, 'Walking through a story of life' and 'Political Status-Long Kesh '71-'76'; again it was a therapeutic process during the long months of isolation, no travel, no golf. The 'story of life' was a lighthearted stroll around Ireland and the golf courses I've played over 30 years, the characters I've met and the little anecdotes which made the journey worthwhile. I took the idea from Albert Speer, Hitler's armaments minister who spent his 20 years in gaol after Nuremburg walking around his exercise yard, but he had a plan, he had a map of Europe on his cell wall and he meticulously marked out his path throughout Europe, in his own mind of course, but he physically did the steps as he walked around the yard, and each day he walked from town to town, quite fascinating when you think about it? So I did something similar in lockdown, playing golf courses from Dunfanaghy to Drumoland, Ballyliffen to Balmoral, Glasson to Galway Bay, Rosapenna to Rosses Point, Portsalon to Portumna, Cairndhu to Castlerock! Three decades of pars, birdies and pints, wonderful Links and beautiful Parkland throughout Ireland and also Germany, Gran Canaria, Fuerteventura, Barcelona, Thailand, Scotland and Malta, and the craic was always mighty amid friendships galore as walked through the story of life!

The second book was actually my Masters Dissertation back in 2011 at NUI Galway; it was a look at life within the Cages during those years in the 70's, and a precursor to this new book, 'Armed Struggle to Academia', a tome of 120,000 words, my major contribution to the literary world!

My love for the 'beautiful game' has endured though the decades even if Celtic's position at the top level of football hasn't, then through my boys I took a second love for gaelic games and now through my grandchildren, another generation pulling on the green and gold of Donegal. But for the past 30 years the little white ball game has been my life, from Dunfanaghy via Cregmore to Galway Bay; the Muckish Ramblers, Kirchhoff, Bogies & Fogies, golf Societies par excellence, the craic has been mighty and the golf wasn't bad either!

I've been blessed in life; two wonderful parents, Annie and Patsy, both at rest on the little hillside in Termon, two sisters, Bernadette, and Winnie who passed recently. She had special needs and spent a lifetime in care but was happy, her passing came suddenly during COVID but not virus related. Padraic, Ciara and Kevin, gave me strength when I needed it most and were always there for me, and I hope I was there for them. My grandchildren: Tiarnach, Rionach, Alanna, Oran, Caolan, Cian, Rian, and of course Oisin, who will always be with us, I think of him every day. Last but not least, like the Lord keeps the good wine to the end, I have been blessed to have met such a wonderful woman at a time in life when it was good for both of us. Was it a match made in heaven if not Mayo or Donegal, well actually in Maspalomas, Gran Canaria.

As I was writing over the past year, four of the guys I was in Long Kesh with have passed: Gerry Cairns, Eamonn Maguire, Jim Scullion and just recently Johnny Burns, who I was lifted with all those years ago in 1972. All good friends who I spent those early years in the Cages with, I hadn't seen them much over the past decades, but there was always a bond and the light never dimmed. It brings our own mortality to the fore, Johnny's death especially was so sad; he succumbed to COVID-19.

When I was a kid I had terrible dreams one night that when you died, that was it forever, millions of years. I think the teacher was talking about life and death in class. I cried and called for my mum but she didn't hear me, and I got a strange feeling in my stomach. Almost 70 years later when I think about it, I still get that same feeling; life is for living, you can't think otherwise. I've lived a lot of life and I feel there is still a lot of living to do. I want the family to be happy, I want to see the grandchildren all grown up, enjoying life and being successful, Donegal to win 'Sam' again and for Mary's sake, Mayo as well. Celtic in their proper place competing in the Champions League, more great scenes like Lowry winning the 'the Open' at Portrush and myself finally lifting the Captains Prize in Galway Bay and Mary the Ladies title. I hope my birthplace of Belfast will become part of our unified country where we share a peaceful future with our unionist neighbours. I always wanted to run a marathon, climb Errigal and play every golf club in Ireland; after the health issues, the first two will remain unfinished business but the third is a realistic target in the retirement years. I've already played almost 100 of the 400 or so courses so we're well on the way. We intend to travel the country playing each course on the list that we haven't visited yet; already in summer '21 post covid year we have visited Tulfarris, Ballykisteen, Woodstock, Dromoland, Kilkee, Tullamore, Esker Hills, even Haggs Castle in Scotland; sure if we played regularly we'd manage them in a decade, now wouldn't that be a nice challenge to deliver on, and for all those who never got the chance to walk through a story of life!

"... I am a sailor, you're my first mate
we signed on together, we coupled our fate
Hauled up our anchor, determined not to fail
for the heart's treasure, together we set sail.

With no maps to guide us, we steered our own course
Rode out the storms when the winds were gale force
Sat out the doldrums in patience and hope
Working together we learned how to cope.

Life is an ocean and love is a boat
In troubled water that keeps us afloat
When we started the voyage, there was just me and you
Now gathered round us, we have our own crew.

Together we're in this relationship
We built it with care to last the whole trip
Our true destination's not marked on any charts
We're navigating to the shores of the heart..."

Glossary of Terms and Abbreviations

AK 47 - Popular version of the Kalashnikov smuggled to the IRA in the early 1980s.

Alliance Party - Middle class, cross community, middle of the road political Party.

Apprentice Boys - Protestant Society set up to commemorate the victory of the Williamite Army against King James II at the Siege of Derry in 1688.

An Phoblacht - Republican newspaper, morphed out of the United Irishmen in 1970. through Republican News which then merged with An Phoblacht in later years, now Online only.

Ard Fheis - Annual conference of Sinn Fein and indeed all Irish political parties.

Armalite - Automatic rifle smuggled into Belfast in the early 70's from America.

Army Council - Directs the IRA during times of war.

ASU - IRA Active Service Unit.

Ballymurphy - Working class estate built after WW2, strongly republican and the home place of Gerry Adams.

BBC - British Broadcasting Corporation.

Bloody Friday - 21st July 1972, 29 car bombs left in Belfast city centre by the IRA, 7 died.

Bloody Sunday - January 30 1972, 14 Civil Rights marchers murdered by the Parachute Regiment.

Bodenstown - The little cemetery in Kildare where the father of Republicanism, Wolfe Tone, is buried and an annual commemoration held in June every year by all shades of republicans.

Bogside - working class area in Derry and the home of Martin McGuinness.

Cage 18 - the Cage in Long Kesh where I spent most of my time incarcerated in the 70's.

Chief of Staff - IRA military Commander.

Clonard Monastery - Republican area near the Lower Falls In Belfast, attacked by loyalists in August 1969.

Crumlin Road gaol – Belfast prison which held republicans from 1845-1996, now a Museum.

Cumann na mBan - The womens section of the IRA.

Na Fianna Eireann - The youth section of the IRA, founded by Countess Markiewicz & Bulmer Hobson in 1907.

Garda Siochana - The police service in the Republic, 'Guardians of the Peace'.

Flying Column - Large IRA groups in the countryside in the War of Independence 1919-1921.

Free State - After the Treaty in 1922 the name given to the new Government & State.

GHQ - Ruling authority within the IRA.

Dail Eireann - The Parliament of the Irish Republic.

Easter Proclamation - Declaration of the Republic read by Padraig Pearse on the steps of the GPO in 1916.

Easter Rising - The military rising against British rule in 1916 which led to a massive change in Irish society, 16 Of the Leaders were executed and changed opinions.

Fianna Fail - the most successful political party in the Republic, formed by Eamonn deValera in 1926, the anti Treaty side in the Civil War who then broke from Sinn Fein to form FF.

First Dail - After the election of 1918, Sinn Fein had 73 MP's elected and proclaimed an Irish Republic and set up the 1st Dail in the Mansion House in January 1919.

Good Friday Friday Agreement - the political deal in 1998 between all political parties which brought an end to the conflict in the 6 counties.

H Blocks - Cellular system built to replace the Cages after the burning of the Camp in 1974, it had a turbulent history, 5 years of the Blanket protest, the Hunger Strike which claimed 10 lives, the great escape in 1983 when 38 escaped, and loyalist leader 'King Rat' shot dead in the gaol, it closed for good in 2000.

Home Rule - For 30 years at the end of the 19th century the main political issue in British-Irish affairs, finally jettisoned at the beginning of WW1.

INLA - The group broke from the Official IRA in 1974 amid a deadly feud, 3 of the Hunger Strikers were from the INLA and were responsible for the killing of Airey Neave at Westminister, a close friend of Margaret Thatcher.

IRA - The major republican group during the conflict, the IRA were formed after the Easter Rising and fought the British in the War of Independence, the two sides of the IRA fought the Civil War and morphed into Fianna Fail and Fine Gael, the rump stayed as Sinn Fein. In 1970 the Provisional IRA formed from a split from the Official IRA and fought a 30 year war against the British.

IRB - Originally formed out of the Fenian Movement in the 1860's, they were heavily involved in the 1916 Rising.

Long Kesh - 22 Cages in a former RAF base near Lisburn, turned into an Internment Camp in 1971 and then became the major holding centre for all prisoners of the conflict, it gained iconic status during the years and personifies the conflict.

Long War - The term coined by discussions in the Cages in the mid 70's which referred to longevity of the struggle against British rule.

Loyalists - Generally referring to the paramilitary groups, UVF, UDA, Red Hand Commandos who carried out hundreds of sectarian assassinations during the conflict.

Maidstone - British Navy ship docked in Belfast Lough turned into an Internment centre in 1971 and which I had the pleasure to spend a period in '72.

Magilligan Camp – an internment camp near Derry where I was interned in ’72.

Maze Prison - The name given to Long Kesh by the British to try and deflect the bad publicity it was getting and where I had the dubious pleasure of spending many years in the 70’s.

Operation Motorman - a massive operation by the British Army involving 30,000 troops and heavy armoured cars to break down the barricades in Free Derry and areas of Belfast.

MRF - British undercover military unit responsible for several assassinations.

NICRA - Civil Rights Movement.

OC - Officer Commanding an IRA Unit..

Official IRA - The rump of the Republican Movement which was left after the split with the Provisional IRA in 1970. Eventually morphed into the Workers Party and Democratic Left.

Oglaigh na hEireann - the gaelic epithet for the IRA and the Irish Army.

Orange Order - A staunchly all Protestant religious organisation .

Partition - The division of the country after the Treaty of 1922.

Peoples Democracy - Student group which marched from Belfast to Derry in 1969 and were attacked at Burntollet Bridge by loyalists and B Specials.

Republican News – Northern republican paper which merged with An Phoblacht in later years.

Provos - A colloquial term for members of the Provisional IRA.

RTE - The state television service in Ireland.

RUC - the armed police force in the 6 counties who morphed into the PSNI after the GFA.

SDLP - Formed in 1970 replacing the Nationalist Party, the leading party of nationalism until the re-emergence of Sinn Fein after the Hunger Strikes.

Sinn Fein - Founded in 1905 by Arthur Griffith, it became the political wing of the IRA during the War of Independence, after the Treaty it split into the two sides of the Civil War and then split again at the founding of FF. In the modern era it was the political wing of the Provisional IRA but eventually morphed into the political part, in Govt in the 6 counties and positioned to lead the Govt in Republic after next election.

Special Branch - Intelligence service within the RUC, PSNI & Gardai.

Stormont - The Parliament in the 6 counties since Partition, suspended in 1972 but brought into use again after the GFA.

Taoiseach - Prime Minister of the Republic.

Tan War - A colloquial name for the War of Independence.

TD - Member of the Dail.

Tet Offensive - The VC offensive against America in Vietnam in 1968 which the IRA tried to copy in South Armagh in the 90's.

Tories - colloquial name for the English Conservative Party.

12th July - Annual commemoration of the Battle of the Boyne by the Orange Order.

Unionists - Pejorative name for those loyal to the Crown in the 6 counties.

United Irishmen - Society which attempted to end British rule in the rebellion of 1798, made up of Catholic Defenders and Presbyterian radicals led by Wolfe Tone.

UDA - The largest loyalist paramilitary group in conflict and responsible for horrific sectarian murders during the conflict.

UVF - Originally formed in 1912 to fight Home Rule, the modern UVF were formed by Gusty Spence in 1966 and conducted a sectarian murder campaign in the conflict.

UDR - Local based British Army regiment in the 6 counties, replaced the 'B' Specials in 1970.

Bibliography

Adams, Gerry; *A Farther Shore*, Random House, (New York, 2003).

Adams, Gerry; *Before the Dawn*, Heinemann/Brandon, (London, 1996).

Adams, Gerry; *Hope & History*, Brandon Press, (Dingle, 2003).

Ahern, Bertie; *The Autobiography*, Hutchionism, (London, 2009).

Aldous, Richard; *Great Irish Speeches*, Quercus Publishing, (Dublin, 2007).

Aldous, Richard/Purcell,Niamh; *We Declare*, Querus Publishing, (London, 2008).

Alonso, Rogelio; *The IRA and Armed Struggle*, Routledge, (London, 2007).

Anderson, Brendan; *Joe Cahill, A Life in the IRA*, O'Brien Press, (Dublin, 2003).

Bell, Bowyer, J; *The Secret Army–the IRA*, Academy Press, (Dublin, 1979).

Beaslai, Piaras; Donnelly,S, *IRA Jailbreaks 1918-21*, Mercier Press, (Dublin, 2010).

Blair, Tony; *A Journey*, Hutchionson, (London, 2010)

Breen, Dan; *My Fight for Irish Freedom*, Anvil Books, (Dublin, 1924).

Brown, Dee, Bury My Heart at Wounded Knee, Pan Books, (London, 1972).

Burke, David; *Deception & Lies-the Arms Trial*, Mercier Press, (Dublin 2020).

Campbell, John; *Margaret Thatcher-the Iron Lady,* Vintage Books, (London, 2008).

Coakley, John/Gallagher,Michael,(Edt); *Politics in the Republic,* Routledge, (London 1999).

Conway, Kieran; *Southside Provisional*, Orpen Press, (Dublin, 2014).

Conlon-McKenna, Marita; *Rebel Sisters*, Transworld Publishing, (Dublin, 2016).

Coogan, T,P; *Michael Collins-Biography*, Hutchionism, (London, 1990).

Coogan, T,P; *The Troubles*, Random House, (London, 1995).

Coogan, TP; *1916-the Easter Rising*, Orion Publishing, (London, 2001).

Comerford, Maire; *The First Dail*, Clarke Publishing, (Dublin, 1969).

Comerford, R,U; *The Fenians in Context,* Wolfhound Press, (Dublin, 1998).

Craig, Patricia; *the Ulster Anthology*, Blackstaff, (Belfast 2006).

Deane, Marion, (Edt); *Belmont Castle-Theobald Wolfe Tone*, Lilliput Press, (1998).

de Breadun, Deaglan; *The Far Side of Revenge,* Collins Press, (Cork, 2008).

Dohery,Gabriel/Keogh,Dermot,(Edt); *Michael Collins-Making of the Irish State, (Mercier, Cork 2006)*

Doherty, Paddy; *Paddy Bogside*, Mercier Press, (Cork, 2001).

Edwards, Ruth, Dudley; *The Seven,* One World Publications, (London, 2016).

Elliot, Marianne; *the Catholics of Ulster, A History*, Penguin Press, (2000).

Ellis, David; *A Winter in Belfast*, Amazon UK, (2020).

English, Richard; *Armed Sruggle,* MacMillan, (London, 2003).

English Richard; *Irish Freedom,* MacMillan, (London, 2006).

Fahy, Desmond; *How the GAA survived the Troubles*, Wolfhound Press, (2001).

Fisk, Robert; *In Time of War*, Gill & MacMillan, (Dublin, 1983).

Fitzpatrick, Maurice; *John Hume in America,* Irish Academic Press, (Kildare, 2017).

Foley, Michael; *The Bloodied Field*, O'Brien Press, (Dublin 2020).

Foster, Roy; *Vivid Faces*, Penguin, (London, 2014).
Foy,Michael/Barton,Brian; *The Easter Rising*, History Press, (UK, 2011).
Friere, Paulo; *Pedagogy of Freedom,* Rowman & Littlefield, (New York, 2001).
Glennon, Kieran; *From Pogrom to Civil War*, Mercier Press, (Cork, 2013).
Greaves, C, Desmond; *Liam Mellowes & the Irish Revolution*, Camelot, (London,1971)
Greg, Patrick; *The Crum*, Gill & MacMillan, (Dublin, 2007).
Harnden, Toby; *Bandit Country*, Hodder & Stoughton, (London, 1999).
Hanley, Brian; *None of the Literary Type-Liam Mellowes*, Teagasc, (Carlow, 2016).
Hart, Peter; *Mick–the real Michael Collins,* MacMillan, (London, 2006).
Henry, William; *Pathway to Rebellion, Galway 1916*, Mercier Press, (Cork, 2016).
Hughes, Brendan; *Up Like a Bird*, Time Warp Books, (2021).
Ingram,Martin/Harkin,Greg; *Stakeknife*, O'Brien Press, (Dublin, 2004).
Jackson, Gen,Mike; *Soldier*, Transworld Publishing, (London, 2007).
Keane, Fergal; *Wounds - Memoir of War & Love*, Harper Collins, (London, 2017).
Keogh, Dermot; *Jack Lynch-A Biography*, Gill & MacMillan, (Dublin, 2008).
Lewis, Rob; *Fishers of Men*, Blake Publishing, (London, 1999).
Lynch, Martin; *Chronicles of Long Kesh*, Oberon Books, London, 2010.
Lyons, F,L; *Ireland since the Famine*, Fontana Press, (London, 1985).
Magee, Patrick; *Gangsters or Guerrillas*, BTP Publications, (Belfast, 2001).
Major, John; *Autobiography,* Harper/Collins, (New York, 1999).
Maloney, Ed; *A Secret History of the IRA*, Penguin, (London, 2002).
Maloney, Ed; *Paisley-Demagogue to Democrat,* Poolbeg Press, (Dublin, 2008).
Maloney, Ed; *Voices from the Grave,* Faber & Faber, (London, 2010).
Maye, Brian; *Arthur Griffith*, Griffith College Publishing, (Dublin, 1997).
Mansergh, Martin; *The Legacy of History*, Mercier Press, (Cork, 2003).
Mitchell, Senator,George; *Making Peace*, Heinemann, (London, 1999).
Morrison, Danny, (Edt); *Hunger Strike,* Bandon, (Kerry, 2006).
Morrison, Danny; *Then the Walls Came Down*, Mercier Press, (Cork, 1999).
Mowlam Mo; *Momentum*, Hodder & Stoughton, (London, 2002).
Murphy, Michael; *Gerry Fitt-Political Chameleon,* Mercier Press, (Cork, 2007).
Mullan, Don; *Eyewitness Bloody Sunday*, Wolfhound, (Dublin, 2002).
Murray,Gerard/Tonge,Jonathan*; Sinn Fein & SDLP*, O'Brien Press, (Dublin, 2005).
McCallion, Harry; *Undercover War*, Blake Publishing, (London, 2020).
MacIonnrachtaigh, Fergal; *Language, Resistance & Revival,* Pluto, (London, 2013).
MacLochlainn, Piaras; *Last Words,* Cahill & Co, Parkgate, (Dublin, 1971).
MacSuibhne, Brendan; *The End of Outrage*, Oxford University Press, (2017).
McArdle, Dorothy; *Irish Republic*, Irish Press Ltd, (Dublin,1951).
McCaffrey, Barry; *Alex Maskey-Man & Mayor*, Brehon Press, (Belfast, 2003).
McCann, Jim; *And the Gates Flew Open,* Glandore Publishing, (Belfast, 1998).
McGarry, Fergal (Edt); *Republicanism in Modern Ireland,* UCD Press, (2003).
McDonald, H; *McGuinness, Martin, A Life Remembered*, Blackstaff Press, (Belfast,

2017).
McInally, C; *Bloody Sunday to Bobby Sands-the Long Revolution*, Connolly Assoc, (Australia, 2020)
McKay, Susan; *Bear in Mind those Dead,* Faber & Faber, (London, 2008).
McKee, William; *Governor-Inside the Maze*, Gill & MacMillan, (Dublin, 2009).
McKearney, Tommy; *Provisional IRA,* Pluto Press, (London, 2011).
McKitterick/Kelters/Feeney/Thornton; *Lost Lives,* Mainstream Publishing, (Edinburgh 2001)
McPhilemy, Sean; *The Committee,* Rinehart Publishing, (Colorado, 1998).
Noonan, John; *What Do I Do Now*, (Dublin 2005).
O'Bradaigh, Ruairi; *Dilseacht-Story of Tom Maguire*, Irish Freedom Press, (1997).
O'Dochartaigh, Niall; *From Civil Rights to Armalites,* Cork University Press, (1997).
O'Shea, Katherine; *Uncrowned King of Ireland,* Nonsuch Publishing, (UK, 2005).
O'Brian, Liam; *Insurrection Memories-1916,* Ardcru Books, trans./E O'Dochartaigh, (Gallimhe 2016)
O'Brien, Justin; *Killing Finucane*, Gill & MacMillan, (Dublin, 2005).
O'Brien, Justin; *The Arms Trial,* Gill & MacMillan, (Dublin, 2000).
O'Dowd, Niall; *An Irish Voice*, O'Brien Press, (Dublin, 2010).
O'Halpin, Eunan; *Kevin Barry, an Irish Rebel in Life & Death*, Merrion Press, (Cork, 2020).
O'Hearn, Denis; *Bobby Sands-Nothing but an Unfinished Story*,Pluto, (London, 2010).
O'Malley, Dessie; *Conduct Unbecoming- A Memoir,* Gill&MacMillan, (Dublin, 2014).
Purdy, Martina; *Stormont-Behind Closed Doors,* Brehon Press, (Belfast, 2005).
Restorick, Rita; Death of a Soldier, Blackstaff Press, (Belfast 2000).
Ross, David; Ireland, *History of a Nation,* Geddes & Grossel, (Scotland, 2002).
Ryan, Meda; *Tom Barry-IRA Freedom Fighter,* Mercier Press, (Cork, 2003).
Ryder, Chris; *Inside the Maze*, Metheun, (London, 2000).
Ryder, Kearney; *Drumcree-the Orange Order's Last Stand*, Methuen, (London, 2001).
Sharrock D/Devenport M; *Man of War-Man of Peace*, MacMillan, London,(1997).
Sinnerton, Henry; *David Ervine-Unchartered Waters*, (Brandon Press, Kerry, 2002).
Stone, Michael; *None Shall Divide Us,* John Blake Publishing, (UK, 2003).
Tiernan, Joe; *The Dublin & Monaghan Bombings*, (Dublin, 2006).
Townshend, Charles; *The Republic*, Penguin, (London, 2013).
Tressell, Robert; *Ragged Trousered Philantropist*, Harper/Collins, (London, 1993).
Uris, Leon; *Trinity*, Deutsch Ltd, (London, 1976).
Walsh, Dermot/McCabe, Ann; *To the Honour of Jerry McCabe*, Blackwater Press, (2006).
White, Captain Jack; *Misfit-A Biography,* Livewire Publications, (London, 2005).
White, Robert, Ruairi, *O'Bradaigh-Life & Times of an Irish Revolutionary*, Indiana Press, (2006).

Chronology

1916	Easter Rising
1918	General Election – Sinn Fein win 75 Seats.
1919	1st Dáil
1919-21	War of Independence
1922	Treaty
1922-23	Civil War
1926	Fianna Fail founded.
1939-45	WW2.
1953	Born in Belfast.
1956	I contact TB, twin sisters die at birth.
1956-62	IRA Border Campaign.
1966	50th anniversary Easter Rising UVF reformed – kill 3 Nationalists.
1968	Civil Rights in Duke St, Derry attacked by RUC.
1969	PD march from Belfast to Derry, attacked at Burntollet. Battle of the Bogside and burning of the Falls. First RUC man killed by loyalists on the Shankill.
1970	Sinn Fein splits. IRA splits into Official and Provisional wings. Tories come back to power at Westminister. Curfew in Lower Falls. Battle of St. Matthews.
1971	First British soldier killed, Gunner Curtis, in New Lodge. First IRA Vols. Killed, Jim Saunders & Billy Reid. 6 months mandatory sentence in Crumlin Road gaol for rioting. Marty Forsythe shot dead. New Years Eve, Interned, Palace Barracks, Holywood, Prison Ship Maidstone, Magilligan Camp & Long Kesh.
1972	Bloody Sunday. Released from Internment after Stormont collapses. First IRA-British Govt Ceasefire. Political Status granted after 1st Hunger Strike. Bloody Friday. Operation Motorman. Arrested by 1 Para on bombing charge, held at Crumlin Road gaol.
1973	Sentenced to 6 years in Long Kesh. First bombs in London at Old Bailey.
1974	UWC Strike. Burning of Long Kesh.
1975	2nd IRA Ceasefire
1976	Released from Long Kesh. Danny Lennon and the Maguire children killed. Joey Surgenor & Frankie Fitsimons killed. Peace People formed. Blanket protest begins.
1977	Moved to Donegal and get married.
1978	Padraic born.
1979	Ciara born. Mountbatten killed at Mullaghmore; 18 Paras killed at Narrowwater.

1980 2nd IRA Hunger Strike.

1981 Kevin born.
3rd Hunger Strike led by Bobby Sands begins.
Bobby Sands elected MP,
Kieran Doherty elected TD.

1981 Ten Hunger Strikers die on protest.

1983 Gerry Adams elected MP.
38 escape from Long Kesh.

1985 Start in Sigro/Kirchhoff.
Anglo-Irish Agreement signed.

1986 Republican Movement drops Abstentionism.

1987 8 Vols. killed at Loughgall.
Eksund intercepted in Brittany.
Eniskillen IRA bomb kills 11.

1988 3 Vols. Killed in Gibraltar.
Brother in law Kevin killed by British Army.
Michael Stone kills 3 at Milltown.
2 Soldiers killed at IRA funeral.

1990 Italia '90.
Marriage break-up.

1993 Shankill bomb and Greysteel.

1994 Oisin born.
World Cup USA.
3rd IRA Ceasefire.

1996 Canary Wharf bomb.

1997 4th IRA Ceasefire.

1998 Good Friday Agreement.

2000 Last prisoners released and Long Kesh closed.

2000 Tiarnach & Rionach born.

2002 World Cup Japan/Korea.
Meet Mary in Gran Canaria.
Alanna born.

2003 Voluntary Redundancy from Kirchhoff.

2004 IT Course at LYIT.
Oran born.

2005 BA at NUI Galway.
Caolan born.
Cian born.

2007 Year at Universita ta Malta.
Dad died.
Rian born.

2008 Engaged to Mary in Malta.

2009 PGDE at NUI Galway.

2010 MA History at NUI Galway.
Mum died.

2011 Graduated as Secondary Teacher with Masters in History.

2012 Teaching in Ireland and Malta.

2012 Superintendent & Invigilator with the State Exam Commission

2015 Oisin left this world.

2016 Open Heart Surgery (1).

2017 Open Heart Surgery (2).
Open Heart Surgery (3).

2018 Brain Hemorrhage.

2020 COVID-19 Pandemic.

2022 Golfing at Galway Bay.

Appendix 1

Vols. Civilians, Friends I knew who were killed in the conflict.

Gerard McAuley, 15, Fianna, August 15 1969, shot dead by loyalists in Clonard, Falls.

Martin Forsythe, 19, IRA, October 24 1971, shot dead by RUC in Belfast city centre.

Jimmy McCollum, 16, civilian, December 17 1971, killed by UVF bomb in bar he worked, Belfast.

Tony Lewis, 20, IRA, March 9 1972, killed in premature explosion in Clonard, Falls.

John Moran, 19, civilian, May 23 1972, killed in loyalist bomb attack on bar he worked, Whiterock.

Norman Campbell, 19, civilian, June 8 1972, shot dead by UDA at his work on the Shankill.

James Doherty, 6, October 1972, shot dead on street in Turf Lodge?

John Donaghy, 18, IRA, October 10 1972, killed in premature explosion in Lower Falls.

Tony 'TC' Campbell, 19, IRA, February 4 1973, shot dead by British Army in New Lodge.

Frankie Dodds, 31, September 9 1973, died in Long Kesh possible effects from beatings by Army.

Jim Bryson, 26, IRA, September 22 1973, shot dead by British Army in Ballymurphy.

Martin Skillen, 21, IRA, August 3 1974, shot dead by British Army in Lower Falls.

Gerard Fennell, 28, IRA, November 8 1974, shot dead by British Army in Twinbrook.

Danny Loughran, 20, INLA & Irish Army, April 5 1975, shot dead by Official IRA in Divis Flats.

John Kelly, 26, IRA, January 21 1975, killed in premature explosion in Belfast city centre.

Danny Lennon, 23, IRA, August 10 1976, shot dead by British Army in Andersonstown.

Tucker Kane, IRA, 1976, killed in road accident on IRA business.

Brian Stewart, 13, October 4 1976, killed by plastic bullet fired by British Army in Turf Lodge.

Frankie Fitzsimmons, 29, IRA, October 16 1976, killed in premature explosion at Gas Works, Belfast.

Joey Surgenor, 24, IRA, October 16 1976, killed in premature explosion at Gas Works, Belfast.

Patrick Smith, ex prisoner, 1976, shot dead by the IRA, Short Strand.

Brendan O'Callaghan, 21, IRA, April 23 1977, shot dead by British Army in Lenadoon, Belfast.

Tommy 'Toddler' Tolan, 31, IRA, July 27 1977, shot dead by Official IRA in Ballymurphy.

Jim Mulvenna, 28, IRA, June 21 1978, shot dead by the SAS in Ballysillan, Belfast.

Henry Corbett, 27, ex prisoner, September 3 1979, shot dead by UDA, Bawnmore,

Newtownabbey.

Bobby Sands, 27, IRA, May 5 1981, died on Hunger Strike in the H Blocks, Long Kesh.

George McBrearty, 23, IRA, May 28 1981, shot dead by British Army in the Brandywell, Derry.

Joe McDonnell, 30, IRA, July 8 1981, died on Hunger Strike in the H Blocks, Long Kesh.

Kieran Doherty, 25, IRA, August 2 1981, died on Hunger Srike in the H Blocks, Long Kesh.

Micky Kearney, 33, INLA, February 17 1987, shot dead during INLA internecine feud at Springhill.

Larry Marley, 41, IRA, April 3 1987, shot dead by the UVF at his home in Ardoyne.

Charlie McIlmurray, 32, ex IRA, 1987, shot dead by the IRA, near Killeen, Armagh.

Kevi McCracken, 31, IRA, March 14 1988, shot dead by British Army in Turf Lodge.

Anthony McKiernan, 44, ex prisoner, 1988, shot dead by IRA in Belfast.

Hughie Hehir, 37, IRA, 1988, shot dead by Gardai Special Branch in Clare.

Brendan Davison, 33, IRA, July 25 1988, shot dead by the UVF in the Markets, Belfast.

Eddie Fullerton, 56, Sinn Fein, May 25 1991, shot dead by UDA in Buncrana, Donegal.

Lawrence McNally, 38, IRA, June 3 1991, shot dead by SAS in Tyrone.

Alan Lundy, 39, ex prisoner, May 1 1993, shot dead by UDA in Andersonstown.

Hugh Torney, 41, INLA, September 3 1996, shot dead in internecine INLA feud, Lurgan.

Denis Donaldson, ex IRA & SF, April 4 2006, shot dead at cottage in Donegal.

Appendix 2

A long list of ex Long Kesh political prisoners I knew who have passed in recent times, many from cancer and possibly related to the CR Gas which was dropped on the prisoners from a British Army helicopter in 1974. In total almost 200 prisoners have passed since, roughly 10% of the 2000 involved in the 24 hour battle for control of the Camp. The British Govt. refuse to release archived files relating to the use of CR Gas or the legality of its use on defenceless prisoners.

Johnny Burns Turf Lodge
Jim Scullion Turf Lodge
Tommy Downey Turf Lodge
Micky Flanagan Turf Lodge
Gerry Cairns Turf Lodge
Sean Fryers Turf Lodge
Hughie Doran Turf Lodge
Tommy Smyth Turf Lodge
Eddie Brophy Turf Lodge
Eamonn Maguire Turf Lodge
Derec MacTomais Dublin
Phil McMahon Belfast & Dublin
Gerry 'Whitey' Bradley Carrick Hill, Belfast
Terence 'Cleaky' Clarke Ardoyne
John 'Juice' McMullan Lower Falls
Dave Morley Newry
Billy McKee Falls
Prionsias McAirt Falls
Frankie Cox Armagh
Kevin Sullivan Whiterock
Tony O Kane 'Madrua Rua' New Lodge
Peter Stewart Bawnmore
Bill Bradley New Lodge
Tony Bradley Falls
Rab O Hanlon Ardoyne & Australia
Bob Haughey Lurgan
Jimmy McGeown Lurgan
Syd Elliot Andersonstown
Jim McGivern New Lodge
Charlie McKiernan Markets
Joe Henry Newry
Seamus Henry Newry
* William 'Plum' Smith (UVF) Belfast

Index